Reviewers' comments on *Astrology, Karma & Transformation:*

"Arroyo's new book reflects a real depth of comprehension and ability to integrate humanistic astrology with Jungian psychology and Eastern philosophy. The simplicity and clarity of his treatment of complex ideas is remarkable; it makes accessible even to the beginner a wealth of understanding...giving meaningful psychological grounding to astrological interpretation."
— *Library Journal*

"This is straight, clean astrology, in modern terms, very well and concisely written. One of the best modern works we have seen."

— *CAO Times*

"You have done a superb job on *Astrology, Karma & Transformation.* It is the kind of book that is going to raise the level of consciousness in the astrological field. I salute you for the depth of consciousness and the insight that is shown in your book."
— **Isabel Hickey**
Author of *Astrology: A Cosmic Science*

"I find it to be superior to any other astrology book I have ever read. It is a remarkable work of extremely meaningful material that is written in a very lucid and practical style, and that is why I tell my students that I consider it to be an absolute 'must'."
— **Robert S. Kimball**
Astrological Researcher & Teacher

"It is not contrived or artificial when Arroyo talks of the horoscope as the map of the soul in its present karmic state. Nothing is forced. The understanding of astrological principles flows harmoniously. In fact, there is not a single sentence or thought in this book that is not honest, reasonable, and fair to the miracle of the human being. In addition to this quality of excellence, there is profound astrological knowledge. This is a superb book, a gift to astrology.

— **Lore Wallace**
Astrology Now

ASTROLOGY KARMA & TRANSFORMATION

The Inner Dimensions of the Birth Chart

Stephen Arroyo

CRCS PUBLICATIONS
Post Office Box 1460
Sebastopol, California 95472
U.S.A.

Library of Congress Cataloging in Publication Data

Arroyo, Stephen.
    Astrology, karma & transformation.

    Bibliography: p.
    1. Astrology. 2. Occult sciences. 3. Develop-
mental psychology. I. Title.
BF1708.1.A77   133.5   76-21588
ISBN 0-916360-04-0
ISBN 0-916360-03-2 pbk.

FIRST EDITION

INTERNATIONAL STANDARD BOOK NUMBERS:
  0-916360-03-2 (paperback)
  0-916360-04-0 (hardcover)

LIBRARY OF CONGRESS CATALOG CARD NUMBER: 76-21588

Published simultaneously in the United States
and Canada by CRCS Publications.

Distributed in the United States &
Internationally by CRCS Publications.

Cover Design & Mandalas by Pacia Ryneal

Book Design & Layout by Kathleen Mullins

Acknowledgements

Although most books do not acknowledge the contributions of editors, proofreaders, and others who helped to give form to a particular book, it is my feeling that these people's efforts are underestimated and therefore deserve gratitude and recognition. A book such as this is born through the joint efforts of both the author and all the other people who help to refine and define the author's intentions. And all of them together, rather than just the author alone, constitute the channel through which a book is brought into being.

Therefore, I want to give special thanks to Joanie Case and Barbara McEnerney for their editing and proofreading, and I am indebted to both of them for a multitude of excellent suggestions about both the form and the content of this book. It is through their deep understanding of not only editorial requirements but also of astrology itself that whatever may be valuable in this volume has been made clear and accessible to the reader.

I also want to thank Pacia Ryneal for doing both the cover art and the mandalas which I feel add a great deal to this book, Dierdre Engstrom for designing the graphics in chapters 6 and 10, and Diane Simon for proofreading and positive feedback.

Finally, I want to express my appreciation to Jim Maynard and Sharon Saltzman for their wide variety of skills, practical knowledge, and encouragement related to the design and production of this book.

A small portion of the material incorporated in this book has been previously published in the form of articles in Dell's HOROSCOPE magazine, Popular Library's AQUARIAN ASTROLOGY, and Llewellyn's ASTROLOGY NOW. We appreciate, therefore, the editors' permission to bring it forth in this entirely revised and enlarged presentation.

To my wife, partner, & adviser Kathy,
   In appreciation for her encouragement, her
practical & spiritual help, and her way of being.

Contents

Introduction

*Without stirring abroad one can know the whole world;
Without looking out the window one can see the way of
heaven. The further one goes, the less one knows.*
—Lao Tzu

Ever since I began to study astrology, an interest which began during
a period of great personal changes and which followed a deep
immersion in the writings of C.G. Jung, I have known that there is more
to astrology than most astrological textbooks ever mention. In other
words, I have always been intuitively aware of the fact that, behind the
symbols and the archaic language of traditional astrology, there lies a
vast realm of potential wisdom, deeper understanding of the very laws
of life, and insights that can lead a devoted student to a more refined
comprehension of the spiritual dimensions of experience. Hence, as I
began to devour one astrological book after another, I immediately
found myself searching for the deeper meanings of the symbols, the
inner significance of this cosmic language which seemed to me to hold
such great potential for spiritual growth and heightened awareness.

As I continued my studies, it became increasingly clear to me that
astrology works with levels of consciousness and dimensions of
experience that are far beyond the understanding of the earth-
conditioned logical mind. It became apparent that only the higher
intuitive mind (what one might call the "eye of the soul") could truly
understand astrology in all its deeper ramifications and significance;
and, year by year, I found that one could indeed sharpen the intuition
through meditation, constant practice, and openness to the point
where one could immediately sense the essential reality which authors
tried to explain verbally in so many books.

In my early studies, however, although I approached astrology with
very little of the skepticism that many people in Western culture have
to overcome in such an endeavor, I was quickly and deeply
disappointed in the quality of thought, discrimination, objectivity, and
spiritual awareness exemplified in the writings of most ancient and
modern astrologers. This disillusionment extended not only to the
works that focused mainly on events, prediction, and superficial
character analysis, but also to those "esoteric astrology" texts which,
although occasionally accurate for some people, are usually rather
ridiculous in their generalizations and preaching, thus bypassing any
discussion of the *essential* meaning of the various astrological factors.
Hence, I feel fortunate that I was soon led to the works of Dane
Rudhyar and to in-depth studies in the fields of yoga, healing, Eastern
religions, and the discourses and writings of many spiritual teachers, in
addition to Jung's incomparable scientific investigations which I
continued to study for many years. All of these pursuits, coupled with
my own increasingly clear perceptions into energy fields, plus a long-

term study of hundreds of highly instructive dreams, and an intuitive synthesis of these many dimensions of life around a central spiritual ideal, eventually led me to a method of understanding and applying astrology with which I now feel quite comfortable.

By this I do not mean to infer that I have developed a "closed system" of astrological "interpretation." On the contrary, such pat approaches soon become rigid and irrelevant, and it is precisely that kind of system that I have found so intolerably limiting. I simply mean that I am now confident that the direction I am pursuing in my own understanding and in my counseling work is the right one for my own growth and, in fact, far more constructively useful for my clients and students than the assortment of untested theories and assumptions that comprise so much of traditional event-oriented or "esoteric" astrology. The falsehoods and unfounded generalizations encountered in so many astrological books are profoundly destructive if applied to individual situations without refinement or sensitive adjustment to the person's level of consciousness. And they are all the more ludicrous when one discovers that even a cursory testing of such statements with complete integrity and absence of self-deception can experientially prove their total irrelevance to real life experience in the majority of cases.

It may interest the reader to know that, when I started my astrological studies, the following transits were in effect: Saturn conjuncting the natal ascendant, Neptune aspecting Venus, and both Pluto and Uranus in Virgo closely aspecting natal Uranus, all by so-called "hard" or "stressful" aspects. I mention this to indicate the fact that astrology for me encompasses not only a full-time career and a way of thinking and pursuing truth, but also that it has been and still is a tool for refining my own nature and inspiring me toward greater heights of immediate experience. This book is the result of the ideas I have gathered while investigating the unifying principles of life and the deeper meanings of astrology. It includes a great variety of topics which either were difficult for me to understand from traditional textbooks during the course of my own studies, or which aren't readily available in books at all. I have made no attempt to write a "cookbook" sort of text, filled with hundreds of set "interpretations," and I am herein assuming that the reader already knows *at least* the traditional basic meanings and characteristics of the signs, planets, houses, and aspects.

In this work, I primarily want to illuminate certain dimensions of astrology. There are many levels of astrological interpretation. What have been neglected in astrological literature are the deeper meanings, the inner dimensions, and the growth-oriented experiential level of interpretation. For those satisfied with prediction formulae, archaic concepts, and simplistic character analysis, this book will be irrelevant. Those will find it useful and informative who still ask such questions as: Why does astrology work? Why was a certain person born with certain aspects in the natal chart? What is the *purpose* of this seemingly difficult time period? Why has a certain person been unable to deal effectively with a certain problem? This book is primarily based on personal and clinical experience, and I have tried to make it as practical as possible. However, due to the subtlety and immense scope of some of the topics discussed, it is also highly speculative in places; for I do not claim to have all the answers to ultimate questions and I certainly make no claim to have attained the heightened spiritual awareness required for definite knowledge of higher dimensions of life. This book is decidedly not a set of rules whereby one can interpret charts in a mechanical way, but rather it is a guide to be used in unison with one's own intuition and personal experience. Specific rules may guide us in the first stages of our astrological studies, but they eventually must be left by the wayside as the Oneness and Love that transcends all our carefully devised rules and laws becomes more and more a living reality that illuminates each individual moment and each encounter with another human being's mystery.

A great danger in any kind of "occult" study is that the student may become lost in the endless peripheral manifestations of the One, rather than seeing everything as simply a reflection or aspect of the central, unifying reality. The quotation by Lao Tzu at the beginning of this introduction beautifully expresses the essential value and truth of *simplicity*, a realization that must become immediately apparent to any astrological practitioner if he or she is ever to begin to synthesize the multitude of factors in any astrological chart into a coherent, meaningful whole. The Oneness that appears at high levels of consciousness becomes the many when it is reflected into the lower levels of being. The further one gets from the central reality, the more diverse and contradictory life appears. However, as one becomes attuned to that center, to that higher Oneness, one perceives with increasing clarity that the birth-chart is a whole, unified, living symbol; that the individual person is not *merely* a composite of many diverse factors, but is a living unit of divine potential. And the growth-processes with which astrology deals (e.g., transits and progressions) are not isolated cycles that happen occasionally to overlap; rather they are all aspects of a unified and developing consciousness operating simultaneously at many different levels and in many different dimensions. Hence, it is my feeling that a student or practitioner of astrology, if he or she is primarily concerned with utilizing such knowledge as an incisive, helpful, individualized art, need not worry about all the different "techniques" of prediction or interpretation that now flood almost all astrological publications. As I often tell my students when they ask me, "Where do I begin when I do someone's chart?", if you understand one factor in the chart *thoroughly*, it will lead you to the center from which all emanates. In other words, just begin talking about something you *do* understand, *relate* that to the person's personal experience and understanding, and then let it flow by itself. As Albert Einstein remarked, if you penetrate to the core of anything, you will eventually encounter the deepest reality and truth.

The simplicity I have been pointing toward is not just an unreachable ideal; it is not something which sounds nice but which in practice is inapplicable and irrelevant. It is a quality that grows from an individual's awareness of Oneness and from an awareness of the infinite potentiality of one's inner life. The mind can be the "slayer of the real," as the Oriental sage put it, in which case it is the enemy of clarity and light. Indeed, one's mind can become so absorbed in the intricate details of a particular chart that one loses sight of the client's wholeness and personal values. In that case, the mind is the enemy of truth and serves only to gloss over the current problem with a mass of confusing details. The client may feel better for a time, since the mind has been distracted into thinking of all sorts of new things. But how long will this relief last before the person is again confronted with the need to face the current situation and to deal with it in a concentrated, in-depth manner?

The mind, however, can also serve as an instrument of the higher self, in which case it helps to illuminate the unfathomable reality of life and individual destiny. The quality of any astrological dialogue depends more than anything upon the purity of mind, the depth of concentration, and the specific life ideals of the counselor. And those who try to dismiss the importance of the astrologer's philosophical or spiritual values, claiming that such an orientation is "mystical," unscientific, or irrelevant to a knowledge of "sound astrological fundamentals," seem to me to have very little understanding of the impact of their work and the responsibility they assume in counseling others. The apparent chaos in some astrological circles nowadays, and the confusion that at times becomes overwhelming in the minds of new students of astrology, can only be clarified by our recognition of the supremacy of the philosophical and spiritual attitudes underlying our work. As Dr. Kenneth Negus wrote in an excellent article:

> Astrology at its best does not concern itself merely with the material and energy that are the primary concerns of the sciences. Only a higher *philosophical* approach can properly deal with the supreme formative forces that make our world and its environs into a cosmos— this is one of the *highest* astrological truths, and a nonscientific one.
>
> *We need to recognize a hierarchy of knowledge within astrology itself.* This means that the philosophical and humanistic levels of astrological knowledge must not only be essential ingredients in astrological studies, but must indeed be granted a transcendent superiority. (from *Astrology Now*, Vol. 1, No. 11, p. 18)

In attempting to point the reader in the direction of this wholeness and simplicity, I do not feel that it is my place to do much preaching about what is true and what is not. The very nature of this book does, however, necessitate that I use my own understanding and values to suggest possible meanings or to discriminate between various factors. In this volume, I have primarily tried to reveal the overall simplicity of astrology by speaking quite often of what I call the "themes" in a chart. This approach to astrology has been expounded by many astrologers: Dr. Zipporah Dobyns repeatedly speaks of the twelve letters of the astrological alphabet to which all chart factors can be reduced; Richard Ideman speaks of the various "dialogues" between these essential factors, thus combining planets, signs, and houses into a coherent whole. I have often used the term "interchange" to describe any of the possible interactions between the essential twelve astrological principles.* I feel that any student of astrology could benefit from this approach—a way of seeing the chart factors which, if taken to its logical conclusion, completely transcends the level of interpretation that classifies everything good/bad or favorable/unfavorable.

The wholeness I have been speaking of is beautifully exemplified in this book by the mandalas for each of the twelve signs of the zodiac drawn by Pacia Ryneal. A mandala is a perfect symbol of unity and concentrated form, and of course many astrologers speak of approaching the birth-chart as the person's individual mandala. Ancient zodiacal mandalas exist from Arab, Hebrew, Indian, Babylonian, Greek, Roman, Tibetan, Sumerian, and European Christian cultures; and these modern mandalas, I feel, incorporate both ancient symbolism and modern intensity in a way that graphically reveals the deeper dimensions of astrological symbols. The time has come to modernize astrology, both in theory and in practical interpretation, and Pacia Ryneal's art is a reflection of this trend toward relevant modernization.

Finally, it must be stated that a book like this (dealing with such questions as karma, reincarnation, and self-transformation) is necessarily based on assumptions that completely contradict many of the unspoken assumptions that underly both "common sense" and most types of astrological interpretation. This is so because, once one sees reincarnation and karma as *facts of life* and once one dedicates oneself to self-transformation based upon a spiritual ideal, all of the traditional labels, meanings, and interpretations of event-oriented astrology are turned inside out. Once one takes this more comprehensive approach, based on the acceptance of a reality higher than what our physical senses perceive, it becomes apparent that most important solutions come not from the outer world, but from within. Instead of focusing on how much ease or comfort we experience in a certain situation or time period, one penetrates into the lessons and growth-potential inherent in all "difficult" experiences and takes the "easy" experiences in stride without losing balance or becoming ego-

---

*Some examples of such "interchanges" should be explained for those readers unfamiliar with this approach to astrology. One example would be the various interchanges between what one could call the seventh and tenth letters (or principles) of the astrological alphabet, all of which are generally similar, although each manifests a bit differently in specifics: Saturn in Libra; Saturn in the seventh house; Venus in Capricorn; Venus in the tenth house; all Venus-Saturn aspects; and, to some extent, all squares between the seventh and tenth houses and between Libra and Capricorn.

Another example would be all interchanges between the fourth and tenth principles: Moon in Capricorn; Saturn in Cancer; Moon in the tenth house; Saturn in the fourth house; all Moon-Saturn aspects; and, to some extent, all oppositions between the fourth and tenth houses and between Cancer and Capricorn.

If any individual chart contains two or more instances of one specific type of interchange, that particular dynamic would constitute at least a minor "theme" in that person's life. If the chart contains three or more, it is likely that a major life theme would be so indicated.

inflated. In such an approach, the convenience and comfort of life in the material plane is not the factor of major importance; rather it is the inner state of being and the process of self-development that holds priority.

For example, if one is born with Venus in square aspect to the Moon, Neptune, Uranus, or Saturn, it's not particularly important that one has some degree of trouble with love affairs or relationships. The important thing is to know what that experience signifies in the larger scope of our conscious growth, what it can teach us, and what its purpose is. In this book, therefore, I have tried to point the reader in the direction of understanding the birth-chart, transits, progressions, and chart comparison factors at a level of depth that will hopefully elicit an inner awakening to personal needs, potentials, and purposes. This is not an easy task, for life is a multi-level process. Although one can know with some confidence that a particular transit, for example, will manifest on the surface in a certain way that most people will recognize and respond to, there is often simultaneously a deeper meaning to that time period, a life-development or change in awareness that may have very long-term ramifications. It is the astrologer's duty and most difficult challenge to elucidate that meaning for the client and to help refocus the client's attention on the *essential* process that is occurring rather than merely on the superficial changes. As Jung has pointed out many times in his writings, that with which you are not consciously in touch happens to you as "fate." It seems to happen *to* you, and you then don't take any responsibility for it or recognize your part in bringing it to manifestation. The more one is consciously in touch with one's inner life, the more astrology offers—not sensational surprises or a way of manipulating fate—but rather a means of clarifying the stages of self-development which we should welcome and use as opportunities for personal transformation.

ASTROLOGY KARMA & TRANSFORMATION

Aries

1

Karma

What happens to a person is characteristic of him. He represents a pattern and all the pieces fit. One by one, as his life proceeds, they fall into place according to some pre-destined design.
—C.G. Jung

The word "karma" is used in so many ways by occultists, astrologers, and others concerned with the universal laws that guide our lives that, in considering the relation of astrology to karma, we should first of all clarify the meaning of the term. Basically, it refers to the universal law of cause and effect, identical with the biblical idea that "Whatsoever a man soweth, that shall he also reap." This law is merely the broader application of our earthly ideas of cause and effect; it is obvious that no one who plants thistles can expect to harvest roses. The law of karma is similar to the law of Newtonian mechanics that states: "For each action, there is an equal and opposite reaction." The only difference between the universal law of karma and the mundane physical law of cause and effect is the scope of existence that each embraces. The law of karma assumes that life is a continuous experience, not by any means limited to one incarnation in the material world. The universal law of karma, then, can be seen as a way of achieving and maintaining universal justice and equilibrium. It is, in fact, one of the most simple, all-encompassing laws of life. It is inseparable from what some have called the "law of opportunity"—i.e., a universal law that places each of us in the conditions which provide the exact spiritual lessons we need in order to become more god-like.

The concept of karma is based upon the phenomenon of polarity by which the universe maintains a state of balance. This is not to say a state of inertia, but rather a dynamic, constantly changing equilibrium. Inherent in this concept is the assumption that an individual "soul" (or "entity" in some schools of thought) has within itself the causal power which eventually bears fruit, the "effects." The faculty which initiates this process is the "will," and the whole structure of the causal phenomenon is called "desire." "Desire" can be seen as the application of the will in such a way as to direct the person's energy toward the manifestation of an impulse or idea.

The whole idea of karma is, of course, inseparable from the theory (or law) of reincarnation. Although some authors have considered karma and reincarnation to be metaphors or symbols of a cosmic process far more subtle than is apparent in the popular conception of the terms, most people who have accepted the teachings of reincarnation and karma as a living reality are satisfied with the traditional, even obvious, meaning of the words. For most people, the process of reincarnation simply refers to the periodic manifestation of immortal beings, souls, or spirits through the medium of the physical world in order to learn certain lessons and to develop specific ways of being as a preparation for a higher state of being (or consciousness). According to the reincarnation theory set forth in the psychic readings of the great clairvoyant Edgar Cayce (now often called "The Sleeping Prophet," after the title of Jess Stern's best-selling book), all "entities" were created "in the beginning" and periodically incarnate in order to learn the fundamental spiritual lessons: love, patience, moderation, balance, faith, devotion, etc. According to Cayce, it is often an aid to spiritual development to have a knowledge of basic universal laws, such as reincarnation, karma, grace, "like begets like," and "mind is the builder." The "law of grace" is the most important in the Cayce psychic readings.

Like Newtonian mechanics compared to modern nuclear physics, the law of karma seems to operate at a rather gross level compared to the law of grace, which, according to Cayce, supersedes the law of karma when one opens oneself to the "Christ Consciousness" within. This "Christ Consciousness" is the human experience of *oneness* which has no *reaction* because it does not take place at the level where the law of polarity (or opposites) operates. Hence, if we accept Cayce's concept of the law of grace, we find that the law of karma is not the ultimate force underlying our lives. Still, it can be helpful to understand karma, what it is, and how it works. Cayce himself has stated that "each lifetime is the sum total of all previous incarnated selves" and that "everything which has been previously built, both good and bad, is contained in that opportunity" (i.e., the present incarnation). Throughout his thousands of recorded psychic readings, Cayce repeatedly stressed that, when a person was experiencing a specific kind of problem or a stressful phase of life, he was simply "meeting self,"—in other words, that the individual was now having to confront the very experience that he had created in the past.

The law of karma at its grossest level is expressed in the biblical axiom "an eye for an eye and a tooth for a tooth."* One cannot overestimate the power of desire as the deepest force initiating karma. Only the separate ego can desire, for the essential self (or soul) is already one with everything and so desires nothing. In essence, the law of karma tells us, "You get what you want—eventually." But, of course, we may not understand the ramifications of our desires until we experience them. For example, a man may desire material wealth. So, in a future time, he is born into a family of astounding wealth and luxury. He now has what he wanted, but is he satisfied? No. Other desires arise immediately, for the nature of the restless mind is to produce desires. In fact, the man may come to realize that his new-found wealth is not only

---

*For those who care to investigate how widely references to karma and reincarnation appear in the Bible, see: Job 14:14; Eccles. 1:11; Jer. 1:5; Matt. 17:9-13 & 16:13-14; Mark 6:15; Luke 9:8; John 3:7 & 1:21, 25; Col. 3:3; Jude 1:4; and Rev. 3:12.

unsatisfying, but even a horrible burden! At least when he was poor, he had nothing to lose; so he was free. Now wealthy, he continually worries about losing what he in fact no longer wants but yet is attached to. The question then becomes: How can one release (or be released from) his desire-forged attachments in order that he can again be free? (The great English poet William Blake called these attachments "mind-forged manacles.") This freedom is the sought-after goal of all paths of liberation and techniques of self-realization.

The greatest wealth of insight about the nature and workings of karmic law is found in the writings and teachings of various spiritual teachers, most of whom are from the Orient and whose teachings therefore are rooted in Buddhist or Hindu traditions. Paramahansa Yogananda, one of the first Eastern spiritual masters to spread his teachings widely in the Western world, wrote a beautiful and inspiring book entitled *Autobiography of a Yogi*, in which we find the following quotation:

> Fate, karma, destiny—call it what you will—there is a law of justice which somehow, but not by chance, determines our race, our physical structure and some of our mental and emotional traits. The important thing to realize is that while we may not escape our own basic pattern, we can work in conformity with it. That is where free will comes in. We are free to choose and discriminate to the limits of our understanding, and, as we rightly exercise our power of choice, our understanding grows. Then, once having chosen, a man has to accept the consequences of his choice and go on from there.

Yogananda further explains how to deal effectively with one's karma and what the proper attitude should be toward one's destiny:

> Seeds of past karma cannot germinate if they are roasted in the divine fires of wisdom....The deeper the self-realization of a man, the more he influences the whole universe by his subtle spiritual vibrations, and the less he himself is affected by the phenomenal flux (karma).

Yogananda was also intimately familiar with astrology, since his *guru* was a master of all the ancient arts and sciences. His comments on astrology and the scope of its relevance are therefore worth considering:

> A child is born on that day and at that hour when the celestial rays are in mathematical harmony with his individual karma. His horoscope is a challenging portrait, revealing his unalterable past and its probable future results. But the natal chart can be rightly interpreted only by men of intuitive wisdom; these are few.

> Occasionally I told astrologers to select my worst periods, according to planetary indications, and I would still accomplish whatever task I set myself. It is true that my success at such time has been accompanied by extraordinary difficulties. But my conviction has always been justified; faith in the divine protection, and the right use of man's God-given will, are forces formidable beyond any other.

In Buddhist tradition, the goal of liberation techniques and spiritual practices is called "nirvana," a term which has not been correctly interpreted by many Westerners seeking to penetrate the depths of Buddhist wisdom. The literal meaning of the term "*nirvana*" is "where the wind of karma doesn't blow." In other words, the only way to achieve spiritual progress is to awaken ("*Buddha*" means simply "one who is awake") to a level of awareness beyond the domain of karma and beyond the planes of illusion. One can gather from these teachings that the only way to deal with karma, *ultimately*, is to rise above it. However, as long as we are incarnate in the physical form, the law of karma affects us in one way or another; and it would thus be extremely useful if we could achieve an understanding of the karmic patterns with which we have to deal in this lifetime, if for no other reason than that it would enable us to face our destiny with grace, acceptance, and fortitude.

An ancient tradition in India goes into great depths in its analysis of karmic law, dividing types of karma into three groups. *Pralabd karma* is considered the fate, or destiny, karma which must be met in the present lifetime. This basic destiny pattern is considered to be fundamentally unalterable, simply a pattern and sequence of experiences which the individual has to deal with in this incarnation. It is stated, however, that a spiritual approach to life, the help of a spiritual master, or simply the Lord's grace may occasionally intervene to lessen the impact of particularly heavy karma, thus making "a sword thrust" into a "pinprick." *Kriyaman karma* is that karma which we are now making in this very lifetime, the effects of which we will have to face at a later time. The primary reason for the sometimes severe disciplines of various spiritual paths is that such control on behavior can help the traveler on the path to refrain from making more karma which would inhibit his spiritual progress in the future. Other than practicing such disciplines, the primary way to avoid creating karma in the present is to refrain from intense desires and attachments, while simultaneously cultivating the proper spirit and detached attitude in carrying out our daily duties. Naturally, maintaining the proper spirit and detachment is very difficult, and it is considered in most spiritual teachings to be absolutely impossible without the aid of meditation. Lastly, *Sinchit karma* is the term given to the reserve of karma that we have accumulated over many lifetimes but which is not specifically active in this incarnation. According to these teachings, we have, over thousands of incarnations, accumulated such vast karmic entanglements that it would be impossible to encounter all the results of past thoughts and actions in one lifetime. We would simply be overwhelmed, physically, psychically, and emotionally. Hence, that portion of our karma which is not allotted to our present lifetime's fate, or *pralabd*, karma is held in reserve. We will, according to these teachings, have to face all of that karma also, sometime in the future, unless a Perfect Spiritual Master relieves us of some of that burden.

A spiritual teacher with a large following in the USA, Meher Baba, likewise elucidates the workings of karma:

> You, as a gross body, are born again and again until you realize your Real Self. You, as mind, are born only once; and die only once; in this sense, you do not reincarnate. The gross body keeps changing, but mind (mental body) remains the same throughout. All impressions (*sanskaras*) are stored in the mind. The impressions are either to be spent or counteracted through fresh karma in successive incarnations.

> You are born male, female; rich, poor; brilliant, dull;...to have that
> richness of experience which helps to transcend all forms of duality.

I doubt whether anyone who is familiar with the accuracy and
profound usefulness of astrology would deny that the natal birth-chart
reveals in symbolic form the individual's primary life pattern: the
potentials, talents, attachments, problems, and dominant mental
characteristics. If this is so, then the birth-chart obviously reveals a
blueprint, or X-ray, of the soul's present *pralabd*, or fate, karma. As I
showed in great detail in my book *Astrology, Psychology, and the Four
Elements*, the birth-chart can be viewed as revealing the individual's
pattern of energy which manifests on all levels simultaneously:
physical, mental, emotional, and inspirational corresponding with the
four elements *earth, air, water,* and *fire*. The *sinchit*, or reserve, karma is
not indicated in the birth-chart, since it is not allotted to this lifetime.
Likewise, the *kriyaman* karma is not indicated either, since we seem to
have some degree of freedom, limited though it may be, in
determining what karma we will create in the present. Hence, I do not
want to give the impression, by speaking of "fate," "destiny," and similar
terms, that there is nothing we can do *or be* in response to our karma
that will change our lives in a positive way. On the contrary, although
the birth-chart shows the karma and hence the restrictions that bind us
and prevent our feeling free, the chart is also a tool that enables us to
see clearly in what areas of life we need to work toward transmuting
our current mode of expression. As Edgar Cayce says repeatedly in his
readings, "Mind is the builder." We become what our mind dwells
upon. If therefore we can subtly alter our attitudes and modes of
thought, if we can attune our consciousness to some higher frequency
by meditation, by not only *having* but also by *living* an ideal, then we
can begin to be liberated from bondage and to breathe freely with the
rhythm of life.

Indeed, as one of the twentieth century's greatest astrologers, Dane
Rudhyar, has emphasized in his extensive writings, events don't happen
to people in nearly as important a way as *people happen to events*.
These four words sum up the possibilities of our spiritual-psychological
development as we meet our karma, whether pleasant or distressing. In
other words, our attitude toward experience is the crucial factor. Our
attitude alone will determine whether, in meeting difficult experiences,
we will suffer (and curse our "fate") or whether we will grow by
learning the lessons that life is teaching us.

The chart therefore shows our mind patterns, our past conditioning,
the mental impressions and patterns referred to by Meher Baba as
sanskaras. The chart shows what we are now *because* of what we have
thought and done in the past. These age-old, deeply-entrenched
patterns are not easily changed. Let this be said without qualification! It
is not a simple matter to change powerful habit patterns merely
through the application of a bit of old-fashioned "will power." Neither
do these patterns essentially change by glossing them over with the
faddish jargon of some of the "New Age" psychotherapies or
philosophies that inflate the ego by encouraging people to assert: "I'm

taking charge of my life; I make everything happen; I now know that I'm making myself suffer; etc." Human spiritual evolution is much subtler than that. The old "where there's a will, there's a way" approach to dealing with one's problems collapses when the challenge is too intense. And the attempt to rationalize one's conflicts and spiritual crises out of existence will only dam the flow of the life energies for a short while, quickly followed by a torrential release of power that starkly reveals the shallowness of pseudo-spiritual escapism. The karmic patterns are real and powerful. Those habits are not going to fade away overnight following a short positive-thinking pep-talk. These life forces must be accepted, acknowledged, and paid due attention.

Self-knowledge and self-realization is a necessary prelude to God-realization; but—in the early stages—a student of spiritual truths or a student of higher forms of astrology often becomes discouraged when his or her new insights into the self reveal so many negative traits, emotions, and habit patterns. It is at this point in the individual's development that great care must be exercised both by that person and by any person—astrologer or otherwise—who attempts to counsel or guide the student. It should be explained that, just as opening a door a small crack and allowing a beam of light into a dark room reveals all kinds of dust in the air and perhaps other dirt that was not previously apparent in the room, so when the first steps toward self-knowledge are taken, whether utilizing the beam of light known as astrology or another illuminating method, the student very often quickly develops a negative attitude toward his or her self, destiny, birth-chart, etc. It should be further explained that, as the intensity of light increases, the student will become even more immediately aware of his or her faults, weaknesses, or negative qualities, but that such awareness is to be welcomed as an indication of greater self-knowledge and definite developmental progress. The student should be encouraged to use such insight as a prod toward taking definite constructive action in the positive transformation of the individual life, rather than as a reason or excuse for fear or anxiety. Further, it can be pointed out to the student that, as the level of self-knowledge increases, the person's karma often begins to manifest on a subtler level since he or she is now open to learning what must be learnt about the self, and hence, there is no longer the need for shocks or dramatic events to awaken the individual from the slumber of spiritual lethargy. As Jung points out,

> The psychological rule says that when an inner situation is not made conscious, it happens outside, as fate. That is to say, when the individual...does not become conscious of his inner contradictions, the world must perforce act out the conflict and be torn into opposite halves. (Aion, p. 71)

Hence, it seems safe to say that a commitment to self-development and self-knowledge not only holds out the promise of aiding the individual to be a more whole, happy, and illuminated soul in the future, but also that such a step often begins to alleviate a great deal of suffering in the present, once the initial confusion and discouragement is overcome.

We can thus see that we all have certain karmic influences that we must meet: we all must reap the fruits of what we have sown. Astrology, by providing us with a blueprint of our attachments, problems, talents, and mental tendencies, offers us a way—an initial step—of not only realizing in a specific sense exactly what our karma is and helping us to work with these confrontations within and without, but also a way of beginning to rise above and gain a perspective on this karma. The idea that the individual birth-chart reflects what we have done in the past is confirmed in Edgar Cayce's psychic reading #5124-L-1:

> For, as given from the beginning: the planets, the stars are given for signs and for seasons and for years; that many may indeed find their closer relationship in the contemplation of the universe. For man has been made a co-creator with the Godhead. Not that man is good or bad according to the position of the stars; but *the position of the stars indicate what the individual entity has done about God's plan in earth activities*, during the periods when man has been given the opportunity to enter into material manifestations.

The birth-chart shows, therefore, the past *creative use* or the *misuse* of our powers. If we accept the idea of the power of the individual's mind and will, then we must also accept the idea that we are responsible for our fate, destiny, and problems as shown in the natal chart. In an important sense, we could then even say that the birth-chart shows nothing but karma. Everything in the chart can then be assumed to stem directly from our past actions, achievements, and desires. Although Saturn alone has been called the "planet of karma" in many writings, this is an oversimplification. Indeed, astrology could legitimately be called a "science of karma"—that is, a way of realizing and accepting one's responsibilities in a precise way.

Specific Chart Factors

In the interpretation of charts, almost any factor can be regarded as karmic or as having karmic implications. However, there are some specific astrological factors that we should pay special attention to in this kind of investigation. Many of these are dealt with later in this book in much more detail, but a brief outline of specific things to focus on should be mentioned here.

Saturn

Saturn, often called the "Lord of Karma," is said by many astrologers to represent the major karmic problem in any individual's life. The planet Saturn has come to be called the "Lord of Karma" not because it is the only element in the chart which symbolizes an aspect of personal karma, but because the position and aspects of Saturn reveal where we meet our most specific and concentrated tests, as well as where we often experience pain and frustration. And, since the popular conception of karma is that all karma is negative and troublesome, Saturn's testing is viewed by many as identical with the action of "karma." This is of course a gross oversimplification, as well as a misinterpretation of what karma really is. It may be more accurate to say that Saturn in the natal chart (especially according to its house position and conjunction, square, and opposition aspects) shows where our "difficult" karma comes into its most specific focus. These challenging aspects of Saturn show crystallized habit patterns of thought and action which inhibit the flow of our creative energy. Such an aspect can reveal the past misuse of a talent or power which we now must discipline and redirect into constructive channels. It is in this area that a radical *adjustment* in our approach and attitude is necessary. Such an aspect (and this could apply to a lesser extent to the quincunx, semi-square, and semi-sextile aspects as well) generates great energy from its inner tension; and we can use this energy to develop greater awareness and creativity. Saturn is the planet of form and structure, and we often find that the planet in close aspect to Saturn needs to be given a new *form* of expression. (See Chapter 5 for more on Saturn.)

Saturn, however, is not the only indication in the natal chart of obstacles that we have to deal with. Almost any over-emphasis, vital lack, or particularly stressful configuration—no matter which planets are involved—can point to an important need for growth and development. The primary thing to realize is that life is *purposeful*, that we have to encounter these various difficulties for a positive reason. As the medium Arthur Ford says:

> The greater the obstacles in the physical body, the more opportunity for a soul to pay off karmic debts and achieve more rapid spiritual growth. The hurdles are stepping-stones if successfully surmounted, and the soul who in flesh body cheerfully meets and overcomes physical handicaps is growing more rapidly than another who seems by earthly standards to have everything to live for. The reward is not in the physical form but in spiritual development, and the more hurdles that are overcome in a physical lifetime, the less often that soul will thereafter need to return to physical form to round off the rough spots in his character. (from *A World Beyond* by Ruth Montgomery, p. 46)

Aspects & Elements

The topic of aspects will be dealt with in detail in Chapter 6, but here we can briefly mention some important points. In interpreting the birth chart karmically, all square (90°) and opposition (180°) aspects show the necessity of coming to terms with our own complexity, with somehow developing that awareness necessary to encompass markedly different approaches to life.* The forces indicated in the square aspect are at cross-purposes and interfere with each other's expression. These forces therefore need to be harmonized within the individual, a process which usually takes years as the person slowly develops new

---

*It seems to me a reasonable hypothesis that, at least in many cases, these "markedly different approaches to life" grow from the individual's having had markedly different sorts of experiences in various past lives. For example, if one were trained as a male warrior throughout one lifetime, and then as a traditional housewife and mother in another lifetime, that soul may be born into this life with, for example, a square aspect between Aries and Cancer planets, indicating the inner tension the person feels even now from such markedly different life-orientations and modes of self-expression.

behavior patterns and greater self-understanding. The forces involved in the opposition aspect reveal opposite, and yet complementary, pulls toward expression that the individual feels most immediately in relating to others. A need to harmonize these polarities is therefore also indicated in these aspects, but the opposition specifically emphasizes the need to develop more awareness of not only one's self but also of other people's desires, expectations, and points of view. The harmonization mentioned above can only occur through the development of a higher awareness of the forces and urges involved. The eminent psychologist C.G. Jung, in his studies of alchemy, often quotes the ancient alchemist dictum: *tertium non datur*, which means that the third factor (which alone can resolve the problem of opposites and personal conflicts) is not given. Jung goes on to explain that a conflict is never resolved on the same level where it arises, but can be resolved only on a higher level, based on a higher perspective and level of consciousness. Hence, the square and opposition aspects show the areas of greatest tension within ourselves but also—a fact which should be welcomed eagerly—the areas of greatest potential growth.

Another factor related to stressful aspects which I have come to pay great attention to is the element, or elements, wherein one finds the most highly stressed planets. Since the stressful aspects can be considered to indicate areas in which we must learn to refine our nature, to make adjustments, and to build new approaches, it follows that any planet (especially any "personal" planet) involved in such aspects should be viewed not only according to its *own* nature and fundamental principle but also according to the element of the sign wherein it is placed. Since, as I have shown in great detail in *Astrology, Psychology, and the Four Elements*, the four elements reveal the actual levels of energy and dimensions of life that the individual can immediately experience, then the element of any sign that contains one or more of these highly-charged, powerfully-stressed planets is inevitably a dimension of life where there is a need for adjustment and refinement. The element where we find such planets shows what kinds of *attachments* and *desires* are strongest for us, what one of the major purposes of this lifetime is, and what areas of life continue to cause us problems and are thus in need of transformation. If a person has a close conjunction or stellium in a particular sign, all parts of which configuration are in a stressful aspect to another planet or planets, then the element of that sign is invariably indicative of the dimension of life the person has to work at in some way, either to express that energy more harmoniously and positively or simply to refine the intensity and grossness of attachment in that area.

Some examples may help to clarify this last point. If the stressed planet (or planets) is in a water sign, there is a need to refine one's emotions and one's mode of emotional expression. A person with such a planetary placement may in this lifetime be expressing his or her emotions in too gross or too compulsive a manner. Some kind of emotional discipline (this is not to say repression!) may be needed to provide the inner pressure necessary to effect a refining transmutation of this energy. The person's instinctive reactions may be either too repressed *or* too uncontrollably dominating; hence, he must learn both to channel his emotional power constructively and to protect himself from outside negative influences without closing off to all of the water of life. The person can also be too attached to emotional satisfaction, putting this before all else.

If the stressed planet or configuration is in a fire sign, it may be necessary to control one's impulsiveness and egocentric behavior, and to develop love, sensitivity, and patience. A refined, disciplined use of the abundant fiery energy is far more effective and creative than mere frustrated gestures of defiance or self-aggrandizement. The person may have to learn how to live in the present and to develop the humility that grows from submitting oneself to a higher will or divine power. Other lessons that may be indicated by a stress on the fire signs are: how to be receptive, how to admit one's weaknesses and deeper needs, and how to ask for help when one is suffering. Fiery people are often too proud to admit that they too have needs; and this tendency, along with excessive attachment to gross *action* as the only way to deal with life, often inhibits their developing an immediate awareness of their inner life.

If the stressed planet or configuration is in an air sign, the individual may need to discipline the thought processes, not only *how* he thinks, but also the manner in which the thoughts are expressed to others. Fantasies, intellectual escapism, unnecessary projections into the future, unrealistic schemes, and the habit of rationalization may have served their purpose by now; and so the person may be faced with the need to restructure this entire area of life and to learn that the intellect is a good servant if properly disciplined but a very poor master. There may be too much attachment to intellectual knowledge, clever ideas, "scientific" proofs, and orderly concepts. This individual should take to heart the fact that a learned person who does not *act* on his knowledge and make it real through immediate experience is no better than a mule with a load of books on his back. The so-called knowledge can become merely a burden, and the person's intellect can turn into a devouring monster whose greed for more and more "knowledge" knows no bounds.

If the stressed planet (or planets) is in an earth sign, there may be too much attachment to the physical senses, worldly values, physical comfort, reputation, possessions, and worldly "wisdom." The person will undoubtedly have to deal with the question of what will really and permanently provide the deep security he or she longs for. The awareness of immediate survival needs (money, food, shelter, etc.) can take such precedence over deeper or more inspiring activities that the person tries to compensate for the lack of joy and enthusiasm in life by working even harder at the endless task of building security, a security which—needless to say—can be destroyed at any moment. A person with this earth emphasis may be so enamored of living and thinking in a "practical" way that he or she never allows a more transcendent or inspiring thought or activity any place in the personal lifestyle.

As one spiritual teacher says, "karma *is* attachment." The birth-chart, therefore, and especially the highly-accentuated components of the chart, shows our attunements—and hence, our attachments, and hence, our karma. Viewing the chart and one's life in this way puts everything in a new light. The arbitrary, judgmental, and false distinctions between "positive" and "negative" features of a birth-chart begin to melt away. There are no longer any "good" or "bad" charts, aspects, or human beings. We are all part of the vast cosmic drama, and—on this material plane—we are all entangled in our own karmic nets. Once this is perceived, the question is: what does one do to *detach* oneself from these karmic involvements and limiting patterns of being? The consensus that I have been able to discern from the teachings of many spiritual masters is that no amount of *wanting, willing,* or *hoping* to become detached or "enlightened" accomplishes very much. One can become detached from one's old habit patterns only by becoming *attached* to something better. For example, if a beggar has only three pennies and he suddenly drops them, he will hurry after them to protect what little he has. However, if, at the moment the beggar dropped his pennies, he saw a $5 bill blowing down the street, he would immediately ignore his pennies and chase after the bill. Hence, we can see that it is not enough merely to become sick of our old self, our old ways of being, and our life-long conflicts. Since the habit patterns of the past exert a strong and constant pull upon us, and since we feel insecure if we stray too far from those habit patterns, we must find something very powerful to become attached to if it is to pull us away from the karmic tendencies. The only thing that is sufficiently powerful and unlimited to effect this detachment is a spiritual force of some type. I leave it to the reader to find the method of attuning to this higher power which is appropriate for his or her state of development. But, whatever the path chosen, the Biblical axiom provides us with sustaining faith: "Seek and ye shall find; Knock and it shall be opened."

"Karmic" Signs

It is unnecessary to discuss here the various characteristics of all twelve signs that may be related to karma and transformation. There are many books of high quality which elucidate what lessons have to be learned and what new attitudes developed for each of the signs.* But I do want to mention here some aspects of three of the signs: Virgo, Pisces, and Scorpio. Of all twelve signs, these three are most *obviously* concerned with crises that can clearly be related to karma. It often seems that Virgo and Pisces people (i.e., those with these signs highly emphasized in their charts, not just people with the Sun in these signs) have to bear far more than their share of burdens, both physical

---

*Cf. Especially *The Pulse of Life & Triptych* by Dane Rudhyar; *From Pioneer to Poet* by Isabel Pagan; and *Wisdom in the Stars* by Joan Hodgson, all of which are excellent and penetrating analyses of the deeper meanings of the signs.

drudgery and duties (Virgo) and emotional turmoil and confusion (Pisces). This is because these signs represent crucial stages in self-development, phases of evolution and growth in which the person must confront the fruits of his or her actions and attitudes. (Note that Pisces, the twelfth sign, marks the end of an entire cycle of life, and that Virgo is the sign of the *harvest!*) Both signs symbolize a process of purification as a preparation for further development. Virgo deals with purification of the ego and of the personal motives behind overt behavior, and Pisces is related to the purification of the emotions and mental images that have accumulated over the centuries. The sign Scorpio can be specifically related to karma because it is during this phase of development that one must honestly face his or her true desires and come to realize the power inherent in them. This is why so many people with a strong Scorpio emphasis have such a strong attraction to mysteries, the occult, "forbidden" areas of experience, and revelations about afterlife. These people are in touch with the most powerfully negative aspects of their being, and their well-known suspicion and lack of trust in others comes from the fact that, since they know how untrustworthy their own emotions and how ruthless their own motivations can be, they naturally assume that other people are similarly motivated. Scorpio is the sign of death and rebirth, and anyone with a major emphasis on Scorpio in the natal chart is torn between clinging to old, compulsive desires purely out of habit and the deeper desire of the innermost self to be reborn.

The "Water" Houses

The so-called "water" houses (Houses IV, VIII, & XII) have been called the "trinity of soul" or the "psychic trinity" and together they constitute another major factor relating to personal karma.* Although the twelfth house alone has been called the house of "karmic liabilities" in traditional astrology, *all* karma is a liability which binds us to the material plane and to a limited level of consciousness. And all the water houses deal with the past, with conditioned-responses which are now *instinctual* and which operate through the emotions, and hence—with karma. At one level, these houses deal with the deepest *yearnings* of the soul, yearnings which by their very nature are at least partly unconscious. The cycle of the water houses shows the process of gaining consciousness through *assimilating* the essence of the past and letting go of the residue which has outlived its usefulness. The emotional waste and exhausted emotional behavior patterns must be purged before the soul can express itself clearly. People with an emphasis on the water houses live within themselves and are extremely hard to get to know (especially if the Sun, the symbol of the individual *self,* is in one of these houses). So much of their life energy operates at a subliminal level; so much of their motivation is influenced by irrational, unexplainable, and often bewildering nuances. Their sensitivities are

---

*Cf. the author's *Astrology, Psychology, and the Four Elements,* Chapter 16, "The Elements & the Houses," for more specific information on each of the water houses.

unpredictable, since one never knows what will activate an old memory, irritate an old sore spot, or energize a troublesome complex. All of these houses, therefore, correlate with the need to attain emotional peace and freedom from the past, and anyone with major emphasis on these houses in the natal chart has a need to bring to the surface the hauntings and fears generated by past experiences and to let these feelings be illuminated in full consciousness.

Richard Ideman, an astrologer who has pioneered in reformulating astrological concepts in relation to psychological terminology, states that the water houses can be indicative of various types of fear: fear of returning to the helpless childhood state (IV), of social taboos (VIII), and of chaos (XII). Where do these fears come from? Obviously, from the past, whether from past conditioning and training of a specific type or from specific kinds of traumatic experiences or shocks. Planets falling in the water houses therefore represent urges toward expression which are colored by karmic patterns, emotional prejudices, or unconscious motivations and fears. They often show the ghosts of the past which still haunt a person, and the fact that they are at least to some degree unconscious explains why these energy complexes so often tend to undermine the conscious orientation to life. These forces, these urges and energies are, so to speak, waiting to be reborn through our conscious effort; and they will not leave us in peace until we face them honestly and liberate that energy through courageous action.

The planets in water houses show what is happening on subtle or subconscious levels; they show sources of in-depth experience in the present lifetime which—although stemming from the distant past—are still alive and constitute a major concentration of life energy. As long as we remain unaware of these aspects of our nature, the energy and psychic functions represented by water house planets are unavailable for *conscious* direction and creative utilization. When these parts of ourselves are made conscious, however, they can come alive with great force. The fact that water house planets often reveal factors in our lives that transcend, overwhelm, or undermine our conscious orientation is to be welcomed, for the ego-consciousness often becomes stuck in limited patterns of expression and therefore needs a periodic confrontation with the deeper sources of life within us. Such an experience can be refreshing; for the "self-undoing," chaos, self-loss, or utter dissolution of the conscious ego-personality experienced by a person with major emphasis on the water houses can open the person to spiritual insight and illumination. A strong emphasis on the water houses may show that these factors in the individual's life are struggling for *recognition*, that is, for acceptance into the light of consciousness. (Notice that the word "recognition" means *to know again*, referring to a past knowledge of the factor indicated, which is at present "forgotten" or unconscious.) The negative emotional effects of stressfully aspected planets in these houses can often be ameliorated by consciously recognizing and attending to the life forces so symbolized, just as the ancients worshipped each of the planets as a deity (i.e., a universal power or law), knowing that the gods' *nemesis* would surely follow if a person arrogantly ignored the demands of stronger forces.

To outline the specific meanings of the water houses, we might summarize as follows. The fourth house reveals the conditioning which links us to this life's family, home, sense of privacy and domestic tranquility, and other related security factors. It is associated with the assimilation of our experience in youth and with the understanding of specific karmic ties with the parents or with other individuals who had a strong impact on our upbringing. The fourth house further represents a yearning for a peaceful environment wherein the individual person may feel protected and nurtured; and those who have emphasis on this house not only tend to feel the need for such an environment themselves, but they also tend toward protective and nurturing behavior toward others. (Note, however, that certain planets in the fourth house—especially Uranus and Mars—diminish the chances that the person will express *tranquility* in this area of life!) The peace for which these people yearn is often sought in a very private lifestyle and/or through detaching themselves from the emotional turbulence of parental relationships either through physical distance or through more subtly coming to terms with their feelings about their parents on an inner level.

The eighth house likewise reveals a strong need for privacy, and the person is usually rather difficult to get acquainted with on an intimate level. However, in contrast to the fourth house type of person, this individual is not satisfied *merely* to have privacy because he also wants *power*. This kind of person is strongly motivated to exert some kind of powerful influence in the world while simultaneously maintaining considerable secrecy; and this motivation is usually of a compelling sort, driving the person to exert himself toward various goals to which he is karmically attached. The eighth house shows past conditioning from previous lives of which we are at times aware, but which still operates instinctively and which derives great emotional power from deeper than conscious sources. Planets in the eighth house show emotional-compulsive tendencies which we try to control and usually keep secret, but which nevertheless exert a formidable power in our lives. It is difficult to *eliminate* these urges through will-power alone, as many people with Pluto, Scorpio, or eighth house emphasis try to do; but these urges can be transformed or regenerated and refined through a commitment to self-reform coupled with intensity of immediate experience. Repression or self-control alone is never sufficient to deal with life-factors shown by eighth house planets. One must give oneself to involvement with others and must learn to take risks now and then in order to allow the energy to flow freely and the deepest feelings and drives to come to the surface. The eighth house can therefore be related to the assimilation of many lifetimes' experiences with sexuality, the values attached to intimate human relationships, and the responsibilities involved in using any kind of power that has an impact on others. The eighth house represents a yearning for the deep emotional peace which will help the person to relieve some of the pressure that compulsive emotions and instincts have exerted for so long. Naturally, this peace and contentment is connected with the soul's longing for ultimate security and tranquility (salvation!), which can be achieved only by becoming free from desires and compulsive willfulness. But relatively few people with an eighth house emphasis realize the true nature of their deeper longings. Instead they often look for ways of establishing emotional peace by trying to *satisfy* the emotions (with money, sex, worldly power, "occult knowledge", etc.) rather than by working at *outgrowing* the powerful grip that their emotions have upon them and thus experiencing emotional peace as a natural by-product of a commitment to self-reform along the lines of spiritual evolution.

The twelfth house, by contrast, reveals influences that are totally and *obviously* beyond our control. It is often clear to the person that he or she will not be able to satisfy the inner longings through any ordinary activity, although this clarity may take years of suffering to develop. The yearning for emotional peace found in the eighth house is still present, but here it is intermixed with an awareness of the need for *ultimate* peace for the soul. Planets in the natal twelfth house symbolize forces which often overwhelm us and which can be dealt with effectively only by redirecting that energy to an ideal that inspires us *inwardly* toward greater self-knowledge and devotion to the Oneness of all things and *outwardly* toward greater generosity of spirit and service. This house deals with the process of assimilating a vast array of experience in all dimensions of life, particularly in our handling of responsibilities toward all other living beings. Through some sort of devotion, spiritual practice, or selfless service, one begins to gain freedom from the results of past actions and their accompanying mental impressions. The contact with a vast panorama of past life experience can also enable the person to express unlimited imagination in the creative arts as well as simply understanding and empathizing with the pains and joys of all living creatures. Both the eighth and the twelfth houses are related to occult and metaphysical studies and practices, suffering at a deep level as a prelude to some sort of rebirth, and an immediate awareness of the realities of psychic and spiritual dimensions of life. The primary difference between the eighth and twelfth houses is that, whereas eighth house planets have to be confronted immediately and worked *through*, twelfth house planets can often be *transcended*. In the first case, one brings to the surface the old tendencies in order to transform them through immediate and intensive involvement, whereas in the latter case, one rises above the problems entirely.

One can deduce from the above comments that planets in the water houses have a powerful impact at subtle levels of being. Their influence is therefore not always obvious and easy to interpret. In my experience, the 4th, 8th, and 12th are the most difficult houses to interpret in a natal chart, for one never knows at what level these energies are manifesting. For example, Saturn in *any* of the water houses can indicate a rigidity at deep levels, a subconscious resistance to emotional expression. In some cases, there is a marked fearfulness, a withdrawn nature, or strong feelings of guilt, obligation, or generalized emotional heaviness that pervade the individual's consciousness. But sometimes these same people have a great depth of understanding of occult or unconscious forces; for example, Sigmund Freud, the astrologer Vivian Robson, and the theosophist Annie Bessant all have Saturn in the twelfth house.

A few other brief examples of planets in water houses should serve to give a more complete impression of what I have been referring to. With the Moon in these houses, the person's sense of inner security or emotional support may be vague or unconscious. Hence, a sense of *order* is often greatly needed to bolster the person's sense of security; and this is perhaps why so many astrologers have the Moon in these houses. They seem to find the support and sense of order they need in such studies. With Mercury in the water houses, intuition rather than a strict logic is the keynote of the mind's mode of operation. Perception and communication is often muddled, but—at other times—extremely subtle and incisive. The mind naturally tends toward deep thinking, and—although obsessive ways of thinking can be present—there is also often a talent for occult, psychic, or spiritual studies or writing. With Mars in these houses, the person is often driven by forces beyond his control, and his strongest aims may not have an easily definable character or goal. The person may be driven to the point of obsession, like Vincent Van Gogh, who had Mars in the twelfth house, or he may channel his passions toward energetically fighting for those in trouble or against his own negative tendencies. This latter approach may lead him to be too harsh with himself, but there is no denying that Mars in the water houses can be an effective stimulus toward self-development.

Venus in the water houses generally shows that the person can't find emotional satisfaction in any ordinary superficial activity or relationship, a fact which is much bemoaned by some astrological writers. However, this very fact may lead the person to explore his inner life more fruitfully or to begin to direct his energies toward spiritual goals as a means of achieving emotional satisfaction. This person needs time alone in order to explore the inner world. With Jupiter in these houses, the religious needs can be satisfied only by tuning in on deeper life forces. There is often an inner generosity of spirit, which sustains the person through hard times and provides inspiration when everything on the surface of life looks bleak. Having any of the trans-Saturnian planets in the water houses frequently indicates a marked psychic sensitivity and/or distinctly active unconscious forces.

In short, planets in the water houses reveal that which cannot be found—or easily experienced in a satisfying way—on the surface of life, but can only be fulfilled in the depths of inner realization. *Any planet falling in any water house can thus be interpreted as an aspect of the person's nature, as a dimension of life experience, which the person can fulfill only by searching within himself.* The individual must become a seeker, an explorer of the inner realms of being, before he gains sufficient understanding of the inner life to enable him to satisfy the yearning he feels. Hence, planets falling in these houses are indicative of aspects of being which are most problematical when the person is spiritually immature, when he has not yet taken definite steps to know and to face his inner nature and motivations. Once he or she has perceived the subtler purpose behind these yearnings and the ultimate reason for this temporary frustration and longing, the individual is well on the way to experiencing the necessary transformation of consciousness.

The Moon

In the present lifetime, the personality is built upon the foundations of the past. Just as the fourth house is at the very bottom of the natal chart, thus constituting the foundation upon which we build our entire operational personality, so the Moon—which traditionally "rules" Cancer and the fourth house which partakes of the identical principle—represents our root feelings about ourselves. The Moon principle is similar to what many psychologists call the "self-image," although the sense of self represented by the Moon is not so much a conscious, visual image as a subliminal, usually rather vague intimation of what we really are. Astrologers have traditionally associated the Moon with the past, whether it is merely the past during this lifetime, and related to early childhood conditioning and to the relationship with the parents (especially the mother), or whether it is correlated with a broader understanding of the past in the context of reincarnation theory. It has been stated in many astrological writings that, whereas the Moon shows the past, the Sun shows the present orientation, and the Ascendant points toward future development. There is no doubt sound reasoning behind these parallels, and—on an abstract level—they are probably quite accurate in most cases. However, everything comes together in the *present*; what we have *been* continues to influence our orientations, attitudes, and actions in the *now*. How we feel about ourselves and what patterns of expression come most naturally and feel most comfortable to us (the Moon) all have a great impact on our *present* mode of living.

Just as the Moon in our solar system reflects the solar light to the Earth and thus focuses the life force toward practical objectives (symbolized by the Earth), so the Moon in astrology represents a general *reflection* of what we have been in the past. *It is an image of assimilated past experience and behavior patterns* with which we now feel comfortable because they are familiar and because we have—in fact—exemplified those qualities in our very being. In other words, the Moon symbolizes—especially according to its sign position—specific mental and emotional karmic patterns which either inhibit or help us in our attempts at self-expression and adjustment to the outer world. If the aspects with the Moon are harmonious, they reveal past conditioning and patterns of spontaneous reaction that can help the person to adjust to life and to society, and to express his or her self. If the Moon aspects are stressful, thus symbolizing an inability to adjust oneself easily to life and/or a negative self-image, these emotional predispositions must be outgrown. It is important to note that the

Moon symbolizes such *spontaneous* reaction and behavior patterns that these orientations are primarily evident in childhood, when one's behavior is rather pure and uninhibited. Hence, the lunar sign and aspects are most immediately effective in the early part of one's life. As one gets older, it is possible to outgrow some of the old emotional patterns, even to the extent that the emotional *blockages* shown in the chart through lunar aspects may no longer have any important meaning. I am not saying that the Moon sign ceases to be important, for that will *always* symbolize a dominant tone in the person's fundamental way of being. But I am emphasizing that the *problems* and *conflicts* associated with Moon aspects and with the expression of the qualities thereby symbolized may be almost totally outgrown, or at least adjusted to in a healthful manner.

Since the Moon is such a complex symbol and since its meanings are so many and diverse, the most appropriate way of explaining them further is to present a schematic outline:

a) The Moon symbolizes the image of oneself that a person sees reflected in his or her dealings with the *public*. Hence, a stressfully aspected Moon can show an inability to *project* oneself harmoniously in order that other people respond in a positive manner. A harmoniously-aspected Moon often shows that one can express oneself harmoniously in dealing with the public and that one has a good sense of what the public likes. (In other words, as one intuitively responds to others *accurately*, they in turn respond in a positive way.) Harmonious aspects with the Moon therefore show areas in which we can project ourselves easily in order to get good feedback.

b) A stressfully aspected Moon often shows a markedly *inaccurate* self-image, for how the person feels about self based on past patterns and past identity may not be an accurate description of the person's true nature in the present. This inaccuracy of self-image is often reflected in such behavior as: taking things the wrong way, being oversensitive, over-reacting to trifles, dressing in a way that doesn't suit the inner nature and true personality, and being too defensive.

c) The house position of the natal Moon shows the area of life activity where we need to get feedback, where we can come to see ourselves more objectively, and where we can tune into a sense of self that can provide us with inner tranquility.

d) The Moon's sign shows how we defend ourselves instinctively. For example, Moon in fire reacts with anger; Moon in air with rationalization, argument or discussion; Moon in water with retreat or emotional outpourings; Moon in earth with endurance.

e) The Moon's sign also symbolizes a mode of expression that comes naturally and a mode of behavior wherein we feel secure; for the Moon sign shows an old pattern of life which is usually fairly comfortable (unless the aspects are too stressful). A few examples: Moon in Capricorn finds security in age, in acting old, in cultivating aged behavior. Moon in Taurus can find security in acting like an earthy peasant. Moon in Leo finds security in dramatic displays or at least in being *recognized*.

f) Since the Moon represents a strong urge to express a mode of being that is a natural and intimate part of oneself, the Moon's sign also shows what you need to express in order to feel *good about yourself*! As Grant Lewi put it, the Moon shows the "heart's desire." The aspects with the Moon simply show how *easily* one can express this mode of being and how easily one can attain this feeling of well-being.

g) The Moon sign symbolizes the practical application of the solar energy and purpose. This is the reason why a Sun-Moon trine, sextile, or—to some extent—conjunction (as well as simply having the Sun and Moon in compatible elements) is such a stabilizing and potentially creative aspect; for in these cases, the solar energy can easily be expressed in a practical way.

From all of the above, it should be clear how important the Moon's sign, house, and aspects are in any consideration of karmic revelations in the chart. There is probably no other factor in the natal chart that can be so immediately related to past experiences and past habit patterns. We should be careful not to oversimplify the association of the Moon with past lives to the point of making statements like: "Well, you have the Moon in Leo, so you must have been an actor in a past life." Such interpretations may be occasionally valid, but they usually have no constructive purpose and may give the client the impression that the astrologer is simply trying to make an impression with sensationalistic statements, a deduction which may be quite accurate. The important thing to dwell on is the need which the Moon symbolizes in *this* lifetime, and the most constructive approach to interpreting charts from the karmic viewpoint is to elucidate the deeper motivations and pressures which the person may feel but which he has no way of identifying or putting in a broader perspective.

In concluding this chapter, we can say that each of us has the opportunity to harmonize within ourselves the diverse manifestations of the universe; and we have the opportunity to accept all other human beings, even those with whom we strike a discordant note on the personality level. Can we live without demanding that all experiences and all human beings harmonize with our attunement? Can we evolve a mature, detached consciousness that enables us to watch ourselves play our allotted role in the cosmic drama? Can we laugh at our complexity, our conflicts, and our inconsistencies? Most importantly, can we have faith that the universe is harmonious and that it is only our narrow vision that sees discord? The answers to these questions will determine to a great extent how we face our karma in this life and what sort of karma we are creating now.

Taurus

2

Transformation

No astrologer—and as well no psychoanalyst—can interpret a life and destiny at a level higher than that at which he
himself functions.
— Dane Rudhyar

There have been periods in history when students of astrology, other
"occult" sciences, and various spiritual paths have been persecuted,
exiled, tortured, and otherwise harassed. During these periods, it
became necessary for such students to develop a secret language, code,
or set of symbols with which they could communicate to each other
without outsiders knowing what was being conveyed. During these
historical epochs, the "occult"—or *hidden*—language served the
practical purpose of insuring the safety of those individuals who were
initiated into such teachings. In the America of the late twentieth
century, however, conditions have—at least for a time and in most
places—changed dramatically. There is still an occasional harassment of
an individual who practices astrology, spiritual healing, or whatever,
but—by and large—the freedom to explore various methods of
personal growth that citizens in a democracy are supposed to enjoy is
becoming more of a reality. In fact, great masses of people have
exhibited a growing interest in all forms of occult, spiritual, and psychic
subjects, as exemplified by the sale of books, attendance at classes and
lectures, and emphasis in the mass media on these topics. Perhaps once
the fad of popular interest passes, we will once more be left with only
the small numbers of serious devotees and dedicated students that can
be found during any age. We should of course not be misled by
numbers alone, thus mistaking quantity for quality of interest.

Regardless of what the future brings in the astrological field, I feel
that two things are certain. First, many serious students of astrology are
yearning for—and are responding to those who are developing—a
new, modernized astrological language. Secondly, many people who
are curious about astrology are quickly turned off to it after reading a
few traditional books or attending a few classes on the subject; and
many of them would probably pursue this interest if astrology were
presented in a modern and constructive way that made it more
accessible to positive-thinking and practical people. Since astrology
today is so often presented in an archaic way based too much on belief
and not enough on real knowledge and understanding, a student must
be pulled toward astrology with great force and must feel an
overwhelming fascination with it to enable him or her to sustain a long-

term interest and involvement. Today it is no longer necessary to keep astrology "esoteric" or "mysterious," although we can still deal with the "esoteric" aspects of astrology in a direct, experiential way, as I am trying to do in this book. The subject in itself has the capacity to instill one with a great sense of awe for the mysteries of the universe. We don't have to add to this mystery. So often, I feel that the effort to keep astrology mysterious is just a game of the ego, as if the person is saying: "Look how smart and insightful I am, since I can figure out all these cosmic mysteries!" In other cases, it is clear that the astrologer or would-be astrologer makes things seem mysterious or unclear simply because of his or her lack of understanding. The more one truly understands through immediate experience (rather than through mere theoretical deduction), the more simple and practical one's expression of that understanding can become. As Einstein said, if you really understand something, you should be able to explain it to a small child. And, as I stated in the Introduction, what is currently needed not only in the field of astrology but also in our entire world-view are simplifying, synthesizing principles. In other words, why should we go on playing egocentric guessing games in astrology when we can deal directly and immediately with the archetypal, structural principles of life itself?

What simplifying, synthesizing ideas about astrology can we begin with? First of all, we should agree that all of astrology—when applied to individuals' lives—deals with transformation. In other words, it is a way of clearly perceiving and gaining a perspective upon the constant changes, cycles, growth and decay periods that characterize all of nature. We should also agree that astrology offers us an *experiential* language, i.e., a language which is most useful if used to describe an individual's inner *experience* of life and its incessant changes.*
Astrology does not *necessarily* symbolize the outer situation or events in a person's life, although it may do so in many instances. But much more often, it will symbolize the inner experience and how that experience fits into the total life pattern. For example, suppose someone "fell in love" as Saturn was transiting in a square aspect to the natal Sun. Very few astrologers would be able to correctly deduce from that configuration alone that the person had in fact begun a new "love" relationship. But any astrologer familiar with the deeper significance of the transits of Saturn would be able to describe to some extent the *meaning* of that experience, how the person would *feel* during it, and the approximate duration of the most intense phase of that relationship. This example shows the need for feedback in astrological work with clients and why a consultation in the form of a counseling *dialogue* is much more specifically accurate and useful than a one-sided "reading."

I stated in the previous paragraph that all of astrology—when applied to the lives of individual persons—deals with transformation. Perhaps it would be useful to be more precise in a schematic form. Astrology, based

---

*Cf. page 79 of *Astrology, Psychology, & the Four Elements*, where I have defined the basic astrological factors in terms of *experience*: the planets as *dimensions of experience;* the signs as *qualities of experience;* and the houses as various *fields of experience.*

upon the planetary configuration being considered, deals with these kinds of personal transformation:

SUN: Transformation of the identity and mode of creative energy expression.

MOON: Transformation of one's feelings about oneself and how comfortable one is with oneself.

MERCURY: Transformation of one's mode of thinking & perception, and of the way in which one expresses one's intelligence.

VENUS: Transformation of one's emotional values and mode of expressing and understanding one's needs for closeness.

MARS: Transformation of the capacity to assert one's will and to know what one really wants.

JUPITER: Transformation of one's beliefs, aspirations, and long-term plans for the future—all of which promise some kind of improvement.

SATURN: Transformation of one's ambitions, priorities, and work structure.

URANUS: Transformation of one's sense of freedom, individual purpose, and personal uniqueness.

NEPTUNE: Transformation of one's spiritual and/or social ideals.

PLUTO: Transformation of the use of one's inner powers and resources, particularly the mind and will power.

We will repeatedly refer to these various kinds of personal transformation in later sections of this book, and those more detailed references should clarify the scope and meaning of the changes thereby indicated. But it should be stated here that, in order to experience these transformations in a healthy and relatively harmonious way, one must have the right attitude toward and relationship with the various energies and powers that the planets represent. There must be a consciously-forged alignment within ourselves between all the aspects of our being in order to be totally open to the endless transformations that life will demand of us. And this alignment—this openness—has a direct bearing on our physical, mental, and spiritual health. As the Jungian psychiatrist Robert M. Stein has written:

> Psychosomatic research has been almost exclusively limited to investigating the mind-body relationship in terms of cause and effect. In contrast to the causal model used in modern scientific medicine, the ancient acausal model of theurgic medicine holds that sickness is a consequence of divine action. A basis of theurgic medicine is that the deity who inflicts the wound is at once both the sickness and the cure. The aim, therefore, is not to combat the disease as in allopathic medicine, but rather to establish a connection, i.e., *a right relationship to the divine power.* (From "Body and Psyche: An Archetypal View of Psychosomatic Phenomena"; *Spring 1976.*)

To use ancient terminology, the planets are the "gods" which we must worship; i.e., it is necessary to pay due attention to these forces within and without us in order to live in a state of health and wholeness. Since, as stated in the above quotation, the "deity who inflicts the wound is at once both the sickness and the cure," we can see that any life *problem* indicated in the individual chart is a hint to us that a better relationship to that universal power or principle is needed. In other words, it is in that area of life that a transformation of some kind is necessary. It is useless to pretend that such a problem is simply an annoyance which can readily be repressed or ignored, an attitude which is all too apparent in the common astrological advice: "Well, don't worry too much about it. As soon as this planet passes into the next sign, everything will be OK again." What is not understood by those who give this kind of advice is that there might not be much of a problem in the *present* if the individual had achieved the proper perspective and integration through *past* learning and assimilation of *past* experience. Whatever conflicts or necessities for decision-making are being stirred up in the present will surface again in the future, although perhaps in a slightly different form, if they are not effectively dealt with now.

In many ancient cultures, the planets were considered to be either actual celestial deities, or at least the embodiments of spiritual forces or agencies. In certain branches of Hinduism, the planets were regarded as the "Lords" which the Supreme Lord appointed to rule over the various regions of creation and to mete out one's karma. In a very real sense, if we can consider a "deity" to be an embodiment of a divine force or universal law, it is easy to take the next step of viewing the planets from the same vantage point as did the ancients: i.e., as symbols or reflections of various universal laws, principles, and forces which could indeed—judging from their power in our lives—be called divine. Further study of various ancient writings from the Orient can also provide us with a more elaborate and detailed picture of not only the structure of the universe but also of the real meaning and mode of operation of astrological factors. For example, the teachings of Vedanta—a popular tradition in India—say that the simple *principles* of one plane govern the *complexities* of existence on the planes below it. What is *one* on a higher plane becomes *many* on the lower planes. Hence, in studying astrology, whether we realize it or not, we are actually studying the higher principles that "govern" all life in the planes below. Hopefully, by understanding the higher principles at work in our lives, we can more easily and harmoniously accomodate ourselves to the cosmic purpose behind our immediate experience.

Sun and Moon Principles

The Vedanta tradition further speaks of many sub-planes of existence between the physical world and the pure causal (or mental) plane. The "Sun worlds" are mentioned first, then the "Moon worlds," and after that numerous sub-zones. In addition, it is often said that the Sun and Moon seen with the physical eyes are mere reflections of the Sun and Moon sources of power on subtler planes. The Vedas and the Shastras, two Indian scriptures so ancient that no one really knows how old they are or where those teachings originated, say that *individual souls come down from the astral regions to this material world along the rays of the Sun and Moon.* Perhaps this is why the Sun and Moon are so important in astrology and why everything in the chart should be related to the person's Sun and Moon signs and aspects. If indeed the soul is an essential *unit* of the divine power, then it is in itself whole and

complete. But when the soul incarnates into the realms of duality, such
as the material world where we always have good-bad, day-night, male-
female polarities, it seems that the soul polarizes according to the Sun
and Moon positions. In other words, it is reflected into two aspects of
being, manifesting as conscious and unconscious, active and passive,
male and female—Sun and Moon principles. The wholeness is lost,
division has begun. In most cases, women are more in touch with their
lunar qualities and men with their solar qualities, although it must here
be remembered that we are dealing with archetypal principles which
do not manifest in a pure form in living human beings. Hence, there are
many men (for example, those with emphasis on Cancer, Taurus, and
Pisces) who are intimately in touch with and able to express lunar
qualities; and there are many women (especially those with emphasis
on Aries, Aquarius, and Scorpio) who are quite comfortable with
expressing the strength and independence characteristic of the Sun.

Although the scientific world-view describes the Sun as immensely
larger than the Moon, it has always seemed to me an especially striking
symbol that the relative diameters and distances of the Sun and Moon
are such that, *when seen from the earth*, both discs subtend almost
exactly the same visual angle (0.5°) and *appear to be the same size*. Not
only does this illustrate that, symbolically, the lunar and solar forces in
our lives are of absolutely *equal* importance, but it also clearly
demonstrates how large indeed even one full degree is when we
observe the sky from the earth.* In addition, the fact that the Sun and
Moon are visually of such equal size should give astrologers even more
reason to consider the Moon sign to be of equal importance with the
Sun sign in any chart and to base their interpretations on a synthesis of
the Sun and Moon positions in relation to each other.

What exactly are these solar and lunar principles? We can again find
the clearest explanation of their psychological significance in the
writings of C.G. Jung. Jung correlates the lunar force with the
archetypal feminine principle and the solar energy with the masculine
principle, just as astrologers and alchemists have done for millenia. He
further defines the feminine principle as *eros*, not in the modern sense
of purely physical attraction but in the broader sense of *relationship* to
other human beings. He then defines the masculine principle as *logos*.

> Woman's psychology is founded on the principle of Eros, the great
> binder and loosener, whereas from ancient times the ruling principle
> ascribed to man is Logos. (from "Woman in Europe"; Collected Works,
> Vol. 10; par. 254)

> Whereas logic and objectivity are usually the predominant features of
> a man's outer attitude, or are at least regarded as ideals, in the case of a
> woman it is feeling. But in the soul it is the other way round: inwardly
> it is the man who feels, and the woman who reflects. Hence a man's
> greater liability to total despair, while a woman can always find
> comfort and hope; accordingly a man is more likely to put an end to

---

*This kind of realization might well serve to prompt astrologers to use smaller "orbs" for
interplanetary aspects once they see that even one degree is twice the diameter of the
Sun or Moon itself and that the 10° orbs often used for lunar or solar aspects are *twenty
times the diameter of the Sun or Moon!*

himself than a woman. However much a victim of social circumstances a woman may be, as a prostitute for instance, a man is no less a victim of impulses from the unconscious, taking the form of alcoholism and other vices. (from *Psychological Types*; C.W., Vol. 6; par. 805)

Woman's consciousness has a lunar rather than a solar character. Its light is the "mild" light of the moon, which merges things together rather than separates them. It does not show up objects in all their pitiless discreteness and separateness, like the harsh, glaring light of day, but blends in a deceptive shimmer the near and the far, magically transforming little things into big things, high into low, softening all colour into a bluish haze, and blending the nocturnal landscape into an unsuspected unity.

It needs a very moon-like consciousness indeed to hold a large family together regardless of all the differences, and to talk and act in such a way that the harmonious relation of the parts to the whole is not only not disturbed but is actually enhanced. And where the ditch is too deep, a ray of moonlight smoothes it over. (from *Mysterium Coniunctionis*; C.W., Vol. 14; pars. 223 & 227)

Although there are great differences between cultures and between generations in terms of what modes of expression are encouraged in the sexual roles (a fact too often ignored by astrologers!), the search for personal wholeness is becoming more and more of a preoccupation among many people in the Western world. In one brief paragraph, Jung concisely describes our current need to develop both sides of our nature (Sun and Moon); and this very development toward personal integration is one of the main areas of life in which astrology can be particularly helpful.

Human relationship leads into the world of the psyche, into that intermediate realm beween sense and spirit, which contains something of both and yet forfeits nothing of its own unique character. Into this territory a man must venture if he wishes to meet woman half way. Circumstances have forced her to acquire a number of masculine traits, so that she shall not remain caught in an antiquated, purely instinctual femininity, lost and alone in the world of men. So, too, man will be forced to develop his feminine side, to open his eyes to the psyche and to Eros. It is a task he cannot avoid, unless he prefers to go trailing after woman in a hopelessly boyish fashion, worshipping from afar but always in danger of being stowed away in her pocket. (from "Woman in Europe"; par. 258)

The concept of individual wholeness is of course an ideal toward which psychological and spiritual growth should proceed. It is certainly not a common phenomenon. In fact, many of the problems experienced between people of opposite sex can be directly attributed to the fact that this wholeness is so often lacking. Again to quote Jung:

It is almost a regular occurrence for a woman to be wholly contained, spiritually, in her husband, and for a husband to be wholly contained, emotionally, in his wife. (from "Marriage as a Psychological Relationship"; C.W., Vol. 17; par. 331c)

As we grow in awareness of our own wholeness, the kind of astrology we do should also grow to reflect this developing unity. Once we have gained a perspective on the sexual roles of our culture through our own experience, then we can begin to see our clients as individual human beings who by their very potential transcend the limitations of such roles. Until we do succeed in gaining this perspective, there will be many situations with which we cannot deal objectively and which we try to resolve by giving advice that is so conditioned by our cultural and sexual biases that it is essentially worthless to the struggling individual who seeks our help. (There is also considerable sexual bias in many astrological traditions, although not as much as some extremists like to believe; for those who say that astrology is "sexist" merely because it speaks of the archetypal male and female principles simply have no understanding of their own potential wholeness.) It may, for example, be quite inappropriate to use the 19th century's rigid astrological correlations for marriage in astrological work with a modern young person. But it would be equally inappropriate to use terms and assumptions which are relevant to many younger people today in a consultation with an older person whose life pattern is more traditional.

The Sun and Moon positions in the natal chart also reflect our experience of the parents and our relationship to them. In this lifetime, the parents constitute, as it were, the concrete and apparent sources of our life, our identity, and our character. Many of the older books on astrology give the impression that we can invariably deduce from the chart exactly what the relationship with the parents is like and how they got along with one another, whether they were divorced or one parent died early, and so on. I have not found it so easy to deduce these specific insights as some writings would lead one to suppose. It is often possible to hazard a guess based on the chart data which turns out to be accurate, but—even in those cases—it really proves nothing and gives no useful insights. It is merely a guessing game. Why should we use psychic energy and valuable time trying to guess something that we can often find out merely by asking the client a simple question? It seems to me that the Sun and Moon positions and especially their aspects usually symbolize one's inner experience of the parents, what the parents as a couple represented to the person, whether they seemed to the person to have a positive relationship with each other, and how the person felt in relating to each of them as individuals. We should be clear about the fact that the birth-chart primarily shows our *experience*, not necessarily the "objective" facts of the situation. For example, I have seen many cases in which, although the parents often fought and eventually divorced, the child's chart has a Sun-Moon trine and totally lacks the traditional indications of a disrupted family life. Seemingly, in such cases, the person is not seriously affected by the parental discord. I have seen other cases of people whose charts contain a Sun-Moon square and numerous other indications of a parental "complex," and yet whose parents were quite happily and harmoniously married for forty years. In these cases, one might assume that the individual *perceived* the parents to represent conflicting ways of being and modes of self-expression (shown by the Sun-Moon square most specifically) which then generated in the individual certain problems in relating to the actual parents, as well as an inner conflict between active and passive, dominant and receptive roles. In the vast majority of birth-charts, the Sun and/or Moon will have both harmonious, flowing aspects and also stressful, challenging aspects with other planets. A close analysis of these chart factors combined with an intimate discussion of the person's deepest feelings will usually reveal that, although the person had (or has still) a harmonious relationship with a certain parent on some levels, there are other levels where he or she experienced great frustration or conflict. For example, if one's Moon is trine to Mercury but square to Venus, the person is likely to have good intellectual rapport with the mother but not easy exchange of love feelings and physical closeness.

The most useful thing we can do in psychologically analyzing the individual's early life from an astrological perspective is to realize that our particular attunement, karma, and patterns of self-expression will inevitably *elicit* certain reactions from others, and particularly from those with whom we live closely day to day. The parents cannot ultimately be blamed for any of our problems, and there is no constructive purpose to such projection of our own responsibilities onto others. I am not inferring that there are no parent-child relationships which need close examination and, sometimes, psychotherapeutic treatment. On the contrary! It seems that we are often born as the parent or child of an entity with whom we have particularly intense karma. But if that relationship itself, rather than just one individual's attitude toward it, is indeed a real problem, then it is invariably necessary to look not just at one natal chart but also at a detailed chart comparison between the people involved. Some people are of such entirely different natures and attunements that they are purely and simply incompatible, and—in these cases—no amount of work at the relationship will make those two people more alike. They may be able to learn how to accept each other more fully and to give each other sufficient space for self-expression, but they still may not want to be around each other a great deal.

A child lives in the parents' energy field. In other words, *the child lives and breathes in the atmosphere that the parents create through their relationship to each other.* Hence, as a person grows older and lives more and more independently from the parents, he may find through this increased perspective that his true nature is not compatible with the parental atmosphere that he still carries around in the form of psychological habit patterns. If this is the case, then that person needs to find and develop his own atmosphere, a mode of living and relating which is conducive to his own total nature. Very often, the sign on the fourth house cusp symbolizes the type of atmosphere an individual requires in order to feel comfortable with himself. A chart comparison, more than just an analysis of the individual chart, can usually reveal whether a person will be comfortable and healthy in the parental atmosphere and whether the conditioning patterns associated with that atmosphere will help or inhibit the person's self-expression. An individual must come to grips with this entire question in order to achieve the kind of detached perspective that enables him to deal objectively and effectively with his own children and to recognize their needs for independent space. If this objectivity is not attained, then the individual will usually repeat the parents' mistakes unconsciously. As Jung writes,

> The disastrous repetition of the family pattern could be described as the psychological original sin, or as the curse of the Atrides running through the generations. (from *Mysterium Coniunctionis;* C.W., Vol 14; par. 232)

Transformation in the Social Context

In American culture, rather than an initiation ritual which would result in the personal transformation required to enable us to sever quickly and completely the childhood ties to the parents and to propel the individual into adulthood, there is only a long, drawn-out period of trying to convince oneself that one is an adult, an independent, self-sufficient being. Instead of sacred words or myths to protect him or her during this hazardous transformation period, the individual has nothing but vague promises coupled with a license to drive a car and to drink alcohol. In the United States, since there is no ritualistic *rite de passage* from one mode of living to another, this process usually lasts throughout the twenties at the very least; and very often, it is never completed, the individual never achieving a full birth from childhood patterns and needs. The cultural ideals in the United States are so high, so unrealistic that no one can ever meet them. Thus, we become a nation of sheep, a nation of lost children playing "grownup." In the U.S., there is no king, no absolute authority outside ourselves. Hence, we have to turn to our own resources. That is terribly frightening to us. We react by searching, often quite desperately, for safety in some social, professional, or familial role. We therefore run away from our own responsibility and try to please *everyone else*, thus avoiding the burden of coming to terms with our own selves and our own ideals. Thus many of us start to die within; and, in later life, we then find ourselves vaguely resentful with no clear object for our resentment. Instead of realizing that we resent our own ignorance, foolishness, and cowardice, we often turn our resentment toward some group, some vaguely-defined segment of our society which either openly flaunts its disregard for our oppressive values or which somehow represents the oppressive social structures that we see as having enslaved us.

In a society where we have to find our own means of initiation and transformation, astrology has a particularly valuable role to play. But we must remember that astrology is not a thing separate from life. It is not a religion in itself, nor is it a science which encompasses all other approaches to human understanding. It is simply a tool, one of many possible tools, which may be used in any number of ways. In our own individual lives, astrology can serve the purpose of guiding us through various initiations, transformations, and crucial transitions. It can provide us with that cosmic framework and meaning which infuses every major experience with deep significance, something which most religions try—but fail—to do. And, in the practice of astrological counseling as a profession, an awareness of social roles, parental influences and ties, and individual needs for going through the archetypal human transformation phases is an absolute necessity for effective counseling. When a person's society or religion fails to provide a means of understanding such important processes and needs, another way must be found. And astrology is one method of understanding to which millions of people look for guidance.

Higher Consciousness

Throughout this book, I will often use the phrases "higher consciousness," "a higher level of awareness," and similar terms. Before proceeding to discuss specific astrological factors, therefore, it would be useful to clarify these terms. Some astrologers have written and said in public lectures that one can ascertain the level of consciousness from the birth-chart, that one can tell—according to certain aspects and planetary positions—whether an individual is an "evolved soul" or an "old soul" simply from astrological data. I feel that this is a gross error, one which not only can mislead a person in his efforts at self-understanding but which also can lead to a judgmental, self-righteous attitude toward other human beings, especially among beginning students of astrology who have not yet developed the sophistication which only practical experience can provide. All of us are simply struggling souls on the path toward greater love and light. We may be at different stations along the road, but we are all on the same road, whether we realize it or not. The birth-chart is a symbolic map of the particular section of the road on which we are journeying in this lifetime. As Dane Rudhyar has taken great pains to explain in his voluminous writings, the birth-chart reveals the structural patterns of life.* The content and the consciousness within that structure are not shown in the chart. Although a spiritually-oriented and psychically sensitive astrologer may often be able to intuit another person's level of consciousness (and in fact would need to be able to do so in refined applications of astrology for self-knowledge), such perception comes from the individual astrologer rather than from the chart alone. Ideally, one can intuitively synthesize the patterns in the chart with a direct impression of the living person in order to achieve an in-depth understanding of that individual. But even if we are sufficiently sensitive to be able to tune in on a person's level of consciousness, we must be extremely careful of basing any judgments on this personal intuition. Rudhyar's statement quoted at the very beginning of this chapter explains why this caution is so necessary; for each of us has limitations, and our level of understanding and our personal values can indeed limit our objectivity and the effectiveness of our counseling.

Assuming that the chart shows the level of consciousness or the level of spiritual development is also a very limiting approach to the individual person. Are we not capable of growing in awareness during

*Cf. Chapter 4 of *Astrology, Psychology, & the Four Elements* for a complete explanation of structural & formative principles.

this lifetime? Let's hope so! I am fortunate to have identical twin sisters ten years younger than I, and I have been able to watch them grow up, individualize, and develop their own lifestyles. They were born in very rapid succession, and their birth-charts are almost identical. Even the Ascendants are within 1½ degrees of each other. According to the astrologers I have heard who claim to judge the level of consciousness from the birth-chart, both of these souls would be seen as having an identical level of spiritual development. And yet, although their charts accurately describe each of them in general ways and psychological characteristics, these women are as different as day and night on the spiritual level. One is particularly spiritually inclined, a vegetarian, interested in astrology, and rather reflective; the other is much more extroverted and—at least at this time—not nearly as interested in these subjects as her sibling.

Since the constructive use of astrology necessitates that we know not only what astrology *can* do but also what its limitations are, I have felt it necessary to emphasize here that the individual's level of consciousness cannot be judged solely on the basis of the astrological data. In addition, although the archetypal karmic *patterns* are clearly symbolized in a birth-chart, the *precise* way those patterns will manifest and the exact karmic encounters that the person will experience likewise cannot be known from the chart alone. The chart can be used as a lens with which our attention is focused and through which our psychic powers are concentrated; and of course some people do have the ability to tune in on specific karmic experiences in great detail through the use of such psychic senses. But that is another method entirely from simply using the birth-chart alone.

So how can we understand this term "higher consciousness"? The best analogy I can think of is that of electricity and a light bulb. As the conscious power (the electrical current) flows more intensely, the awareness (amount of light) increases. A very unconscious soul may be likened to a 15 Watt lightbulb, an average sort of person to a 60 Watt bulb; a student of one of the higher forms of meditation may achieve, perhaps, the level of 200 Watts. A Perfect Spiritual Master (called in India a *Sant Sat Guru*, or true saint) may be a channel for such infinite power and light that even the analogy of a Trillion Watt lightbulb is insufficient to symbolize such a level of consciousness. As our conscious power flows with more concentration and purity, our own light of awareness may increase from a 75 Watt level, let us say, to a 200 Watt level in one lifetime. The main point to realize, in spite of the awkwardness of this insufficient analogy, is that our birth-chart shows *that structure of life potential that is enlivened and, hopefully, illuminated by our level of awareness.* If the light of awareness is cultivated, nourished, and allowed to develop, then what is shown in the chart in archetypal outline form may be expressed in a more and more refined and positive way in everyday life. If we can allow this to happen, that is true growth—psychological and spiritual—and that is true transformation.

Gemini

3

Keys to Transformation: Part I

Uranus & Neptune

...be cheerful, sir.
Our revels are now ended. These our actors,
As I foretold you, were all spirits, and
Are melted into air, into thin air:
And, like the baseless fabric of this vision,
The cloud-capp'd towers, the gorgeous palaces,
The solemn temples, the great globe itself,
Yea, all which it inherit, shall dissolve,
And, like this insubstantial pageant faded,
Leave not a rack behind. We are such stuff
As dreams are made on; and our little life
Is rounded with a sleep....
—Shakespeare in *The Tempest*

In the past decade, a great deal has been written about the meaning of the trans-Saturnian planets: Uranus, Neptune, and Pluto. It would be impossible for me to condense all these suggested meanings in the scope of one or two chapters, and—indeed—that is not my main purpose here. In this chapter, I will try to clarify the functional significance of these planets—i.e., the dynamic quality of life changes and personal transformation symbolized by these planets as these energies and dimensions of experience are immediately felt by the individual. One is often told in astrological writings or lectures that these planets refer simply and solely to group qualities, generational differences, or "mass karma." While these planets undeniably are related to these factors, the psychologically-oriented astrologer-counselor needs to know the meaning of the trans-Saturnians in the individual life, from a practical, experiential viewpoint. These forces, after all, can only operate through a particular group if they act through the individuals comprising that group. Since I feel that Uranus and Neptune are generally better understood and are explained more clearly in available astrological books than is Pluto, I have devoted the entire next chapter to discussing Pluto in some depth, whereas this chapter treats all three trans-Saturnian planets as a group of related transformative energies, with particular emphasis on Uranus and Neptune. Through the "influence" of these transcendent forces, a human being experiences great changes in his thought patterns, level of consciousness, lifestyle, and capacity for self-expression.

It is my feeling that the trans-Saturnian planets most immediately influence the deepest psychic life of the individual. However, the power of these forces is often so great that they burst out of their psychic confines, as it were, into the world; therefore, they manifest as changes in the physical world as well. One school of thought in modern astrology (that deals with human development in terms of soul growth) holds that the trans-Saturnians will only powerfully influence a soul which has to some extent awakened to spiritual truth. These planets' energies, it is said, affect our subtle bodies—but only when the soul has reached the stage of evolution where these are ready to be awakened. It is theorized that, as the Age of Aquarius advances, more and more souls will be influenced by the trans-Saturnians; and these planets will have the effect of starting the soul on a "higher spiral" of development. I certainly agree that the trans-Saturnians refer to a "higher vibration" (or at least to more refined and penetrating forces) than do the seven planets of ancient astrology. I also concur with the idea that the level of awareness of the individual affects how the trans-Saturnians' "influences" will be experienced. But I feel that it is too vast a generalization to state that only "highly evolved" souls are responsive to the energies of these planets. One might more correctly say that a more aware person is capable of being a channel for the expression of the purest, most refined, and most constructive manifestations of these forces, as is the case with all the planets. But by no means can we assert that destructive revolutionaries are unresponsive to Uranus, Mafia members to Pluto, and drug addicts to Neptune. These people are surely expressing one aspect of the trans-Saturnians' power in their lives, although obviously not the optimum mode of expression.

Uranus, Neptune, and Pluto symbolize forces that constantly prompt change (and, hopefully, growth) in our consciousness. The eminent astrologer Dane Rudhyar has referred to the trans-Saturnians as "ambassadors of the galaxy." In an article published in "Astroview" magazine, he states:

> Any organic system or cosmic unit is subjected to two contrary forces. There is the pull which draws every part of the system to the center (for instance, the pull of gravitation); but there is also the pull exerted by outer space, which actually means by a larger system within which the first system operates.
>
> Every planet of our solar system and every living being on Earth is to some degree affected by the pressures and pulls which reach us from the galaxy; we are also affected in an opposite direction by the gravitational power of the Sun, center of our system.
>
> Saturn, however, represents a basic line of demarcation between these two opposite forces, galactic and solar. The planets inside of Saturn's orbit are mainly creatures and vassals of the Sun; while the planets beyond Saturn are what I have called many years ago "ambassadors of the galaxy." They focus upon the solar system the power of this vast community of stars, the galaxy. They do not completely belong to the solar system. They are within its sphere of influence to do a job, to link our small system (of which the Sun is the center and Saturn's orbit the circumference) with the larger system, the galaxy.

That the trans-Saturnian planets are the symbols of cosmic (or *galactic*) forces which impel (and, in actual experience, often *expel*) the individual to grow and to join his consciousness with greater, more comprehensive forces of life is revealed in numerous ways. First, the trans-Saturnians, as observed from the Earth, move slowly; therefore, each remains in one sign of the zodiac for many years. Thus, we find entire generations of men and women experiencing generally similar changes, although the specific focus of the changes differs from person to person, according to the house positions and aspects with other planets.

Secondly, we can see in chart comparisons how the cosmic evolutionary forces operate through individual persons, coming to a specific focus in the relationship of one person to another. The perennial "generation gap" is a good example of how the trans-Saturnian planets correspond with the experience of pressure toward growth and more inclusive consciousness. There is often a rather painful awakening to our need to develop a more open and wholistic approach to life that results from in-depth contact with people of different generations. In a chart comparison between two people born a few decades apart, the outer three planets will fall not only in different signs in the individual charts, but also usually in different houses of the other person's chart when one uses the chart comparison method of placing one person's natal planets in the other person's natal chart. In other words, if I place my 2nd house natal Pluto (which is in, say, 2° Leo) at 2° Leo of my father's chart, it may fall in any of his natal houses; but it is very unlikely that it will fall in the same house where *his* natal Pluto is located. On the other hand, if I place my natal Pluto at 2° Leo in the chart of a person whose age is within a few years of mine, the chances are great that my natal Pluto will fall in the same house in his chart where his natal Pluto is located. We can thus see that the types of major changes prompted by close relationships between persons of quite different ages are likely to be of an entirely new order, affecting both people in totally new ways and pressuring them to transform or radically alter their approach to specific areas of life. To further clarify this point, suppose the natal Uranus, Neptune, or Pluto of a person 20 years older or younger than myself falls in my 9th house; there would then be the strong potential for that individual's influence upon my ideals, beliefs, religious orientations, and plans for self-improvement (9th house) to be revolutionizing (Uranus), refining or spiritualizing (Neptune), or profoundly transforming (Pluto). In a situation like this, therefore, the Uranus, Neptune, and Pluto energies affect both people in new and challenging ways. Encountering people of different generations, therefore, can be more difficult than relating to our peers, since such relationships necessarily jolt us out of our old patterns of thought and behavior in some sphere of life. Such relationships necessitate that we grow in order to become more inclusive (one could say "cosmic"). Hence, relationships with people of different generations often threaten us and often require a great deal of effort. We may have to face some kind of pain in the area indicated or some form of anxiety as we are challenged to transform our attitudes; but, as Jung wrote, "There is no coming to consciousness without pain." Some of us of course do welcome challenges and opportunities to learn from those who have a different perspective on life and a markedly different variety of life experience. If we can remain open to life and to new learning, based to some extent on our awareness of the value of other people's experience, these challenging encounters with others of different generations will be welcomed and even enjoyed.

The basic personal factors in any individual's life are always the same. These essential forces, or dimensions of life, have existed in all human beings throughout the ages. They motivate distinct orientations in an individual's conscious life, although the degree to which they are admitted to conscious awareness depends greatly upon not only the interrelationship between these factors within the individual (symbolized by the "aspects") but also upon the environmental influences and cultural norms at a particular time and place. Astrologically, these forces (which are, I repeat, the essential *personal* factors in any individual's conscious life) are symbolized by the Sun, Moon, Mercury, Venus, and Mars.* Jupiter and Saturn constitute an intermediary step between the personal planets and the transpersonal, impersonal forces of the trans-Saturnians, since they so often have to do with our participation in society and with socially-colored norms, beliefs, and ambitions. The signs, houses, and aspects in which we find these seven planets indicate the particular ways in which these forces operate in an individual. The factors symbolized by these seven planets are, to some extent, modifiable through conscious experience and by the concentrated use of the will.

Uranus, Neptune, and Pluto, on the other hand, are totally beyond conscious control, just as the actual planets are markedly beyond the Earth. Therefore, a person cannot control the energies of these planets at all. But he can control his attitude toward their influence in his life. He can modify his conscious orientation toward the manifestations of these greater forces. In terms of their function, Uranus, Neptune, and Pluto, as stated above, always prompt change in the area of life affected. This change will usually come harmoniously and without too much disruption if these planets are in "easy" aspect with the other seven planets. However, if the trans-Saturnians are in stressful aspects with the other planets, the change will be more difficult to "handle." That is, we will experience difficulty in mastering the situation; and we may be overwhelmed by these forces, for the trans-Saturnians symbolize energies that are far more powerful than any of the other planets. Willpower and determination alone are never enough to cope with these energies.

For example, if one of the trans-Saturnians is in a square aspect to another planet, these forces are at odds with each other. Necessarily, something's got to give. We can sometimes resist the increasing pressure for change in our lives for quite a long time; but, eventually, we come to realize that such resistance is in effect resistance to that which would make us more whole and, thus, more human. This resistance is, therefore, ultimately self-defeating. An example of such a "stressful" aspect in the natal chart appears in the horoscope of Meher

---

*Cf. Page 86 in *Astrology, Psychology, & the Four Elements* for a complete schematic outline of the personal, collective, and transpersonal factors represented by the planets.

Baba, an Indian teacher revered by his devotees as an incarnation of God. In fact, Meher Baba himself, when asked if he was God, replied, "Who else could I be?" In Meher Baba's chart, we find the Sun in the first house in square aspect to a conjunction of Pluto and Neptune in the fourth house. (The Pluto-Neptune conjunction is also in quincunx aspect to the Moon in the ninth house.) Therefore, the sense of conscious identity (Sun especially strong in the first house) in Meher Baba was at odds with the powerful forces represented by Pluto and Neptune (in the fourth house—the fundamental roots of one's being). With such great energy generated in this tense aspect, something had to give. What "gave" was the sense of being an individual, separate entity. The Sun factor, therefore, became a channel through which the greater forces could manifest. The Moon became (symbolically) a factor for the dissemination and focalization of these forces. If we realize that Neptune symbolizes in part "mystical" consciousness and that Pluto represents potential spiritual rebirth, we have the symbolic key to the kind of cosmic energies that were manifesting through this great teacher. The house positions of the Sun and Moon (the channels through which these forces operated) reveal in what areas of life such influences manifested. The Sun in the first house (the house of identity) is an apt symbol for one who so completely identified himself with life's creative power. The Moon in the ninth house (the house of religion and truth-seeking) provides a symbol of a spiritual teacher.

This example demonstrates how the trans-Saturnians in a natal chart are to be interpreted. The focalization of the changes in one's life, due to the pressure of greater forces "desiring" manifestation, can be pinpointed by examining the close aspects with Uranus, Neptune, and Pluto. The trans-Saturnians, therefore, act through us by activating, as it were, the psychological factors represented by Saturn, Jupiter, Mercury, Venus, Mars, Sun, and Moon. It is as if the energy flows from Uranus, Neptune, and Pluto through the channels symbolized by the other seven planets. The aspects involved provide a key to this flow of energy. (See Chapter 6 for more on these aspects.)

Since Uranus, Neptune, and Pluto move through the ecliptic so slowly with reference to the Earth, they do have specific effects upon particular generations of human beings. These influences are altered according to the culture prevailing in a certain area. Aspects to the trans-Saturnians in the natal chart, therefore, reveal how an individual is attuned to the forces of change manifesting not only within himself, but also during a particular era. With respect to the social environment, therefore, and in relation to the various currents of social change at a specific time, we may ask: Will the person be an arch conservative, a total revolutionary, or somewhat more moderate? Is he in tune with the forces of change in his times and open to the messages from "the ambassadors of the galaxy"? Or is he opposed or indifferent to these birth pangs of a new consciousness?

In addition to the natal house positions and aspects, the transits of Uranus, Neptune, and Pluto are also highly significant. These will be dealt with in some detail in Chapter 9, but it might be mentioned here that transits of these planets over sensitive points in the natal chart are the most penetrating and far reaching of all transits; and their ultimate effects are the most comprehensive and long lasting. In the following sections of this chapter, I will briefly describe the meaning of each of the trans-Saturnian planets, and I will also mention how transits of these planets are experienced by the individual.

Uranus

The planet Uranus symbolizes a force that manifests as sudden changes of life pattern, sudden alterations of consciousness, flashes of insight, and quick bursts of new ideas and original conceptions. Uranus can be conceived of as a channel through which powerful forces flow into awareness with electric rapidity. Uranus also manifests as impulses toward independence, rebellion, the erratic, the unconventional, the original, and the unexpected. The "influence" of Uranus does not make a person particularly stable; but it does make him a channel through which new ideas may be born. When Uranus is strong in a chart, that factor symbolized by the planet (or planets) in aspect to Uranus is electrified, magnetized, highly energized, and, if all goes well, illuminated. We, therefore, see that Uranus "acts" electrically, in sudden impulses. This power is needed to burst through the Saturnian ego defenses and the thought barriers of the conscious mind. Contrary to some views, Uranus doesn't always act destructively. It manifests as destruction only when there is resistance to its influence. Since some form of resistance is usually present, however (especially if Uranus is involved in stressful aspects), a transit of Uranus is often experienced as highly disruptive.

By transit, Uranus cuts away the old and revolutionizes one's way of being in the area indicated. It brings sweeping changes that have the effect of reorganizing (often disorganizing at first) one's consciousness in order to permit new growth to come forth. Psychologically, it bursts into awareness in the form of whatever ideas, feelings, and realizations were subliminal—i.e., just below the threshold of consciousness. Its transits, therefore, are inimical to repression of any kind. If an individual has been living in a repressed manner, a mode of life in which vital elements of his or her nature have been blocked, neglected, or ignored, it is almost certain that a transit of Uranus by conjunction, square, or opposition to one of the personal planets will bring to the surface with great immediacy an intense confrontation with these parts of the person's nature. Uranus always speeds up the rhythm of nature; and hence, an individual experiencing one of these transits is often "wired," excitable, restless, and driven by an overwhelming desire for change and freedom. Uranus, at its best, is the great liberator, the awakener, the illuminator which stirs up the person's inner and outer life with such intensity that things are never the same afterwards. This planet may be likened to the mythological figure Prometheus, who stole fire from the gods and thus enabled human beings to extend the reach of their knowledge. Most people have the urge during transits of Uranus to act out their needs for excitement, freedom, and experimentation. They will often make radical moves to change what they perceive to be a stifling life situation. A small percentage of people, however, will experience Uranus transits almost totally on an inner level, during which they will subtly revolutionize their attitude, understanding, and mode of self-expression in the areas indicated. Their outer life will frequently reflect this new, awakened approach to life, but in these cases it is by no means always readily apparent. During Uranus transits, the individual often has an impulse to run away from life situations which are seen to be inhibiting or frustrating to his individualistic self-expression. But it is sometimes a more constructive approach, assuming that the life situation is fundamentally sound and vitally flexible, for the person to experiment with radical changes within the confines of the old situation, whether it be a marriage, job, or whatever. The broadening of self-understanding that can result from such a challenge is often far greater than would be gained from merely throwing over the old and jumping excitedly into the new and different. This is of course not to deny that a total revolution or repolarization in some area of life is sometimes necessary.

In many cases, the influence of Uranus can be defined culturally, for Uranus starts where Saturn ends. Saturn marks the boundary of personal ego consciousness, symbolizing the collective, cultural norms and standards (a kind of cultural "super-ego" in Freudian terms). Saturn is, thus, rigid and contracted. Uranus, on the other hand, bursts through this old structure with revolutionary impulses; and the rigidity of the Saturnine boundary usually causes it to crack and be rent asunder. The psychological manifestations of the Uranian forces as experienced by the individual are not only quite comprehensible, but also even invigorating to the mind that is open to the new. In ancient astrology, the planet Mercury was known as the messenger of the gods, a term which sounds quite similar to Rudhyar's description of the trans-Saturnian planets as "ambassadors of the galaxy." Mercury was at that time associated with the creative faculty in human beings. Of course, ancient astrologers—as far as we know—had no knowledge of the existence of Uranus. Still, many of the alchemists were aware of a creative function deeper (or higher) than the level of the rational mind, which is the primary meaning of Mercury in modern astrology. These alchemists associated this creative activity with the occult meaning of Mercury as the unifier of opposites. From our modern perspective, we might well wonder if they were referring to the function of Uranus but had no such planetary symbol to express what they experienced. This hypothesis seems all the more likely in light of the fact that numerous modern astrologers are now asserting that—in contrast to the ancient Greek version of Mercury's exaltation and dignity in Virgo—Mercury's exaltation should be considered to be in Aquarius, the Uranus sign.

Dane Rudhyar, in his profound and inspiring book *Triptych*, refers to Uranus as "the creative power of the universal spirit." Rudhyar says that Uranus refers to the stage of personal "transfiguration" and that "the transfigured individual has become a focal center for the release of the power of the Universal Mind." He also states that Uranus can be conceived of as "the Voice of God," "the creative power of the mystic Sound that, according to the old tradition of India, pervades all spaces...." The "power of the universal mind" is evident in the extraordinarily quick perceptions that accompany a Uranian attunement. This comes from the ability to gain knowledge and insight from other dimensions through a heightened psychic sensitivity. Uranus represents intuitive insight and the extension of the rational process beyond the barriers of space and time. The experimentation toward which the Uranus energies urge an individual comes from this inner sense that there are no boundaries to human knowledge; it comes from the inner faith that an individual has the capacity to understand life in a more comprehensive way and that he or she has the divine *right* to pursue this knowledge, no matter what conventional wisdom may dictate. (Naturally, many Uranians become so absorbed in the excitement of discovery and experimentation that they commonly go to extremes in their attitudes and opinions, in which case they are given to fanaticism, utter disregard for tradition, and willful obstinacy.) This "intuition" of which Uranian people are capable is not incompatible with logic, however. Grant Lewi pointed out over thirty years ago that Uranus operates in a very logical way, but that the logic works so fast that it appears to be intuition. He also wrote that Uranus represents the extension of perception into realms of superconscious mentality, which we can interpret as the ability to tune in on the universal mind's archetypal level of knowledge. Once one goes past the boundaries of Saturn and ventures into the realms of Uranus and Neptune, all dualities, all oppositions perceived due to limited "logic," and all separate forms begin to disappear. There begins at that point to be a merger of dichotomies, which in Uranian perception manifests as seeing things to be *both and* rather than *either or*. In other words, the opposites of the materialistic logical mind are seen together in one flash of immediate perception, as parts of one whole, comprehensive perspective on life.

The house position of Uranus shows us where one can potentially *experience* and *use* this awakening power, where sudden changes, insights, and a feeling of needing broad personal freedom are felt most immediately. This house shows where one has an urge to depart from conventional norms of expression, and where one will often reject tradition and useless encumbrances in order to do so. If one has Uranus in an angular house, there will be an especially strong urge to act out one's unconventionality in an obvious, dynamic way. If Uranus is in succeedent or cadent houses, on the other hand, the person may have just as strong an urge toward revolutionary or unconventional impulses, but he may put those feelings to work in his everyday life in a subtler way, while perhaps appearing quite conservative on the surface.

Neptune

The planet Neptune symbolizes a force that is entirely beyond our control, for it is beyond the fringes of reason or of anything comprehensible to the logical mind. The only way Neptune can be truly understood in its essence is to surrender to it; for it is, by definition and function, beyond boundaries. It is only when we merge with it—i.e., become boundary-less ourselves—that we can know it. Hence Neptune is associated with mysticism, mystery, a sense of oneness, spiritual development, and inspiration. It is also said to represent formlessness, illusion, dissolution, imagination, and idealism. To me, the most useful way of describing Neptune's essential meaning is to say that it represents the urge to lose one's self in another state of consciousness (whether "higher" or "lower" consciousness) and the urge to escape from all limitation, from both the limitations of material existence and its boredom and the limitations of the personality and ego. Naturally, one can seek to escape through either self-destructive or personally constructive activities. A Neptunian person may be evasive or escapist, or he can be very perceptive of subtleties and extremely compassionate (or a mixture of both!).

An individual's experience of Neptune's "influence," symbolized by the natal configurations, house position, and transits, is often characterized by a sense of confusion, being uncertain, "up in the air," and "spaced out." At least this is how it is often felt when the individual is just beginning to face it consciously and before the person is sufficiently "grounded" to be able to keep his psychic balance. This confusion results in part from the common attitude that demands that any new experience "fit" neatly into our preconceived mental categories. However, one cannot ever succeed in putting boundaries on Neptune. How can that which is boundless and formless by its very nature be brought within our limited concepts and life structures? In other words, the confusion or "spaced out" feeling so often experienced in relation to Neptune develops chiefly when one is resisting the inevitable disintegration and dissolution of some pattern in our life or some aspect of our personality. This negative side of Neptune's manifestation is also much more apparent, as mentioned above, when one is not grounded in the material world. One might say that, unless one has come to terms with the pressures, realities, and obligations of Saturn, one is not sufficiently grounded to handle the intensity and disruption of any of the trans-Saturnian planets. In other words, one has to take the insights and freedom of Uranus and the inspiration and idealism of Neptune and *make them real* by bringing that awareness down to earth, testing those far-out inclinations, and incorporating them into our everyday life.* Failure to work on this integration inwardly with great honesty and diligence will often bring about either a tremendous feeling of discontent or, in some cases, psychological disturbances which can eventually lead to a large scale disintegration of the personality.

An excellent example of the need to have one's feet securely planted in practical reality as a complementary balance during any spiritual or

---

*This is especially necessary if one's natal chart contains a close aspect of Saturn to Uranus or Neptune, particularly the conjunction, square, or opposition.

psychic work is found in C.G. Jung's autobiography *Memories, Dreams, Reflections.* In that book, Jung writes of how, when he was experiencing the most intense phase of his "confrontation with the unconscious"—during which time he was encountering and communicating with numerous archetypal figures and beings—the only thing that got him through this total transformation in his consciousness was the fact that he could always look back and see that he had a certain place in the world, together with specific professional and familial duties. Without such a solid anchor to hold him to the earth, he felt that he might have easily been tossed about and psychically devastated, much as a small boat is totally helpless in an oceanic storm. We can see how possible and how destructive such devastation can be by witnessing the results of many people's experiments with psychedelic drugs, which artifically forced open psychic channels to the intense vibrations which the trans-Saturnians represent. Many of these people experienced spiritual and psychic realities which profoundly changed their lives; but most of them, since they were so young and therefore without a solid grounding in the world of practical realities and duties, had great difficulty integrating these profound insights into their still unformed personalities. The struggle to integrate such glimpses of higher realities into the developing personality structure necessitated a marked transformation of consciousness and lifestyle, which in many cases did prove to be ultimately fruitful and creative. But arriving at the other shore, after being tossed about on the waters of the collective unconscious, was not at all an easy task; and almost anyone who experimented extensively with these drugs can tell of others they know who never reached the other side or who are still, after many years of effort, trying to find something stable they can grasp onto for support.

In any birth-chart, that factor symbolized by a planet in close aspect to Neptune is highly sensitized and refined. This sensitivity often manifests as a susceptibility to illusion, self-deception, confusion, or even disintegration in that dimension of life; for Neptune inclines a person toward an unrealistic idealization of, or fantasy about, a particular area of life. But these very problems can lead the individual to a fruitful search for a solution. During this search for answers, when the person comes to know that he or she is in fact learning about a higher reality through experiencing *disillusionment,* a Neptune aspect can then indicate a practical and positive idealization and indeed a spiritualization of the factor indicated. The significance of Neptune in one's spiritual seeking is explained more in Chapter 6; but, since it is so rarely properly understood and clearly explained in astrological textbooks, a couple of things should be mentioned here. We have said that Neptune dissolves the old highly ordered patterns of consciousness. Thus, we are made aware of the limitations of our usual perceptions and of the fact that there exists something greater and more comprehensive than what we have presumed. This intervention in our lives of a more unified (however insubstantial) "something" is received by some people as a profound spiritual mystery or as an act of "grace." I have personally found Neptune to be in either conjunction, square, or opposition (the so-called "bad" aspects) with the personal planets or the Ascendant in the chart of every individual I've seen who is actively pursuing some kind of spiritual path as his or her main life's work. Evidently, these "stressful" aspects are not so "bad" for spiritual seekers. One might suppose that the energy generated by such aspects is necessary to prompt an individual to *act* on his spiritual inclinations and to strive with greater effort in that area of life. C.E.O. Carter has likewise found these aspects with Neptune to be more indicative of artistic creativity and spiritual progress than the so-called "easy" aspects with Neptune. In his book *The Astrological Aspects*, a treatment of aspects which I feel contains more gems of insight than any other book on the topic, Carter writes the following concerning the "inharmonious" aspects between Venus and Neptune:

> In some respects, these seem to lead to more definite results than the trine and sextile, for they bestow a divine discontent, and a constant restless seeking for an ideal which is not easily realisable on earth. This is particularly so in matters of the affections. The ideals are indeed very high, and there may be a persistent dissatisfaction both with things and persons, varying from a petulant or peevish attitude, to a noble aspiration and persistent endeavor to seek for a fuller realisation of inner visions.
>
> ...The inharmonious combinations are frequently found in the nativities of great artists. Although the good aspects of these two planets are naturally more favorable for happiness and easy conditions, it seems that, so far as achievement, moral character, and artistic ability go, the inharmonious aspects are in no way inferior to them; in fact, they may be better inasmuch as they may produce more energy. (p. 119)

This "divine discontent" spoken of by Carter is indeed often found in those who have almost any of the conjunctions, squares, or oppositions of Neptune with the personal planets or the Ascendant. This discontent comes from the fact that Neptune sensitizes or tunes one in to the reality of the unseen, immaterial forces of life. When one senses that there is in fact a subtler, higher plane of being which is accessible to human consciousness, it is often difficult to patiently live a mundane existence in a material world that increasingly looks and feels like a prison. It seems to me that the key to forming a right relationship to the Neptunian force in our lives is to realize that no satisfaction or liberation will come from our constantly seeking the ideal for which we yearn *in the outer world,* and that it will only come when we accept responsibility (Saturn!) for making our lives ideal through our own creativity and devotion. In other words, we have to turn within, we have to live the ideal in order to make it real. There is no use in always looking unrealistically for the perfect situation, whether it be the perfect job, the ideal marriage, or the picture-perfect home with beautiful scenery all around. Neptune inclines one toward getting hung up on pictures, on images of perfection, toward which one then wants to run to escape from the pain of everyday life. Naturally, an extremely sensitive person may *need* to live in an environment or to have a type of work which at least does not deplete his or her psychic energy through constant stress. But to insist that everything be perfect before we will live it to the full—before we will commit ourselves to it completely—is an attitude which insures that we will never feel any inner peace.

It has been stated in some astrological writings that Neptune represents our sense of obligation to society and to other people, manifesting as guilt feelings in extreme cases. This is no doubt the way many people experience the Neptune energy, and one might even say that Neptune in this case shows a channel through which we have to pay off certain karmic debts to others. However, this correlation with Neptune is only half-accurate, since the inner motivation behind these feelings and this behavior is not explained. Does one feel obligated to others for no reason? Is it in all cases simply a karmic debt which we subliminally feel we owe to others? Or is there a more general explanation? It seems to me that such a feeling of obligation to society, to humanity, or indeed to any suffering human being or animal comes from the fact that we sense our oneness with all other living creatures. If one feels intensely that he or she is the *same* as any other human being (or even that we are in essence one with animals as well), how can one withhold help to anyone in need? It is not really generosity to give to another who is in essence the same as myself. It is rather an immediate obligation; and, if I don't fulfill this sense of obligation, I may indeed feel quite guilty. This tendency toward identifying with all other people, however, although it is no doubt a fine spiritual quality, must be related to practical facts; or else one leaves oneself open to being manipulated, used, and even exhausted by the demands of others. For it is a rare person who does not in fact need some kind of help, some kind of aid. Just because we sense that we are one with the greater whole of all life does not mean that we have the energy or the resources within us to sustain all other living creatures. We must realize that God also has a part to play. He will play His part, regardless of what we do, so we needn't take on His responsibilities. So often, we find Neptunian people pouring out every ounce of their vital force in the futile attempt to satisfy their insatiable sense of obligation to others. This is a misunderstanding and a misapplication of spiritual ideals, often accompanied by various forms of self-delusion about one's high level of spiritual development. Neptune is perhaps the most subtle planet of all in its mode of operation, and stressful aspects of Neptune to the personal planets often indicate that the person has a subtle form of "spiritual egotism."*

---

*This "spiritual egotism" is especially common in cases where the Sun is involved with Neptune in conjunction, square, or opposition; for the Sun is symbolically related to the ego and the conscious sense of identity. These same aspects of Neptune with any of the "personal planets" or Ascendant can also manifest as a definite form of "spiritual ambition," a phenomenon most common in people whose charts include Neptune squares since the square aspect by nature often connotes ambition of some type. Naturally, such ambition can be directed either into fruitless attempts to gain spiritual power or worldly power in spiritually oriented groups, or into disciplined and consistent forms of spiritual practice based on devotion to an ideal rather than to one's own glorification.

We can gather from all of the above that the nature of the Neptunian influence for each of us is dependent upon our attitude toward it, upon the value that we attribute to it, and upon how we fit experiences of subtlety into our life structure. If we welcome the onrush of Neptunian energies into an open mind and soul, we can experience heightened spiritual perception, imagination, and inspiration. Archetypal images can be seen, and timeless realities can be felt. As Dane Rudhyar writes, Neptune is "at every level, the healing and sustaining power of the wholeness of the whole." Rudhyar further states:

> ...to him whose soul has become a hallowed shrine for the living God, whose circumference of self includes potentially the whole universe, whose mind establishes its formulations in terms of the reconciliation of all opposites, leaving nothing outside of its all-inclusive multi-dimensional logic—to him God answers as Grace. (from *Triptych*)

By house position in the natal chart, Neptune indicates where this potential for grace, for tuning in on transcendental influences, touches one's life most immediately. But it shows only a *potential* for experiencing grace or spiritual realities. One can of course experience non-material forces and psychic sensitivity either constructively (which Dr. William Davidson called the "angelic benediction," referring to a form of higher protection and guidance) or self-destructively (possession, deception, or dissipation of one's energies). Precisely how the subtle Neptunian energy and dimension of life will be integrated into our entire life structure depends in great part upon how honest, courageous, and practical we are. One must be *grounded* in the Saturnian reality to fully appreciate and utilize the uplifting aspect of Neptune's dimension of life. As we mentioned earlier when speaking of C.G. Jung's confrontation with the unconscious and his gratefulness that he was grounded in the material world of work and duties, one must have integrated the Saturnian necessities into a healthy attitude toward all of life if one is going to be able to open oneself to Neptune's influence without dissolving into chaos. How can we appreciate the value of boundlessness if we have not established a life pattern within definite boundaries?

The qualities required to become a channel for the highest manifestation of Neptune's principle are quite rare, for—after all—can any of us claim to be free of self-deceptions, unrealistic fantasies, or desires to evade harsh reality? For that reason, the house position of Neptune in the natal chart indicates for most of us an area of life and field of experience which we tend either to idealize or to escape from, usually motivated by little understood promptings from the unconscious *or* superconscious mind. It is in that field of experience that we look for an ideal, that we believe what we want to believe; and the urge to escape from confronting that area of life, I feel, often comes from the subliminal fear that confronting it harshly and immediately will reveal the emptiness of our self-deception. Hence, we often prefer to remain in the dark, to maintain our sense of mystery rather than risking the realization that what we have idealized for so long is not really as valuable as we have wanted to believe. It seems that we often identify some area of worldly experience with our most profound spiritual longing; and the result is confusion. Acute discrimination (Virgo!—the opposite sign from Neptune's sign Pisces) is required to enable us to clarify for ourselves what is *really* related to our spiritual growth and what is merely an area of life which we have hoped (perhaps for lifetimes) would fulfill our spiritual longing and loneliness.

I have often wondered whether Uranus, Neptune, and Pluto in the natal chart are related to the expression of knowledge gained either in previous lives or between earthly incarnations. Uranus is known as the planet of insight, originality, and genius. From where does this insight and new knowledge come? Neptune reveals a visionary and imaginative capacity and a sense of mystical oneness which are obviously aspects of experience remote from the material realities of everyday life. Perhaps a contact with Neptune in the chart shows a vague stirring of innate mental images or experiences that we have encountered before, perhaps between lifetimes in other dimensions? Perhaps a contact with Uranus shows an attunement to knowledge that was fully assimilated long ago and which is only now being tapped for expression in this lifetime. Chapter 11 will, I believe, shed some light on this question, for the Edgar Cayce psychic readings extensively explore the relation of planetary attunement to the soul's experiences between lifetimes.

All of the trans-Saturnian planets represent levels of consciousness wherein we become rather impersonal. All of them deal potentially with subtler dimensions of life and transformative energies. All three are related to types of psychic powers, so-called intuition, "ESP" and similar kinds of sensitivity. But each is different; and no one of them alone can be called *the* planet of "intuition" or psychic power. From a spiritual viewpoint, all the trans-Saturnians deal with higher planes of being, with the following differentiation:

Uranus represents *mental understanding* of higher levels, levels of consciousness where dualities are united in the *living* truth.

Neptune represents an *emotional attunement* to higher levels, a yearning for and infatuation with higher planes of being.

Pluto represents a *commitment to act* upon our needs for transformation, to incorporate the higher levels of consciousness into our very being, knowing that all desires and attachments will have to be brought to the surface and purged and that all our true motives will have to be faced. At this level of consciousness, one is no longer satisfied with mere knowledge or infatuation; one wants to bring all one's mental and emotional resources to bear in the transformational process.

Cancer

4

Keys to Transformation: Part II

Pluto

Though the seas threaten, they are merciful,
I have cursed them without cause.
—Shakespeare in *The Tempest*

Most astrologers agree that the planet Pluto symbolizes a dimension of life that is so complex and has such deep sources that an aura of mystery surrounds the meaning of this planet in any individual birth-chart. Since its discovery, there have been many attempts to clarify the meaning of this planet; and, although astrologers are able to find many different meanings useful for their particular purposes, and although many articles have been written about the "influence" of Pluto on "mass karma" and mundane events, I have not been able to find any explanation of this planet's significance for the *individual* human being and his psychological make-up which I could regard as complete. It seems there is always something hidden about Pluto, something subtle and difficult to conceptualize in ordinary logical terms. Everything connected with Pluto is slightly out of the ordinary, a bit eccentric, and indicative of a realm of cosmic immensity that boggles the mind. This is true not only of the planet's function astrologically, but also of the movement of the planet itself.

The orbit of Pluto, like the orbits of all the other planets, is an ellipse, but Pluto's orbit is considerably more elliptical than that of any other major planet in the solar system. Whereas the orbital planes of all the other major planets lie within seven degrees of the plane of the Earth's orbit, or the "plane of the ecliptic," the orbit of Pluto is inclined fully seventeen degrees to that plane. The mean distance of this planet from the Sun is nearly 40 "astronomical units," the "astronomical unit" being the mean distance of the Earth from the Sun, or roughly ninety-three million miles. Accordingly, a distance of forty astronomical units amounts in round numbers to 3,700,000,000 miles. The orbit of the planet is so pronouncedly elliptical, however, that its distance from the Sun varies to the extent of some 1,800,000,000 miles, the minimum distance being equal to about 2,800,000,000 miles, or a trifle less than that of Neptune, and the maximum distance, to approximately 4,600,000,000 miles, or nearly sixty-five percent greater than that of Neptune. Like the other planets, however, Pluto revolves around the Sun from west to east — that is, in a counter-clockwise direction. Its period of revolution around the sun is about 250 of our years; hence a "year" on this "world" is

equal to *two and a half centuries here on the Earth!* Pluto is now
approaching the perihelion point in its orbit, or that closest to the Sun;
but it will not pass that point until the year 1989, when it will be at a
distance from the Sun only slightly less than that of Neptune
(2,800,000,000 miles). Pluto will then be nearest to the Earth as well as to
the Sun and in the most favorable position generally for observation
from the Earth.

It is an interesting circumstance that if its orbit lay in the same plane as
that of the orbit of Neptune, Pluto at perihelion would be slightly within
the orbit of Neptune. As a result of the high mutual inclination of the
orbital planes of the two planets, however, their orbits do not intersect at
any point, although *at its closest approach to the Sun, Pluto is actually a
bit* (approximately half an astronomical unit) *nearer to the Sun than is
Neptune.* According to Dr. Franklin of the Haydn Planetarium in New
York City, Pluto will move closer to the Sun in its orbit than Neptune on
December 11, 1978 and will remain there until March 14, 1999. Many
astrologers have commented on this period, linking it to crucial changes
in the world's cultural development. Dane Rudhyar specifically points
out that this passage of Pluto closer to the Sun than Neptune has a
stimulating or "seeding" effect at the deeper levels of collective
consciousness. He writes:

> Pluto can be said, in one sense at least, to symbolize the seed falling
> into the humus made of the dissolved and chemicalized remains of the
> ending cycle of annual vegetation (the product of a Neptunian process
> of dissolution); it can be related also to the "Descent to Hell" by Christ
> before his resurrection. As Pluto therefore cuts into Neptune's orbit, a
> process of release from the past and of impregnation by a nucleated
> vision of the future can symbolically be said to occur. Indeed such a
> period in every revolution of Pluto around the Sun is, historically
> speaking, unusually significant.

> These periods often witness a repolarization of the collective
> unconscious and the ideals of mankind along lines which, in one way or
> another, stress factors deeply rooted in human nature and thus
> common to a large section of mankind.

Marc Edmund Jones has written that this historical phase of Pluto's cycle
"marks the overall and complete revolution of just about everything on
the globe." Zipporah Dobyns further clarifies what she sees as the
meaning of this period:

> This period re-emphasizes the Scorpio quality of the last quarter of
> this century.... Pluto will be in its own sign from the mid-1980's to the
> mid-1990's. Humanity is being notified that it is time that we learned to
> share the resources of the planet. The key meaning of letter 8 of our
> astrological alphabet, whether Pluto, Scorpio, or the 8th house of a
> chart, is the need to learn self-knowledge through the mirror of close
> peers, and to learn self-mastery out of respect for the rights of others.

The idea that Pluto's "influence" is growing stronger in the period
mentioned above is confirmed in the psychic readings of Edgar Cayce,
for he stated earlier in this century:

> ....these (influences) are a development that is occurring in the
> universe, or environs about the earth—Pluto.... It is gradually *growing,*
> and thus is one of those influences that are to be a *demonstrative activity*

in the future affairs or developments of man, *towards the spiritual-minded influence*....

These (individuals) in the present, as might be said, are merely the (ones) *becoming aware* of same. Rather, within the next hundred to two hundred years there may be a great deal of influence (of Pluto) upon the ascendency of man; for it's closest of those to the activities of the earth, to be sure, and is a *developing* influence, not one already established. (Reading 1100-27; quoted in Margaret Gammon's *Astrology & the Edgar Cayce Readings*, p. 46)

One of the most remarkable things about Pluto is that its meaning encompasses many opposite qualities, about which we shall speak in more detail shortly. But simply to study the planet from the astronomical viewpoint leads one inevitably to confront measurements that range from the most minute to the incomprehensibly vast. For example, Pluto is approximately of the fourteenth stellar magnitude, which means that it is around one sixteen-hundredth as bright as the faintest star easily visible to the naked eye on a clear, moonless night. This minute level of brightness, together with its rather small size, are two factors that are quite deceptive, for the power represented by Pluto far surpasses its physical attributes. It seems apparent that *anything connected with Pluto (or with the sign Scorpio or the eighth house) cannot accurately be judged from its appearance, nor can it be understood from mere observation of surface characteristics.* Our conception of the vastness of our planetary system (and thus of the nature of human beings as well) has been greatly expanded by the discovery of Pluto. Astronomers used to think of our solar system as being sixty astronomical units in extent. Now, they see it as a third again as large, or eighty astronomical units in overall diameter, and possibly larger since it is known that the Sun's gravitational field extends far beyond Pluto. The solar system is now considered to be of such dimensions that light—which travels in a vacuum at more than 186,000 miles per second—requires some eleven hours to go from one extremity of the planetary domain to the other. It has recently become clear to increasing numbers of astrologers that the potential expansion of consciousness which Pluto symbolizes *in the individual chart* is a perfect parallel to the expanded awareness of the vast scope of the solar system itself which Pluto's discovery prompted.

Pluto operates at such a deep level and with such subtlety that research into the charts of "famous" people doesn't help us much to understand Pluto's significance. After all, we can't usually know what inner problems or profound experiences shaped these peoples' lives. Hence, the most important research with Pluto has to be done in relation to our own birth-charts and those of close friends. Whether considered in relation to individual experience or collective phenomena, Pluto always symbolizes a form of *extremely concentrated power*. This power is so intensely concentrated that the physical shape or size of Plutonian phenomena (like the planet itself) is irrelevant. For example, the atomic bomb is usually considered to be a Plutonian source of power. The amount of energy released from one such bomb is overwhelming in comparison to the bomb's physical size. As mentioned above, the planet itself exhibits this characteristic; for, although smaller than the Earth, its "influence" affects life on Earth in a proportion far greater than its size would indicate. Plutonian power, therefore, is derived from a source that is beyond or within the physical form through which the power emanates. The great energy of Pluto comes from a source that is not at all obvious and which we might call transcendental. This is the reason that Plutonian energy always manifests in terms of opposites, for that which is truly transcendent can only be understood by ordinary consciousness in terms of opposites: the light and the dark, the joy and the suffering, the spectacular show followed by the inevitable backlash. For example, nuclear energy and large scale use of chemical pesticides have been referred to as Plutonian phenomena. Both are sources of great power, and we have all seen the obvious results they can accomplish. But both have also been used in such a way as to bring about the negative, destructive aspects of such forces: radiation poisoning and genetic damage, and chemical poisoning of the soil, food, and water. Pluto therefore symbolizes a kind of power which can be used creatively only when the user is sufficiently spiritually-oriented, for spiritual evolution and in-depth healing are the only areas of experience wherein Pluto's forces can be utilized without a negative backlash.

The Transits of Pluto

The function of the Plutonian energy can best be shown by looking into the meaning of Pluto's transits to important points in the natal chart. Although Chapter 9 will discuss these transits in more detail, it is necessary to touch upon them here in order to clarify the essential principle which Pluto represents. Pluto's transits are ordinarily concerned with the death and destruction of the old, this destruction being necessary in order to make room for the new. C.E.O. Carter writes that "all eliminative processes are Plutonian, including those advocated by what is called Nature Cure." Advocates of the Nature Cure method of healing believe that, in order for the person to be healed, all poisons, toxins, and other impediments to the flow of the life energy must be eliminated, thus allowing the natural healing forces to rebuild (or regenerate) the body. Carter says that a boil is a good example of Pluto's action on a small scale, since it *brings to the surface* that which must be eliminated. This same Plutonian force began to be active on a larger scale at the same time Pluto was discovered, as seen in the Freudian approach to psychology (bringing to the light all "repressed" psychic material) and in the rise of Nazism (bringing to the surface the unsuspected demons that lurk beneath the facade of "civilization"). Transits of Pluto have a similar influence, bringing to the surface that which is ready for elimination and destruction.

For example, one of my clients came to me a few years ago on the verge of psychological collapse. He was paranoid and hysterical at the time, though he is usually extremely self-contained. He said he was having all sorts of paranoid fantasies about his lover. When we looked at the ephemeris to find out what transits were happening at that time, the experience he was going through was immediately clarified. Pluto, by transit, was in an exact square with his natal Venus. Hence, I explained to him that Pluto's transits had the effect of destroying old patterns of thought and behavior, as well as eliminating all sorts of psychic residue that were preventing his growth. Since Pluto was in square to Venus, his experiences naturally were affecting his emotional life and close relationships. It was as if all the fears, ideals, fantasies, and expectations he had about love relationships had been immediately and forcefully brought to the surface and were being purged and eliminated in spite of this person's conscious wishes. This explanation helped him to get some sort of a perspective on what was going on deep within him, although he of course still had to go through the full range of emotional experience. He seemed somewhat relieved after the consultation; and, a few days later, he told me that he was making an appointment with a psychiatrist in order to help him get in touch with these deep feelings. Things calmed down somewhat after this transit passed; but, when Pluto turned retrograde and again came into the square with natal Venus, the same sort of experiences started up again, though this time with much less force. The third transit of Pluto (direct again) in square to his natal Venus marked the end of this very long and difficult period of emotional transition. By the time the whole process was over, he was much clearer about where he stood in relation to his girl friend; he decided to put off marriage for the time being; and he seemed much more content with his everyday emotional life. In addition, all of his values, whether concerning love, marriage, money, or aesthetic preferences, underwent a total transformation. Judging now, from the vantage point of a few years later, it is apparent that this one experience, although at the time painful and confusing, opened up doors to new insights and indeed to an entirely new outlook on life which are still today deeply affecting his everyday attitudes.

This is one point about the transits of the trans-Saturnian planets that cannot be over-emphasized: the long-term ramifications of these crucial change periods will not become apparent until we have the clarified perspective which only time will bring. The changes that happen during these periods are so intense and so concentrated, while at the same time their full implications on the total life are so subtle, that it is simply impossible for most individuals to assimilate within a short period of time the complete meaning of this transition from one phase of life to another. It may often take as long as ten years for a person to fully grasp what indeed was happening on the deeper levels during these transformative phases. At the exact time of the mathematically precise transit, one has no perspective on what is happening. One often simply feels that the rug has been pulled out from under him, leaving him disoriented and with the realization that, while the old is being irretrievably left behind, there is no place to stand, no firm and familiar guidepost to hold on to. It is a very insecure feeling, and it is often accompanied by simultaneous physical and/or psychological symptoms of disintegration. It often seems to me that the actual experience of these transits (i.e., the transits of any of the trans-Saturnian planets) is not nearly so stress-producing as the resulting panic, fear, and anxiety which quickly ensues in most people. Since human beings are creatures of habit and therefore rarely inclined to give up the old and familiar security of past patterns of life, they usually resist such changes—which only has the effect of increasing the inner pressure and tension. The only thing that can get us through these periods with some degree of psychic balance left intact is a firm, unshakable faith in the wisdom and the order of life itself. This faith has to be based on real knowledge of universal laws, for a sham faith that one clings to primarily out of fear inevitably collapses as soon as a real challenge is confronted. This is one of the greatest values of astrology, for it can lead the individual to discover real and reliable knowledge about the universal laws which shape our life experience. It can give the individual a heightened perspective on his experience, a detachment which can eventually grow into wisdom.

Hence, although some astrologers hold that Pluto transits always bring about some kind of "separation" from people, things, or activities, we can see from the above example that Pluto operates on a level that is far deeper than that of mere transitory phenomena. I am not saying that large-scale outer events never accompany such a transit. I *am* emphasizing that, whether or not there are obvious, external changes at that time, the *meaning* of the experience is never starkly obvious; for the changes at the deepest psychic level are so long-lasting and so profound that the analytical mind cannot grasp their true purpose. In the above example, a "separation" did take place, but it was on a deep emotional level, through the elimination of life patterns that were no longer serving a useful purpose in the person's inner development. He was, therefore, "separated" from self-defeating and inhibiting psychological patterns, although his relationship with a particular woman developed markedly in closeness and in depth, and his capacity to understand his own emotional needs and thus his ability to relate to other people more meaningfully grew at a rapid pace. Hence, although Pluto transits often coincide with the absolute and total end of an old phase of outward activity or an overt mode of self-expression, they inevitably show us inwardly that it is time to let go of an old psychological pattern or approach to life which no longer serves any creative purpose.

This same idea is stated by Dane Rudhyar in his book *Triptych* when he refers to Pluto's influence as bringing about a "freedom from bondage to forms and substances no longer useful to the individualized spirit...." Pluto, by transit, therefore symbolizes *the power to release the more enduring from the transitory,* whether it be the soul from the body at death or the individual self from the old shell of personality and ego. Transiting Pluto brings to the surface hidden or subliminal conditions in order that this energy can be released from the old shell and *transformed into a new source of consciously-usable power.* The action of transiting Pluto always deals with both the light and the dark, the old and the new. Hence, while it often brings to the surface the remnants of the old in order that they can be eliminated, it can also bring to light what the inner self has learned and make manifest the essence of being which endures.

Reincarnation & Karma

Seen in the light of reincarnation and the law of karma, the influence of the planet Pluto might be clarified. For example, transiting Pluto has the effect of destroying and eliminating old psychological patterns, which can be seen as the residue from past life thoughts and actions. If each person (or soul) has lived many lives in many different bodies, it seems reasonable that the memory and impressions of all these lives' actions and thoughts still lie in the unconscious mind. It then follows that such subliminal patterns of thought and action might easily become activated in our daily lives and interfere with our functioning as free, fully conscious entities. The transits of Pluto, therefore, serve to speed our evolution by severing our attachment to the old and making room for the new. In traditional psychological terminology, these unconscious conglomerates, which, according to Dr. C. G. Jung, contain a definite "psychic energy" of their own, are known as "complexes." These complexes are alive and still influence the conscious life of individuals by means of various subtle—yet insistent—feelings. In relation to the theory of reincarnation, these concentrations of psychic energy can be seen as the results (or "karma") of past thoughts, desires, and actions. Pluto's transits, therefore, often seem to wipe out much of this karmic residue in a particular area, allowing the individual a greater possibility of expressing himself thereafter as a psychologically free agent. The fantasies, paranoia, and hallucinations that sometimes accompany Pluto transits are thus the result of this psychic residue being stirred up and forcefully pushed to the surface.

In mythology, Pluto was always connected with the "underworld." Just as the god Pluto held Persephone in the underworld, so the Pluto force in the individual horoscope symbolizes those old patterns and psychic wastes which hold us down and have to be eliminated.* In Greek mythology, Pluto was regarded esoterically as identical with Hades and Dionysos. As the scholar Kerenyi states, Hades and Pluto were both considered to be "cover names" for Dionysos. (*Eleusis*, p. 40) The fact that the subterranean wine god Dionysos and Pluto were regarded as identical gives us a clue to why people behave so compulsively under the influence of alcohol; for the liquor stimulates and stirs up the old, usually unconscious compulsions. Kerenyi writes that Persephone was "seduced by her father, the Subterranean Zeus, Hades, or Dionysos...." This subterranean Zeus is identical with Pluto, and the fact that this deity is called Zeus reveals what overwhelming power was attributed to him.

---

*Pluto's connection with the "underworld" seems to be borne out by people's experiences during Pluto transits; for in some cases, either things or people disappear from sight as if they were taken from the earth's surface into the underworld; in other cases, one has old things or people one was once involved with *reappear;* sometimes there is a disappearance and later reappearance during the long period of Pluto's repeated transits of a particular point. And the connection with the underworld is also borne out in cases where a person experiences contact with the criminal element during this time. Patricia Hearst is a good example of both types of occurrences since she disappeared into the underworld as Pluto was nearly conjuncting her natal Moon. Contacts with the criminal underworld are also common when someone is born with strong natal aspects involving Pluto and the Sun, and sometimes with other personal planets also.

For the Greeks, Pluto was regarded as the antithesis of the Sun God Apollo, hence as an irreconcilable enemy of all new life. This interpretation corresponds with astrological factors; for the Sun in the individual chart shows what we're assimilating and in what area of life our innermost self is expressed, whereas Pluto shows what aspects of the personality must be eliminated before the self can grow and in what area of life we express old, compulsive ways of being. As mentioned above, Pluto was correlated with the divine power living within the earth (the subterranean Dionysos), he who holds the keys to great riches, as well as he who gives and then takes away life-giving forces within all natural forms. This polarity between life and death, light and darkness, the new and the old reveals how closely Pluto is connected with the most profound life processes, active at the deepest levels of experience. In this light, Pluto may be seen as identical to the overwhelming, impersonal power of the earth, what Jung calls "chthonic power"; and the ruthlessness and cruelty often associated with Pluto is starkly evident in nature where survival of the fittest is the rule and where the strong and sly prey upon the weak and slow. There is of course a natural law guiding this process, but it does not lessen the terror and horror that we often feel at the impersonal cruelty of nature in the material plane. Perhaps this connection of Pluto to the deeper power of the earth was what Cayce was referring to when he said that Pluto is closest to the activities of the planet earth?

If one wants to get a better feel for what this chthonic earth power is, I would suggest that one follow the hint found in a particular Greek myth, in which any place where a large fig tree grows was regarded as a point on the earth's surface where one could have easy access to the Plutonian power below. One could sit underneath such a tree and tune in on this energy in order to become familiar with its raw power. For millenia, the fig tree has been regarded in many cultures as the symbol *par excellence* of the earth's fertility and its ability to bring forth life even in a desert. In fact, one of the many unusual astrological "coincidences" of my life was the fact that I used to go up to a high hill in Northern California in order to sit and meditate under the towering branches of a huge, ancient fig tree. I was always powerfully impressed with the intensity of energy that emanated from that area, as if I was descending into the primeval mists of prehistoric times, times when one could still experience cosmic powers and energies with great immediacy. Even on a day when the outside temperature was 110°, the temperature under the fig tree was many degrees cooler. The trunk of that tree was over four feet in diameter, and the diameter of the entire tree measured from the outer branches must have been at least fifty feet. The odd thing is that I had never heard of the Greek legends about the fig tree's correlation with Pluto at that time. When I did come across these myths a short time later, it seemed to me that not only was the ancient legend based upon a real energy that could be experienced but also that it was especially appropriate since my progressed Moon at the time was in the natal eighth house and aspecting natal Pluto.

One of the paradoxical aspects of Pluto's nature is that its symbolism incorporates both the old life forms which are ready to be eliminated *and* the very power that will shatter those forms and effect this type of psychological-emotional surgery. This seeming paradox may be understood when we see that the Pluto energy is contained within the old forms and that it simply needs to be activated (for example, by a powerful transit) for the energy to release and thus bring things to the surface rapidly and compellingly. An analogy would be the sprouting of a seed; for the rigid, concentrated form of the seed is indeed destroyed when the latent seed power begins to stir. As the seed receives the moisture and warmth it needs for the potential energy to unfold, the seed's form is split asunder and indeed is used for food in order to nourish and sustain the new growth. We might take a lesson from this analogy in that, while the old life patterns and forms are destroyed and eliminated from one's present mode of living during a Plutonian period, the energy released from this transformation (even if in the form of pain and deep agony) is the very energy which will nourish us and enable us to push onward toward new growth.

Pluto's House Position

We can say, therefore, that Pluto's position in the individual birth-chart reveals the old ego, or the old shell of the personality which is still active and which still embodies a considerable concentration of psychic energy. As long as this energy remains unconscious and inextricably connected with old patterns of life, it acts as a psychological complex which promotes *compulsive* and *obsessive* patterns of thought and behavior in our conscious life. It is only when this energy is freed from the confines of the old shell—the shell which we have now outgrown—that it can be consciously used to help us manifest the essence of the solar individuality, the new way of being which is necessary for our development. Pluto in the individual chart therefore symbolizes (by house position) the deep-seated psychic impressions resulting from past desires and actions, which now manifest subtly as obsessions and compulsions that have no rational explanation. In other words, the true nature of the original desire is no longer clear to us; yet we are still at the mercy of this inclination, and it often makes us miserable. Pluto's house position therefore also shows where one is living out an old desire or pattern of behavior and where the results of that overwhelming urge are often creating pain and suffering.

Another way of putting this is that we are most intensely meeting our karma in whatever area of life is symbolized at Pluto's house position. Although Saturn is often said to be the planet of karma, this is an over-simplification. Saturn does reveal *specific* karmic tests and specific needs for self-discipline. But the essence of the law of karma, as the clairvoyant Edgar Cayce puts it, is "meeting self." And Pluto's house position shows the field of experience wherein we are meeting our old self and our past desires. The suffering often necessitated by the confrontation with this old self is a clear example of how difficult it is to live up to the ancient axiom "Know thyself." Pluto in the individual chart thus reveals what work we have to do at deep levels of our being, what patterns of being we have to let go of, eliminate, or reject. The reason Pluto is often said to represent a "higher octave" of Mars is not only that both are extremely powerful and assertive influences, but also that both planets reveal in any particular chart specific directions that this energy should take. Whereas Mars represents the energy we have to do work in the world, Pluto represents the energy necessary to do work in the underworld, i.e., at the deeper levels of each person's psychic structure.

Whatever house Pluto is found in is highly energized, for it is here that one is in immediate contact with a deep reservoir of concentrated power. This great power can be used to assert one's desires willfully, ruthlessly, and obnoxiously; or it can be harnessed as positive will and mind power and used to elevate one's higher qualities. Whatever house Pluto is in will show where one is inclined to try to impose his or her will on others, but it is also in this area of life that one can make the most dramatic strides toward personal development. There is great energy at one's disposal in whatever area of life is indicated by Pluto's house position, and this energy can lend depth and thoroughness, insight and power of concentration to those fields of experience, if the energy is utilized with full consciousness. Pluto's house position also indicates the area of life in which the individual may feel isolated and lonely, for in this area the person prefers to remain buried in his or her own interests. This can indicate a certain anti-social quality due to the fact that one is impatient and demanding in this area of life. This impatience arises from the deep feeling that one's identity (an identity carried over from the past) is threatened, that everything related to that particular field of experience is collapsing and being destroyed at the foundations of one's being. Here again we see the polarity between the Sun (one's true identity in *this* life) and Pluto (an old pattern of identity from the past, still subliminally active). The old identity is being destroyed, a process that has to be undergone in order for the person to experience a new way of being.

A few examples may help to explain this connection between Pluto and a resonance with a past pattern of life. Pluto in the first house is one of the most difficult Pluto positions to have in a natal chart. Here, the person usually experiences an almost continual identity crisis throughout his or her first twenty-five years or even longer, an experience that severely affects the person's self-image. But where does this feeling come from? I feel that this factor is only explainable in terms of reincarnation and karma. As an example, two people I know were told by reliable clairvoyants about past lives, the influence of which are very active in their present lives. Both people have Pluto in the first house, often known as the "house of identity." One person was said to have been a slave in the past, and this demeaning experience could surely account for her lack of self-confidence and her periodic identity crises since childhood. The other person was said to have been in Atlantis where he was subjected to all sorts of cruel "scientific" experiments, which had a devastating effect upon his sense of identity. Again, this could easily account for his identity problems in this life. Another person, who has Pluto in the fifth house of his natal chart, was said to have been the head of a large household and to have wielded a great deal of power over other people. This tendency carries over into this life as an inclination to "lord it over" others and to forget that they have their own desires and rights. (Remember that the fifth house correlates with the lordly sign Leo.) Another example, the clairvoyant Edgar Cayce, said in his own psychic reading that he had once been in a position of social authority, shaping the lives of thousands of people when he was a priest in Egypt. This explanation corresponds to Cayce's natal Pluto being in the tenth house of authority, and anyone who reads Cayce's biography cannot fail to notice how often he had clashes with those in authority during *his* lifetime.

We can gather from the above examples that Pluto's house position shows a past pattern of life that is carried over into this life. The power from the past is still there; but, evidently, the time has come to use that power in a new way. The time has come for that old pattern of life to die and for a new way of being to develop. At this point, one might well ask how this new way of being can develop when each of us is chained to the old? I can only answer that one must consciously *let go* of the old and open oneself to the influence of others so that one can learn new attitudes toward that area of life. This letting go is especially difficult for Plutonian and Scorpionic people, for they hate to let go in any way since they fear that the resulting openness will make them vulnerable and thus will be giving the power they want to keep into the hands of others. How can one have the faith to let go if one has no trust in others, in one's own motivations, or—indeed—in life or God? This is the dilemma which any person faces if he or she has a strong accent on Pluto, Scorpio, or even on the eighth house in the natal chart. We might say therefore that the first step in dealing with this type of problem is to learn to *trust*, primarily by taking the risk of opening oneself now and then and coming to realize that one can handle whatever ensues, even if it does bring pain with it. One of the contradictory qualities of Pluto is that those who have emphasis on this planet (or its sign or house) are often so courageous and fearless of suffering in their approach to outer life activities and challenges; yet these are the same people who are often terrified of encountering the pain of their own deeper feelings.

This process of learning a new approach, of refining one's mode of self-expression and the use of one's will power, has often been called "regeneration." Hence, we can say that Pluto's house position reveals the area of life where a complete regeneration must take place. This regeneration changes willfulness, compulsiveness, and ruthlessness into a consciously-usable power of great intensity which then manifests as penetrating insight, understanding of subtle forces (often resulting in knowledge years ahead of its time), and the use of the will to promote creative actions. The Pluto energy can also be directed into healing channels. In fact, many people who specialize in healing merely by laying on of hands or through other systems of healing by touch have a prominent Pluto in their charts. It should be emphasized that the Pluto energy is so effective in healing because it is simultaneously an outgoing, forceful power *and* a receptive sensitivity.

The following sections provide hints and guidelines for interpreting the meaning of Pluto in the various natal houses. Please keep in mind that these are only guidelines and are meant primarily to elicit insights in your own mind related to the person whose chart is being examined. How positively or negatively the various potentials are being expressed is up to you to judge.

Pluto in the first house: In the first house, the house of identity, Pluto indicates that the person's sense of self must be totally changed. Although these people often have a deep and penetrating understanding, their insecurity and reserve prevents them from expressing it freely. They desperately need to listen to others' opinions of them in order to generate a new feeling about themselves; but their very defensiveness about their sense of identity often inhibits this openness. Cooperation at a deep personal level is so difficult for them that they often wind up lonely and, in some cases, even alienated from friends and family. If the Pluto energy is used creatively here, the person can exhibit powerful concentration, a dedication to higher spiritual or social ideals, and a remarkable depth of insight into life's deeper meanings.

Pluto in the second house: Here there is an overwhelming desire to have control of one's material resources as an aid to achieving peace of mind. The very orientation toward controlling or *possessing,* however, is the source of inner turmoil. Pluto in this house indicates that one's attitudes toward owning or toward possessing things or people must be transformed in order to achieve a regeneration of values. Pluto here also indicates that compulsive expenditures can be a source of difficulty, in which case one needs to discipline that tendency. A person with this position of Pluto is, however, often extremely resourceful in his or her efforts to build some kind of material security; and there can be an understanding of the deeper kinds of energy which money represents.

Pluto in the third house: Pluto in this house indicates a person who is compulsively thorough in all matters of communication. This person wants to be absolutely sure that ideas are being clearly transmitted. This can manifest as a rather irritable way of speaking with others, or it can be transformed into a creative ability to get to the depths of human interaction. People with Pluto here may also have great energies which they can direct out their hands in healing work, and they often are naturally talented in all forms of research.

Pluto in the fourth house: Here the Plutonian compulsiveness operates within the home and within the emotional depths of the person's psychological life. There is a strong urge for security and for a place of rest and retreat where the person is able to control *exactly* what is going on in the environment. This can indicate a home life which is subject to all sorts of upheavals and battles due to willfulness and obstinacy. Pluto here indicates that a total reorientation is needed in one's deepest feelings about one's self and in one's sense of security, inner peace, and contentment. It can also indicate deep insight into other people's emotional needs and an ability to penetrate into the unconscious mind.

Pluto in the fifth house: Here there is a strong compulsion to "be somebody," to express one's individuality in a big way. Often these people's desires to be best and to be recognized as best are thwarted, thus leading to painful re-evaluations of the need to be so great. If the energy motivating the compulsion is transformed into a consciously-usable and practically-applicable power, the person then can pioneer into new areas of creativity with unusual depth. Their creative work may be way ahead of its time, but the power and thoroughness of the work will insure its eventual acceptance. Close emotional relations with children or lovers also serve to help these people learn about themselves in essential ways, although the compulsive element of such relations should be eliminated. The key with this position of Pluto is that the person must learn to be content with his lot in life and must learn to use his great energy to *do* something special rather than just wanting to be known as someone special.

Pluto in the sixth house: Here in the sixth house, Pluto indicates someone who either wants to serve and help others or at least wants to *feel* as if he or she is a helpful person. There can be a compulsion to serve others, often in ways that are not appreciated by those being served. This person will often do best to work by and with himself, directing his reformative energies towards his own personal transformation. This position of Pluto also indicates that matters of personal health, or a particular serious illness, can be instrumental in producing great changes in one's attitudes and a purification of one's values. In some cases, it also seems to indicate talent in the healing arts.

Pluto in the seventh house: With Pluto in the seventh house, the individual will find marriage and close relationships the dominant field within which his own personal transformation can take place. Often there are compulsive and painful emotional problems with close relationships. Although this person wants to give others a lot of freedom and desperately wants to be liked, he often finds himself unable to establish a true rapport with others. Co-operation becomes difficult, especially when the person finds that he is involved with people who wield a definite power in his life. With this position of Pluto, a marriage can be long-lasting, but only if the person accepts the personal changes required to make it work.

Pluto in the eighth house: Pluto in this house reveals a compulsion to influence the world through the use of power, whether through socially-approved channels of authority or through deep psychological forces or occult power. There can be an inclination toward manipulating others and toward insisting that others change themselves according to this person's values. Like those with Pluto in the sixth house, this person will do best to let others simply be themselves and to concentrate on learning how to use power for his or her own personal transformation. There are often painfully compulsive experiences in the area of sexuality. The key to the resolution of this entire complex is that the person needs to totally reorient his use of all power: physical, mental, social, emotional, and spiritual.

Pluto in the 9th house: With this position of Pluto, there is a compulsion to have and to express strong beliefs and ideals that can guide the person's way of life. Manifesting negatively, this can take the form of dogmatism, self-righteousness, and a need to convert or convince others that they are the ones who know the truth. In order to transform this tendency, these people should realize that, as C. G. Jung wrote, one person's salvation is another's damnation; and they should let go of the desire to prove their beliefs to themselves by preaching to others. With this Pluto position, we also often find that, as the years pass, the person has profoundly deep experiences which serve to re-orient his or her attitudes about God, truth, and the value of human life.

Pluto in the tenth house: The compulsiveness of Pluto here often takes the form of an impatience toward authority: a resentment against those in authority, or an overwhelming drive to establish oneself as outstanding in some way that will be recognized by others. These people can often attain the position in the world which they seek, but it usually involves a long and somewhat painful re-evaluation of their true motives and values. Hence, those with this position of Pluto need to totally transform their attitudes toward wordly success, authority, and reputation. Ideally, it symbolizes an ability to see beyond the outer forms of "authority" and hence to develop a deeper sense of responsibility about wielding authority.

Pluto in the eleventh house: Here, Pluto manifests as a compulsion to be accepted by other people and as a need to achieve certain objectives that are consciously not very clear. Often, certain fixed ideas have to be changed in order that a re-birth can take place in the areas of one's ultimate desires and sense of purpose. The emphasis upon the future sometimes takes such precedence with these people that the present is neglected. Those with this position of Pluto in their natal charts should learn to rely upon themselves, rather than upon others, for their fulfillment, knowing that their deepest hope for the future will be fulfilled only if it encompasses an entire transformation and clarification of their *own* creative purpose within the framework of social needs.

Pluto in the twelfth house: With this position of Pluto, the person must transform the quality of his or her emotional life by an adherence to some belief or transcendental truth which has the effect of liberating the self from a morass of confusing emotions. Often, this re-orientation will require long periods of loneliness and abstention from social interaction; for dealing with other people often has the effect of again stirring up the old, troublesome emotions that the person is trying to transcend. They should be careful not to allow one-track emotional guilt patterns and feelings of self-persecution to gain the upper hand. The key to this orientation is to establish definite spiritual attitudes toward all of life. Once this spiritual transformation has progressed to a certain point, the individual can develop the capacity to experience the unity of all life which lies beneath outer forms.

In any house, the Pluto energy can be tapped to make way for an impersonal—yet controllable—heightened consciousness and for the will power to direct that awareness into creative activities. As with Saturn, the negative aspect of Pluto has been over-emphasized; for the real power of Pluto only becomes negative if we are seeking to interfere with its work.

The Aspects of Pluto

In my experience, the aspects involving Pluto are among the most difficult factors in any chart to understand, for one never knows on what level the potential is manifesting. Although the nature of Uranus is often referred to as "unpredictable," it seems to me that the action of Pluto is even more unpredictable. In many cases, it seems to make little difference whether the aspect being considered is a "harmonious" or an "inharmonious" one. In fact, as one begins to investigate the aspects of any of the trans-Saturnian planets, one sees that the so-called stressful aspects are often found in the charts of the most creative and spiritually-aware people. Our evaluation of the meaning of various aspects, therefore, really depends fundamentally upon our own philosophy of life and the particular individual purpose that we value most highly. If our primary purpose is to have a life of ease and *absence* of major problems (but also, therefore, absence of challenges toward growth and creativity), there might be some justification for approaching aspects in the traditional way of labeling them hard/soft, good/bad, stressful/easy. But if we have the capacity to see life's possibilities with more complexity and depth, then it becomes much more difficult to categorize various types of human experience according to simplistic, *a priori* types. The fact most obvious to me is that, if one assumes that there is indeed a creative intelligence from which all life manifestations emanate, then every life experience is *guided by* this higher intelligence and has a specific purpose. How can we question this purpose? To do so is to reveal our own intellectual arrogance, for it is a bold step to think that we have the capacity to know better than the Architect of this universe. Outlined in Chapter 6 is a more holistic and—I feel—more constructive approach to aspects than is commonly found in astrological textbooks. Some of the above questions are considered further in that chapter, as is more specific material about Pluto aspects. But there are some basic points about these aspects we can clarify here, since they are related to the characteristics of Pluto already discussed.

Aspects of Pluto to another planet in the individual chart show how *easily* one can use the Pluto energy and how easily one may undergo a Plutonian regeneration. A similar type of development and transformation may, for example, be indicated by both the trine and the square between the same planets, but the person may forcefully resist the change when the aspect is the square. When the aspect is more harmonious (for example, trine or sextile), it seems that the person often has an inner knowledge of why this particular change is necessary, and hence he accommodates himself to the necessary changes more readily. Specifically, it often seems that those with Pluto in trine or sextile to their Sun or Moon (or at times to other personal planets) have an innate understanding of natural processes of growth and transformation. They often seem to take for granted the fact that life is always demanding that we leave behind the old and open ourselves to the new. This does not mean that such people never experience any pain related to Plutonian changes, but simply that they know and accept the fact that the pain they do experience is a necessary part of life.

The fact that a similar type of transformation may be indicated whether the aspect with Pluto is a traditionally "hard" or "easy" aspect can be illustrated by the following example. (Note that it is primarily the person's *approach* to dealing with the required changes that is indicated most specifically by the relative harmony or disharmony of the aspect itself.) During a consultation with a thirty-year-old man a few years ago, we were talking about his emotional reactions and general emotional state when he made the following statement: "I find that I am always having to re-form my feeling states, to consciously change my immediate reactions to many different situations." This particular person at that time had very little knowledge of astrology and certainly no in-depth familiarity with Pluto aspects. And yet, a glance at his chart revealed that he was born with Pluto in a close trine to the Moon! What better symbol could we have of the exact experience he had just described? But the key point here is that he was *aware* that he was continually making a *conscious* effort to effect the reforming and transforming of this part of his nature. It was not something he resisted or was especially troubled by. It was perceived to be simply a regular transformative experience in his everyday life which he fully accepted as necessary, although he was unaware of the astrological symbolism for this process. Someone else with Pluto in conjunction, square, or opposition to the natal Moon might experience the same need to alter his or her spontaneous emotional reactions in order to cope with and adapt to everyday life; but a person with these particular aspects might see it as more of a problem and might tend to resist initiating the effort to make the required changes.

Pluto in any aspect to a personal planet means that there is an increase of consciousness due, a re-birth of sorts, with respect to that part of oneself symbolized by the other planet. This increase of consciousness may be regarded as especially necessary for one's growth if the aspect is a conjunction, square, quincunx, or opposition. In other words, the dimension of experience symbolized by the planet in aspect to Pluto needs to be transformed into a higher or more conscious level of expression. Among the more dynamic aspects, the conjunction, square, and quincunx usually indicate an inner tension and challenge which we can either accept as something we must face with full intensity and commitment, or which we can try to avoid or run away from. The other "dynamic" aspect involving Pluto, the opposition, usually indicates that compulsive, demanding, and willful tendencies interfere quite regularly with the development of certain relationships in our lives. The other planet involved and the houses wherein the planets fall usually give enough information that the specific type of relationship where this problem is focused can be understood. It is my experience that people with Pluto oppositions very rarely realize the fact that it is their own subtle demands—demands that the other person be different from what he or she truly is—that create the relationship problems. In fact, since Pluto by nature is usually indicative of a certain complex of compulsive, unconscious tendencies, it is not surprising that the majority of people with whom I have dealt cannot immediately identify with the compulsive behavior patterns indicated by Pluto in their charts. It is only when people have taken definite steps toward an honest—even ruthless!—self-examination that they become conscious enough of their own deeper feelings and motivations to be able to relate to the meaning of Pluto in their own charts. And the tension of the "difficult" Pluto aspects can then generate the ability to express the Pluto energy in a particularly dynamic way.

Trines and sextiles *can* mean that one easily expresses the Pluto energy in a creative way; but this is not necessarily always true. These aspects do show that the channel is open for the expression of that energy; but, if the energy is still unrefined, still unregenerated, these aspects can simply mean that one can rather easily express the negative, compulsive side of Pluto's power. For example, I once had a consultation with a woman who has Pluto in her ninth house in exact trine to her Moon. Pluto in the ninth house can signify rigidly compulsive opinions and beliefs that have been carried over from a past incarnation; and this is one of the usual meanings of Pluto in the ninth until a transformation of one's ultimate beliefs has taken place. This particular woman repeatedly defeated her groping attempts at growth by clinging to these rigid beliefs. There was no logic to her ideas, nor were they based on any kind of personal revelation or intuition. Her pattern of believing and the resulting opinions seemed to be simply a kind of past conditioning from which she had difficulty freeing herself. No matter how dissatisfied with her present life she was, and no matter what alternative ways of dealing with life were presented to her, she was always able to call upon some inflexible belief which she could use as an excuse for not taking any risk or personal responsibility to change her life. Hence, even though the aspect with Pluto in this case is a "harmonious" one, it seems to indicate merely that she is able to express her self-defeating attitudes and opinions with comparative ease. It is only when she has gone through a transformative process in this area of her life, when she succeeds in leaving behind these inhibiting compulsions, that this trine can begin to manifest creatively.

Pluto aspects can also give us a clue about how a person uses his or her will power and concentrated mental power. Although one must be careful in applying general principles to an individual person, I feel certain that the conjunctions, squares, and oppositions *tend toward* a willful sort of behavior, in which the person will often try to overpower the will of another person rather ruthlessly. These same aspects, however, can also show the potential for developing an extremely powerful inner strength and courage, *if* the individual succeeds in becoming aware of his or her tendency toward a misuse of power and brings it under conscious control. If the Pluto power is expressed creatively, the person can exhibit great self-discipline, unshakable dedication to spiritual development, and a strong sense of resourcefulness.

Another insight into the meaning of Pluto and its aspects became apparent to me when I was listening to a lecture by Richard Ideman, a well known astrologer and lecturer. He related Pluto to the concept of "taboo" and to the fears that people experience in relation to such socially-forbidden realms. This concept of "taboo" is a very useful one, for it explains a great deal about not only Pluto but also the significance of the eighth house and the deeper nature of the sign Scorpio. For example, it has become clear to me that Scorpionic and Plutonian people are particularly susceptible to paranoia in one degree or another. One of the reasons for this deep inner terror is, as I mentioned earlier, the fact that such people don't readily *trust* other people or their *own* feelings and motivations. But another reason for this paranoia and the behavioral and relationship problems resulting from such fear is that the person often feels guilty about breaking social, moral, or familial taboos. There is an extremely intense attraction-repulsion conflict which Plutonian people feel about taboo areas of life. And, whether they actually experiment directly by acting out their interest in these taboo areas of life or whether they merely think about such things but repress the desire to act them out, these people are often troubled by feelings of guilt and by the inner conviction that they will have to pay for such transgressions. It seems to me that the people who refuse to confront their true desires through some kind of direct action are the ones most likely to suffer from the inner stagnation, negativity, and paranoia which can flourish in a severely repressed individual. At least if the person acts out his or her true desires, the taboos and the emotional attachments to those activities are brought into the light so that the person can begin to take full responsibility for his or her deeper feelings.

How can we take this concept of "taboo" and apply it to the understanding of specific aspects with Pluto? In all aspects involving Pluto—especially the conjunction, square, and opposition—the individual feels the pressure to confront a certain taboo. This forbidden area may be sexual, religious, ethical, familial, social, or a combination of some or all of these areas of life. The first impulse in most people is to try to control this tendency by repression. However, many people eventually find that this pent-up transformative power impels them to confront the taboos and to break through their restrictions. It seems to me that some sort of break-through is usually necessary in order to achieve in conscious life the transformation shown as potential in the aspect configuration. The taboos must be confronted since all the psychic garbage, fears, attachments, and negativity have to be brought to the surface in order to be outgrown or transmuted. How can one escape from a prison if one has no knowledge of the structure of the prison, how the various locks work, when the guards are off duty, etc.? Everything must be faced with great immediacy. Some people who have the "stressful" aspects of Pluto to the personal planets sense the over-whelming power of that subterranean force and become terrified of being overpowered by it and of losing control (a control which they don't really have to the extent that they think anyhow!). They often respond to this fear by trying even harder to ruthlessly manipulate others, to repress their emotions with an iron will, and to deny the existence of this force. This kind of response of course merely increases the tension already being felt and ultimately aggravates the problem. This kind of repression, by the way, often manifests eventually as the person acting like one "possessed," i.e., acting in a compulsive manner and driven by forces which are totally unconscious. The person *is* in fact possessed. He is possessed by an intense desire which he refuses to acknowledge. As long as he continues to function assuming that "where there's a will, there's a way," this "might makes right" attitude will cause him no end of trouble. In fact, the reason Pluto, Scorpio, and the Eighth House are so connected with transformation is that they have to do with the power of desires, the desires which forge our attachments, the desires that still motivate us compulsively. Getting to the heart of these feelings, penetrating to the source of these desires and their implications can illuminate not only our everyday experience but also the karmic patterns of this lifetime.

Leo

5

Saturn: Its Nature & Cycles

One moment of patience
May ward off great disaster;
One moment of impatience
May ruin a whole life.
— *Chinese Proverb*

Until recent years, the planet Saturn was usually referred to in most astrological books as a "malefic" influence, a dimension of experience that most people would rather not face but which merely had to be endured for no positive purpose whatsoever. However, a constructive trend in the development of modern astrology is that many authors in the past decade or two have referred to the more positive, growth-promoting meanings of Saturn.* Since this more positive approach is currently becoming more wide-spread, I do not feel that it is necessary to present all the rationalizations which could be used to convince the reader that Saturn does indeed have many positive meanings. However, I do feel that the actual function of Saturn, especially as it transits through the various houses of a chart and aspects the various natal planets, can be further clarified. This clarification is especially needed in outlining Saturn's impact on psychological and spiritual transformation. Let us first briefly state some of Saturn's most important general meanings. Saturn can be viewed as:

A. The principle of self-preservation and contraction, which can manifest purely as defensive, fearful attitudes or as a conscious striving toward the achievement of one's ambitions in the world and a fulfilling of one's duties and responsibilities. It can thus indicate a personal contraction of being inward toward greater self-reliance and inner strength.

B. The principle of form, structure, and stability; hence, it is related to law, cultural and social traditions, the father, and all authority figures.

C. The principle of *time* and of learning through immediate experience which comes only from repeated lessons in life. Hence, this principle leads to many of the commonly-mentioned Saturnian qualities: seriousness, caution, worldly wisdom, patience, practical economy, and conservatism. Saturn is correlated with the Greek god of Time *(Kronos)*, who metes out strict justice impartially and impersonally, but also with very little mercy. Saturn is also related to *crystallization*, i.e., the old patterns of life and personality that get more rigid over time. The learning that takes place over time *may* cause

---

*Among these more positive approaches are the following books: *The Transit of Saturn* by Marc Robertson; *The Horoscope as Identity* by Noel Tyl; and one that shows especially deep insight into the psychological meaning of Saturn with great originality and clarity, *Saturn: A New Look at an Old Devil* by Liz Greene.

Saturnian people to be closed off from life and hence self-oppressive, skeptical, wary of anything new, and hesitant to reveal their true feelings. But the same kind of experience can lead other people to develop a sensitivity to enduring values, an appreciation and capacity for moderation, orderliness, and efficiency, and—in some cases—a detached, peaceful wisdom.

D. The urge to defend one's life structure and personal integrity; and the urge toward safety and security through tangible achievement.

E. According to Dane Rudhyar, Saturn refers to a person's "fundamental nature," the purity of one's true self. It seems that Saturn has come to have such negative meanings in the minds of many astrologers and students of astrology because most people do not live in terms of their fundamental nature, but rather in terms of fashions, social patterns and traditions, and ego games. Hence, Saturn is often experienced as a "stern reproach" or as a challenging act of "fate" in order that we begin to heed the needs of our fundamental nature within. Saturn is indeed a rough task-master, as many of the old books say, but it is particularly rough when we have deviated from manifesting our true nature.

F. Psychologically, Saturn represents a dimension of the ego-complex which can and usually does become rigid with age—in other words, that deeply ingrained group of behavior patterns and attitudes which can tie a person in knots of fear. Saturn is also correlated psychologically with what Jung calls the Shadow, i.e., those parts of ourselves which we block, fear, or about which we feel guilty; and hence we project those qualities onto others. Saturn has been said to symbolize the Achilles heel in the armor one wears before the world, the instinct of withdrawal from life. But, as Rudhyar points out, it also signifies the deep-rooted ambition to actualize the potentialities inherent at birth. This ambition is felt as an *inner pressure* to become or to achieve something definite according to our inner pattern of potentialities.

Of all the general meanings of Saturn, probably the most important is that Saturn represents *concentrated* experience and learning which comes only through life in the physical body, in the material plane. Through the resistance of matter and through the pressure of being incarnate in the physical body, we have the opportunity for developing a greater level of concentrated understanding and greater patience in our attitude toward life itself. Saturn is often said to "rule" the dense material plane. When one incarnates into the physical world, the energy field is constricted and thus *concentrated*. That is why an earthly life is such a good learning experience, for here we learn through *depth* of experience, concentrated work, and through seeing the immediate results of our actions. The pain, tension, and pressure of earthly life therefore has an evolutionary and developmental purpose. The material plane is, as the poet T. S. Eliot writes, the point of intersection of the timeless with time. Saturn is the planet of time; and, through the Saturnian experience of living in the material world, where everything moves so slowly and where we have to work so hard to make anything happen or to grow in any way, one can make the greatest spiritual progress. It often seems to go too slowly, and our patience is tested at every point along the way, but persevering through the inert resistance of matter clearly shows us what is enduring and what isn't, where we meet the tests and where we fail. Saturn's action clearly shows us the cost of our desires and attachments; it starkly reveals the limitations of our ego; and it shows us that a highly concentrated consciousness and in-depth understanding are the main things we can take from this world when we leave it. It shows us the value of work, for all the wonderful beliefs and ideals ever thought of by human beings are of little value if they are not applied to everyday life through effort. Saturn's pressure should therefore be taken as a helpful push toward doing the work that we need to do in order to develop at a deep level, rather than as something to dread and to try to escape from.

Saturn's heat and pressure are needed in order that we can develop what Buddhists call the "diamond soul" or "diamond body," which is a way of saying our fundamental, innermost nature. However, Saturn alone, without love and lightness, is rigidity and death. When mental and emotional fixations and blockages result from the extreme expression of Saturn's principle, the negativity that builds up crowds out the true Love essence and energy of life, and the soul starves and withers since it then lacks the very water of life. Hence, complementing Saturn is Jupiter (and—in some cases—Neptune). For we need not only effort (Saturn) but also grace (Jupiter/Neptune), not only immediate experience and reliance on proven facts (Saturn) but also faith (Jupiter/Neptune). Effort and grace operate simultaneously; they are two sides of the same coin. Through effort one opens a channel through which grace may flow. Without one's making that effort, the grace doesn't readily come into the person's life. However, it should be pointed out that an individual rarely makes any effort in the field of spiritual growth unless grace prompts him or her to do so. Hence, there is little grace without effort; but neither is there effort without grace. So we see that Jupiter and Saturn as well as Neptune and Saturn symbolize complementary pairs which should be related to each other in any work with birth-charts.

Saturn should not be *over*-emphasized, for—in many ways—the action of the trans-Saturnians is much more powerful and deeply transforming than Saturn. Saturn shows us the true nature of the material plane, the influence of necessity in our lives, how things really are from the practical, objective viewpoint. But the trans-Saturnians show us what is possible on planes of being and levels of consciousness that totally transcend the material world. Saturn leads us to experience the *limitation* that is an inherent characteristic of the material world. Hence, any time Saturn in the natal chart is activated, one has to deal with the fact of limitation in some dimension of one's life. In other words, one learns that—on this plane—you just can't *have* everything, and neither can you *be* everything that you might have fantasied. The trans-Saturnians, on the other hand, point us toward planes of being and dimensions of experience that are characterized by their being *unlimited*. They are vast; they hold out the promise of unlimited growth.

From the viewpoint of spiritual progress, Saturn is of the greatest benefit in two ways. First, it shows us slowly but surely what the reality of the material world truly is, once all of our wishes, hopes, fantasies, self-deceptions, and desires are out of the way. Secondly, the Saturnian experience of the material world *tests* us in every step we make in our development. Saturn allows no room for self-deception, escapism, or rationalization. Saturn tests how concentrated our spiritual growth really is and how concentrated our consciousness is. Through Saturnian experiences, we have to answer the question: "Now that the chips are down, does our supposed spirituality or self-knowledge enable us to meet this karma with grace, acceptance, and patience?" It seems to me that many souls are "religious" between incarnations, when they are dwelling in various subtler regions of creation that awe the mind with their light and splendor. But the ego submerges that awareness of higher realities as one grows and develops during an earth incarnation, and so only those who have achieved a truly concentrated focus of their life energy toward a spiritual ideal can retain a *clear* attunement to the higher levels. Only those who are truly devoted to the spiritual aspect of life and who are beginning to transcend the ego and worldly attachments can still maintain that high orientation in the midst of the pressures of the earth plane. Most people have some subliminal stirrings of memories (Neptune) of higher planes or of "dream-worlds," "heavens," or of a state of being that was better and more completely satisfying than what they feel in the present. But the memory is usually out of focus and has the effect in most cases merely of making the individual discontented and unhappy. According to the spiritual teachings of many times and places, only some type of concentrated meditation can enable us to retain the perception of the ideal with a clear focus. That process should begin now, in this very lifetime; and, by constant practice, one can increase the focus of attention on the higher levels of consciousness day by day. Hence, one might say that Neptune represents the urge to escape from the limitations of the material plane and to merge with a greater, more refined Oneness. But it is Saturn that has shown us the need to seek that escape, to find that way toward increasing Oneness and liberation!

Saturn in the Natal Chart

Saturn's meaning in the individual birth-chart can be very complex, but there are some specific points that we can outline in relation to Saturn's position in signs and houses. The aspects with Saturn will be treated later. Saturn's position according to sign may be analyzed most easily by referring to the element and quality of the sign wherein it is placed. I will not repeat here the ideas that I put forth in my book *Astrology, Psychology, & the Four Elements*, but anyone interested should refer to pages 140 through 143 of that book for a detailed explanation of Saturn in the various elements. Saturn's meaning in the quadruplicities may be briefly outlined as follows:

In **CARDINAL** signs: Saturn here has to do with organization and utilization of one's energies. A primary mode of active energy expression (either water, earth, air, or fire) tends to be blocked or held back, indicating the need to stabilize that type of self-expression and to work at developing that quality through effort.

In **FIXED** signs: Saturn here is almost always indicative of strong willfulness and rigid habit patterns that block the flow of the love energy of life. Here, the expression of the *essence* of the life force, the innermost self, and one's essential vitality must be restructured. There is often a lack of trust, and usually a lack of true givingness and love. This may of course be compensated for, but the tendency is present nevertheless. This may sound like a large generalization, but one only needs to ask oneself: "Have I ever met anyone who has Saturn in Taurus, Leo, Scorpio, or Aquarius who is truly a giving person, who is spontaneous in expressing affection, and who is flexible in meeting the needs of others?" Such people are rare indeed!

In **MUTABLE** signs: Saturn here has to do with the need to restructure one's mental patterns and the thought currents' mode of operation. The mind often tends toward negative thinking, worry, and opinionatedness, stemming from past life training or conditioning. Here, the person must reorganize the way he or she thinks, as well as the way he or she applies mental energy toward understanding and ordering everyday experience.

We can further explore Saturn's significance according to its sign and house position by outlining a few more specific principles. Each of the following concepts may easily be applied to an individual's personal chart. Their application is especially valuable in analyzing the house position of Saturn, and it is in that area of interpretation that the relevant meanings stand out most clearly. This is so because each house denotes a specific field of immediate experience with which most people can identify quite readily. Applying these principles to the sign placement of Saturn, however, often requires more insight and knowledge of one's deeper psychological nature and energy flow.

A. Saturn in the natal chart shows where you're too attached and rigidly ego-centered, so that you try to control yourself in that area of life in too extreme a way; hence, you often react defensively in that area of life since you are tied up in a knot of negativity. Hence, one must experience some hard lessons in that area of life in order to wear down the walls of defensiveness and egocentric attitudes.

B. As one spiritual teacher has written, "Duty and responsibility (Saturn) is the dam that holds the mind in check." Hence, that area of the chart wherein we find Saturn is an area where we experience specific karmic duties and responsibilities which serve to help us discipline our minds and desires. This discipline in turn helps us to begin to take responsibility for our own actions, desires, and involvements in this area. The discipline may for a time be experienced as frustration or inhibition, but—as every counselor or psychotherapist should know—frustration may be therapeutic in that it throws the person back on himself, thus giving him the opportunity to develop an inner strength by drawing on his own deeper resources.

C. In the natal chart, Saturn symbolizes a point of great sensitivity, an area of life where one may strive to overcome limitation through a serious, thorough, efficient approach. (Or the person may react by building a wall around himself in that area of life for self-protection, thus insuring that a deepening negativity will develop over the years.) Saturn can indicate where feelings of inferiority, self-consciousness, or oppression afflict us, thus eventually causing resentment and bitterness if the challenges are not appropriately met. However, if one accepts the challenge of Saturn to work at *building a new structure* and set of attitudes in that area of life, then Saturn's position can reveal where we can experience some of the deepest satisfaction in our entire lives.

D. Saturn's position reveals gravity's hold over you, where you find experience to be weighty and important, where you therefore often feel like working harder in order to establish security and stability. It is here that one must adjust to the practical necessities of life, in spite of any fear or anxiety that may be felt, by putting in extra effort and taking on extra responsibilities.

E. Saturn's position shows where you are especially sensitive to social norms and expectations, where you need social approval and/or want to live up to some standard of success or recognition. In many cases, the person will *act* as if he or she absolutely rejects social roles or norms in the indicated area of life, but such behavior should not always be taken at face value since the person is often in fact reacting to fear of failure in that field of activity. Since the person feels that area of life to be so deeply important, the individual may want to avoid it entirely or to reject it completely rather than facing the fears and taking on the weighty tasks it requires.

The Aspects of Saturn

Saturn's aspects *in the natal chart* show how well one is attuned to the earth plane and to the practical necessities of everyday life. These aspects reveal whether or not it is easy for the person to adapt to social life, to immediate practical requirements, and to the culture's norms and standards. Saturn is the great teacher about practical realities and the laws of the earth plane, for Saturn inevitably teaches patience, moderation, temperance of extremes, duty, and work. These aspects, however, are not limited in their scope of significance merely to social involvements, for they also show whether or not one's self-expression in some area is inhibited by one's own sense of propriety and acceptability. In other words, one's perception of what is socially acceptable and what is not may be inaccurate. One may inhibit oneself in a certain area due to the feeling that it is not quite right or proper or acceptable, and yet the objective situation may pose no real inhibition to that mode of expression. To state this another way, what we may feel as a restriction imposed upon us by society may in fact be a self-imposed restriction due to past karma. This sense of inner restriction may in fact serve a growth-promoting purpose. It is true that many stressful aspects with Saturn often manifest as an individual's feeling—and sometimes acting—at odds with conventional standards of propriety and authority, but one must look into the deeper psychological and spiritual meanings of these aspects if one is really to understand the reasons for these feelings and this behavior.

One might accurately say that Saturn's principle, when manifesting negatively, is simply fear. Hence, the stressful aspects of Saturn usually indicate that, at least until the person has adjusted to and outgrown this tendency, the person has the opportunity to come to terms with a specific kind of fear through consciously disciplining and stabilizing the expression of the energy indicated by the planet in aspect with Saturn. By realistically confronting that innate tendency toward blockage and fear, one can begin to reformulate the personal attitude and habit patterns in that area of life. So often, when we face a fear head on, with full willingness to do what is necessary to transform that dimension of our lives, the threatening and dark nature of that which we have feared dissipates, revealing just another life challenge and just another aspect of our own being which we have become accustomed to regard with excessive caution and anxiety. A few examples of traditionally problematical aspects should serve to clarify these points.

Saturn, conjunct, square, or opposite Moon or Sun: Often a fear of expressing what one truly is in very essential ways; fear of criticism or of being wrong or inadequate often leads to a fear of trying anything new. One must stabilize and structure one's sense of self and one's self-image in a new way, in the light of one's *current* abilities, achievements, and strengths rather than in reference to past errors, faults, or limitations (i.e., one's karmic inheritance). One must take responsibility for one's self with new courage and learn to take some risks in self-expression and mode of life in order to realize most deeply what one *is* capable of doing or expressing. Projection of one's fears onto *others* is a common manifestation of the opposition aspect.

Saturn conjunct, square, or opposite Mars: One may have a fear of self-assertion, sex, or taking risks in these areas, which the person may try to compensate for by over-emphasizing sex or ambition. The application and expression of the assertive and instinctual energies need to be restructured and disciplined, which—in many cases—the person accomplishes by dedicating self to some highly specialized sort of work in which he can be highly energetic and through which a great deal of physical-sexual energy may be sublimated.

Saturn conjunct, square, or opposite Mercury: There is great attachment to being intelligent and knowledgeable, and great importance is placed on intellectual competence. These feelings can often be causally related to the fear of being considered stupid, slow-witted, or inarticulate. Hence, although this aspect does in some cases indicate a severe mental blockage, manifesting as speech inhibition, slow learning and reading, or a poor capacity for using language precisely, the more common manifestation in my experience seems to be that the person works harder at (and often succeeds at) learning definite skills and facts in order to prove his or her intelligence and competence. This effort may of course be carried so far that the person becomes rigidly opinionated and mentally arrogant, which obviously can lead to more Mercury problems in the clear exchange of ideas with others. The key here is that the person needs to restructure and stabilize the mental faculties and mode of intellectual expression without veering onto the course of rigid adherence to limited concepts or opinions.

Saturn conjunct, square, or opposite Venus: Here there may be fear of closeness, fear of being vulnerable if one gives of one's affections too freely. In many cases, this can be related to one's early life experiences with a cold parent, but in other cases it seems to be solely a lingering karmic tendency from a past life. The person will often hold self so distant from others that he insures through such behavior that the loneliness he feels in the present will also be part of his life in the future. In other cases, the person seems to become determined to face all aspects of human relationship, especially love relationships, with great concentration and with a strong sense of duty and reliability. But even in this approach to dealing with the problem, there is often evident a certain coldness or aloofness which still elicits rejecting behavior in many cases. In all instances of this aspect, the approach to giving, loving, and receiving with others needs to be redefined and restructured, and it seems to be the usual case that specific disappointing or painful love experiences are necessary to prompt the individual to re-examine this area of life more closely.

What we have said thus far about the aspects of Saturn has dealt primarily with the traditional "stressful" aspects. It is usually more necessary and more fruitful to deal with these aspects in some detail rather than the more harmonious ones since they represent areas of experience wherein the person must make definite adjustments and put in some definite effort. But the harmonious aspects of Saturn deserve some attention, although there is only rarely present the rigidity and fearfulness in these cases that one finds in instances where the more dynamic "stressful" aspects are present. Basically, one might say that the harmonious aspects of Saturn show in most cases that it is relatively easy for the person to adapt to the practical realities of life in the area indicated by the planet in aspect to Saturn and by the houses involved. There may still be considerable caution and reserve, but it is usually a positive sort of prudence and common sense rather than a crippling inhibition. The individual with such aspects seems to have an excellent sense of *timing* and organization of the energies involved, and the discipline indicated is felt by the person to be a necessary fact of life rather than a harsh restriction. The energy represented by a planet in harmonious aspect to Saturn still flows rather smoothly, although it is toned by some degree of caution and practical experience and therefore slowed down to the point where the person is able to be rather matter-of-fact in his or her approach to that area of life.

Since Saturn's principle is by definition the polar opposite of *faith* (Jupiter), almost any aspect of Saturn (whether harmonious or inharmonious) can show an area of life where we lack confidence. One of the most positive implications of *any* Saturn aspect (especially one involving a "personal" planet or the Ascendant) is therefore the knowledge that we can in the indicated area slowly develop a new level of confidence. We can build this confidence based on the realization of what our real capabilities are, as shown by the testing process of time, work, and experience. In other words, by realistically appraising the results of our efforts from the vantage point of seeing the fruits of our labors after years of work, we can determine with some objectivity whether we have misjudged our capabilities or whether we should henceforth consider what were *potential* talents now to be proven facts. The test of time and experience can thus *help* us to develop a real, enduring confidence based not on hopes, self-delusion, or ego-inflated notions but rather on immediate facts. A remarkable inner strength can develop from Saturn's pressure, a strength that comes in part from knowing that we have done the required work, earned the results, and taken full responsibility for our own development. One might gather from the above statements that the interpretation of Saturn in the natal chart should always be tempered by an awareness of the importance of *time*, for what an aspect with Saturn means right now is not necessarily what it will mean a few years from now. It may be difficult now, but that same energy potential may be extremely rewarding a few years from now. Likewise, although many books give the reader the idea that Saturn is invariably depressing and blocks all self-confidence, the fact is that the very configuration with Saturn that denotes lack of confidence in one's youth is the same configuration that can indicate a particularly solid and unshakable confidence in later years. It all depends upon how we deal with the challenge which Saturn always presents in our lives.

The Transits of Saturn

Throughout many occult and religious traditions, great emphasis has been placed on seven-year cycles, in relation to physical growth, psychological development, world events, and spiritual evolution. The Edgar Cayce psychic readings are filled with references to these seven-year cycles, especially in relation to health problems. According to these readings, human beings can change most conditions that they truly desire to change—physically, mentally, and spiritually—within a cycle of seven years. If the Cayce readings are as accurate in this idea as they have proven to be in many other areas, then there is apparently almost no limit to the renewal and regeneration that can be accomplished by an individual on all levels of being. A few quotes from Cayce's readings can serve to illustrate his approach to these cycles:

> For, have ye not heard how that constantly there is the change, and that the body has in a seven-year cycle reproduced itself entirely? No need for anyone, then, to have *any* disturbance over that length of period, if—by common sense—there would be the care taken. But if your mind holds to it, and you've got a stumped toe, it will stay stumped! If you've got a bad condition in your gizzard or liver, you'll keep it—if you think so!
>
> But the body—the physical, the mental and spiritual—will remove same, if ye will *let* it and not hold to the disturbance!
>
> (#257-249)
>
> ...were an anatomical or pathological study made for a period of seven years (which is a cycle of change in all the body-elements) of one that is acted upon through the third eye alone, we will find one fed upon spiritual things become a light that may shine from and in the darkest corner. One fed upon the purely material will become a Frankenstein that is without a concept of any influence other than material or mental.
>
> (#262-20)

> Such conditions (muscular strains) need not be expected to be cured in a day, a week, a month, or a year...it requires seven years for resuscitation, change, or eliminations.
>
>   (#1710-10)

> Here we find the necessity for care, for exercise, for constant checking up on the bodily activities...the body-physical alters in its expression continually, and by the end of a cycle of seven years it has entirely replaced that which existed at the beginning of the period seven years ago. Replaced with what? The same old tendencies multiplied, the same old inclinations doubled—or eradicated?
>
>   (#2533-6)

Another more modern reference to seven-year cycles by a non-astrologer is found in the research of Dr. Daniel J. Levinson. Dr. Levinson is Professor of Psychology at Yale School of Medicine, and he presented his thesis of life cycles at a symposium sponsored by the Menninger Foundation. In his conclusions, Levinson finds that no life structure can last longer than seven or eight years. Since Levinson is a psychologist, his calculations were based on the psychological development of hundreds of people studied over a period of years.

Dr. Levinson's findings were used as a primary source by Gail Sheehy in her best-selling book *Passages: Predictable Crises in Adult Life.* In this book, after interviewing hundreds of people concerning their state of mind and their personal values at various stages of life, she outlines certain life-periods that seem more often than not to be times of crucial choices, changes, and rapid development. It will not surprise most astrologers that these various ages, found through interviews and research to be significant times of life for most people, coincide with the approximate periods of life when transiting Saturn is conjunct, square, or opposite its natal place. If one were to combine the square and opposition of transiting Uranus to its natal place with the Saturn transits, one would have an even more complete and accurate outline of the major change periods in most people's lives than Sheehy has found. This is of course nothing new to astrologers. In 1940 Grant Lewi published his book *Astrology for the Millions,* which pioneered into a better understanding of the Saturn cycles and which provided its readers with a powerful astrological tool which could be practically applied to their individual lives. In that book, Lewi clearly outlined the very transition or "passage" age periods which readers of Sheehy's book are now heralding as an important psychological "discovery." In addition, C. G. Jung pointed out many years ago that most important psychological crises were accompanied by transits of either Saturn or Uranus. I do not, however, want to belittle the work that Levinson and Sheehy have done, for anything that further introduces the concept of life *cycles* into the awareness of the general public is a positive trend. And, in fact, I feel that astrologers can benefit from reading Sheehy's book, since it clearly shows how men and women tend to react a bit differently during the various crucial periods, the awareness of which might lead the astrological counselor to emphasize certain facets of experience during a specific transit with women, and other areas with men. Sheehy, in fact, often expresses the experiential meaning of these crucial phases of life very clearly:

We are not unlike a particularly hardy crustacean. The lobster grows by developing and shedding a series of hard, protective shells. Each time it expands from within, the confining shell must be sloughed off. It is left exposed and vulnerable until, in time, a new covering grows to replace the old.

With each passage from one stage of human growth to the next we, too, must shed a protective structure. We are left exposed and vulnerable—but also yeasty and embryonic again, capable of stretching in ways we hadn't known before. (page 20)

The illusions of the twenties, however, may be essential to infuse our first commitments with excitement and intensity, and to sustain us in those commitments long enough to gain us some experience in living. (page 88)

If any readers are unfamiliar with the general meaning of the conjunctions, squares, and oppositions of transiting Saturn to its natal place, I refer them to Lewi's, Tyl's, and Robertson's books on the subject. Since there is so much good material on this topic already in print, I feel that it is unnecessary to duplicate it here. However, I would like to mention some ideas and key concepts which I have found to be especially useful in counseling and in understanding the various types of Saturn cycles. I do not mean to imply that the transits of Saturn alone should be considered in evaluating important change periods in the individual life, for any astrologer working in an in-depth way would undoubtedly look at all the transits of the outer five planets, important new moons and their aspects, and perhaps the progressed Sun and Moon. We will, however, talk about transits other than Saturn's and also progressions in later chapters. The fact remains, nevertheless, that Saturn's cycles provide us with a particularly complete and useful symbol of human growth, achievement, and maturation.

Traditionally, Saturn is the great teacher, and—more so than with the transits of any other planets—transits of Saturn, especially close conjunctions, squares, and oppositions to natal planets, are often experienced as periods wherein we are being taught specific lessons about life. In some cases, this experience prompts people to say such things as: "It is as if Saturn were speaking to me, whispering in my ear, telling me what I now *have* to do in order to outgrow this present condition that is beginning to feel so confining and frustrating." Any transit of the outer five planets in close aspect to natal planets can be experienced as our getting "messages" from these living "gods." The energies of the other planets are often experienced more as impulses or as compulsions, whereas Saturn is often experienced as the archetypal teacher whose lessons carry great weight and importance. I remember when Saturn transited in opposition to my natal Mercury quite a few years ago. It was a period of profound learning, as if I were being instructed very deliberately and systematically by some higher power who knew exactly what I needed to learn and who would not alleviate the mental pressure I felt until I had paid sufficient attention to his lessons. At times, the mental pressure became so intense that I felt like I was going to explode from all the incredibly profound insights I was being given. Saturn's influence is always felt as an urge to make things

definite and concrete, and so I felt the need to write down what I was being shown. The result was that, by the time this transit passed about a month later, I had accumulated pages and pages of notes to which I referred many times for guidance during confusing periods in my life. Although many books predict a time of mental depression during Saturn's transit of Mercury, it was for me a time of profound and inspiring revelation. The point I am trying to make here is that one can, by opening oneself to Saturn's superior objectivity and wisdom, tune in on very precise and specific lessons about how one is approaching life during the major transits of Saturn.

The Saturn Return

I have above emphasized the periods of approximately seven years which coincide with the conjunctions, squares, and oppositions of transiting Saturn to its natal place. There are almost always major *adjustments* called for at these times, revisions of attitudes, important decisions, alteration of how much responsibility one is taking on or how one views those responsibilities, and sometimes radical changes of lifestyle, profession, work structure, and personal life. Of all of these transits, the Saturn return (at the approximate ages of 29 and 58) has received the most attention in astrological writings. Unfortunately, the treatment of those crucial periods has often been rather on the negative side, emphasizing how difficult those periods are often felt to be. Therefore, it is appropriate that we explore the Saturn return here a bit more deeply. It should be noted that many of the concepts outlined below are also applicable to some extent to other transits of Saturn to its natal place as well.

The first thing to clarify when speaking of the Saturn return is that the quality of the entire experience and the extent to which it is felt to be a "difficult" time depends entirely on how one has lived during the previous 29 years, how much one has worked efficiently toward achieving specific goals, how much depth the person has built into his understanding and creative pursuits, and to what extent the individual has expressed or suppressed his or her "fundamental nature." One cannot deduce the answer to all of these questions solely from the birth chart, for people are capable of working with and adjusting to the potentials shown in the natal map. However, one can get some useful hints by looking at the position of natal Saturn and its aspects. If the natal chart reveals considerable stress associated with Saturn and therefore with the practical requirements of life, it is much more likely that this individual has had some difficulty in dealing with life's practical necessities; and therefore the person may experience the Saturn return as a time of increased stress as he or she is shown what further adjustments have to be made in order to fulfill the life pattern and potentials. If, for example, someone is born with Saturn in a close square, conjunction, or opposition to one of the "personal" planets, that individual will probably find that whatever conflicts or problems are so

indicated will come into an even sharper focus during the Saturn return, thus necessitating some sort of definite action in facing up to these concerns. As long as the action is postponed or the need for it repressed, the pressure of the Saturn return will not let up. But once the problems have been faced, no matter how painful such confrontation may be, there is often a noticeable alleviation of pressure and worry. If, on the other hand, the person has natal Saturn in primarily harmonious aspects with other planets—and especially if natal Saturn is in harmony with the Sun and/or Moon—it is likely that the individual has incorporated Saturnian qualities and an awareness of practical requirements and duties into his character over many years; and hence, the lessons of Saturn will come as no surprise or shock and may well be experienced as a time of confirming and solidifying many of the life-orientations that the person has slowly been developing for years. If, as is often the case, the individual has both harmonious and inharmonious aspects with natal Saturn, constructive developments and growth of confidence may come in one area of life during the Saturn return, at the same time that the person is being challenged to confront some other problematical dimension of life.

The first cycle of Saturn through the natal chart, during the first twenty-nine years or so of life, is primarily based upon *reaction* to past conditioning, karma, parental influences, and social pressures. During that period of life, one is usually rather unconscious of who and what one is in a fundamental way. But then, at the first Saturn return, it often seems like an old debt is being discharged and many old karmic patterns and obligations are rather suddenly removed. At that time, one can experience a profoundly complex state of being; for there is simultaneously a feeling of unalterable *limitation* in one's life structure and a feeling of inner *freedom* that in some cases is accompanied by exhilaration and inspiring joy. The sense of limitation arises from the fact that one becomes aware to a greater extent than ever before of what one's destiny is and therefore what one *has* to do from here on out. No longer are there seemingly endless opportunities and alternatives; you now know that you've made your experiments and lived out your youthful illusions, but that from now on you have to work at fulfilling your role in a vast drama, even if you have no idea how you have come to be assigned the part you're now playing. Your responsibilities to yourself and to others are now seen with sharpened clarity, and perhaps some of these responsibilities feel heavy and confining. But, at the same time, you can experience a profound inner *freedom* resulting from the realization that you are no longer bound by *old* obligations, fears, and inner restrictions. This feeling of unlimited inner freedom is also based on a clearer understanding of your real needs, capabilities, and creative potentialities. If you are the kind of person who has been waiting during your youth for the time when you could really find yourself and begin to express yourself with assurance and marked influence, your waiting is over. Now is the time to act, to work, and to live in the present with acceptance of your destiny and joy in the knowledge that your path is now clear. This transition period doesn't happen all at once; in fact, it

may take place over a period of two to two and a half years surrounding the date of the Saturn return. But if you always felt thwarted in childhood and adolescence, feeling perhaps that you were just serving time and having to endure things that were neither fulfilling nor controllable, you could at this time mobilize your energies with great power, ambition, and even a sense of relief that your waiting is over and that now you can begin to mold your own life with some degree of awareness. As Grant Lewi put it in *Astrology for the Millions,*

> You stand freed, when this transit is past, of many erstwhile inner restrictions. You will have swept your nature clean of dead wood and cleared the decks for action that now proceeds less impeded by internal complexes and personal difficulties. You will, in short, have matured— "put away childish things" — and you will be ready to take your place in the world as an adult.
>
> *Saturn's transit of his own place is the most important point at which free will operates in the life, untrammeled and as free of circumstances as it ever will be.... You will not stand so free again. The choices you make are yours: make them wisely, for here it is that your free will in a very real sense forges your fate for a long time to come, if not indeed for the rest of your life.*

Hence, if one confronts the first Saturn return with great courage and honesty, then during Saturn's second 29-year cycle one is more conscious, more able to initiate action without being inhibited by fear and anxiety, and more capable of taking responsibility for oneself and one's experiences. If one successfully tunes in on his or her true destiny as an individual soul during this period, one can thereafter live more in the present, with the greater patience gained from having submitted to his or her inner law with full awareness and acceptance. During this time, one's potential for worldly success and authority are often consolidated in some direct way, and one is given specific insights about the role one is to play in the world from that point on.* Saturn's natal house and the natal house which is ruled by Saturn are usually areas of life that are further defined with deepened understanding at this time. And there are usually noticeable physical changes, as would be expected since Saturn has such an affinity for material existence. Not only are there often physical signs of age manifesting as health problems that make one realize his or her physical limitations, but also the individual's center of gravity (Saturn!) shifts in such a way that one begins to notice that he has a deeper reservoir of energy available to him. The person's general

---

*A study of famous people and their experiences at the time of the Saturn return can quickly confirm this astrological tradition. For example, Gertrude Stein, whose Saturn return happened while she was 29 years old, wrote the following in *Fernhurst:*

"It happens often in the twenty-ninth year of life that all the forces that have been engaged through the years of childhood, adolescence and youth in confused and ferocious combat range themselves in ordered ranks—one is uncertain of one's aims, meaning and power during these years of tumultuous growth when aspiration has no relation to fulfillment and one plunges here and there with energy and misdirection during the storm and stress of the making of a personality until at last we reach the twenty-ninth year, the straight and narrow gate-way of maturity and life which was all uproar and confusion narrows down to form and purpose and we exchange a great dim possibility for a small hard reality.

"Also in our American life where there is no coercion in custom and it is our right to change our vocation so often as we have desire and opportunity, it is a common experience that our youth extends through the whole first twenty-nine years of our life and it is not until we reach thirty that we find at last that vocation for which we feel ourselves fit and to which we willingly devote continued labor." (p. 29-30)

energy level may be noticeably less than when he was in his early or mid-twenties, but the energy available now is more concentrated, not so scattered, and it is a more reliable and steady sort of energy flow. The center of gravity shifts from the head, neck, and chest areas to the pelvis and abdomen. What was just in the person's head before becomes a more integral part of the entire body, i.e., of his real life experience. Hence, the person finds that he doesn't need to use so much energy as when he was younger. The energy is naturally conserved and steadied, and it is up to the individual person to learn how to live with and utilize this new mode of energy flow.

Saturn's Transits of Other Planets

Since the quality of energy release is similar in all Saturn transits, no matter which natal planet may be involved, and since *all* Saturnian transits are experienced as a personal reaction in some dimension of the individual's life (shown by the natal planet involved) to the basic principles and lessons of Saturn, I feel that it is sufficient here simply to outline some key phrases and concepts that I have found to be useful in understanding these transits, rather than treating each transit separately. As I have tried to make clear earlier in this chapter, the conjunctions, squares, and oppositions of transiting Saturn (indeed of any transiting planet) are the most important aspects to be aware of; and it can also be said that the transits of Saturn to the "personal planets," to the Ascendant, or to its own natal position are almost always noticed by the individual in some obvious way, whereas the Saturn transits to Jupiter, Uranus, Neptune, and Pluto are only *sometimes* easily correlated with experiences or feelings of which the person may be immediately aware. How aware the person is of the meaning of these latter transits depends in great part on how conscious the person is of his or her inner life and also on the position, power, and aspects of these planets in the natal chart. I have personally observed some extremely important experiences to take place when Saturn was transiting in exact (or almost exact— within 10') aspect to Jupiter, Uranus, Neptune, or Pluto; but it is also the usual case that the deeper *meaning* of anything that may happen during *these* transits is not fully apparent for a number of months or even years. The following basic principles may be applied to any transit of Saturn; the key concept simply has to be related to the dimension of life experience represented by the planet being activated by Saturn.

A. Saturn always slows down the usual rhythm of nature in the area indicated; but, by slowing things down and making one feel at times like "When will this ever end?", it concentrates our experience, makes us live in the present, and helps us to focus our energy and to concentrate and conserve it.

B. Saturn transits deepen and focus one's attention and awareness, while at the same time making one more detached and objective. For example, Saturn aspecting Venus shows that you can become more detached and objective in your attitude toward love, but also that you can during this time develop a deeper ability to give and to receive love, because you are more focused in the here and now and more aware of exactly what you are doing, whom you're sharing love with, and what it means to you.

C. Saturn transits often feel like the "hand of destiny" is reaching into your life in the area indicated, making things happen, and forcing you to face your fears in that area. Facing these things may be difficult and may seem quite harsh at times, but it is a necessary step in realization if you are to build a more secure and realistic approach to experience in that area.

D. Saturn transits often reveal to the individual what *must* be done and decided if one is to live with full integrity and in accord with the responsibilities felt toward one's own self.

E. Saturn transits pressure an individual to make the indicated dimension of experience more definite and concrete; and this more realistic approach to that area of life is usually prompted by one of two methods of testing one's attitudes and priorities in that field of experience. Either the person feels that he is being tested *by circumstances* to see if he measures up to certain standards; or the individual feels an *inner* urge to examine that area of life to see if it meets his new-found values and personal requirements. This testing may be experienced as limitation or frustration, depending on the individual's scope of awareness, as the person learns that he can't have everything. But such pressure can prompt the growth of self-reliance and inner strength in the area indicated.

F. Saturn transits can help you to build up your confidence in the area indicated, based on the realization of what your real capabilities are and upon what you have earned through effort. Once you know your capabilities more realistically, you can proceed to take more responsibility for your own life.

G. Saturn transits tend to moderate whatever is excessive in one's life, whether excessive pride in some area of life, excessive activity, excessive attachment, excessive dependency, or even excessive (i.e., unfounded) faith.

Saturn Through the Houses

The key concepts mentioned above (Sections A through G) can also be applied in the understanding of Saturn's transits through the various houses of the natal chart, with the following distinction: Saturn's transit in exact aspect to a natal *planet* symbolizes the process of defining a specific *dimension of the personality* and shows what one feels to be most authentically an essential aspect of one's true self; whereas Saturn's transit of a natal *house* represents a period of defining one's approach to an entire *area of life experience and activity.* Very often, the changes represented by Saturn's transits of the natal houses are more publicly noticeable than Saturn's transits of the natal planets, although there are many exceptions to this general rule. If a person is born with any planet "accidentally dignified", i.e., natally located in the house with which it is associated, the period when Saturn is transiting that house will be especially important and powerful; for Saturn will then conjunct the particular planet during the same period when it is in the house related to that planet. In other words, if one is born with Venus in the 7th house, then when Saturn conjuncts Venus it will also be in the 7th house, thus giving us two separate symbols of a similar process of defining and structuring one's awareness of companionship and love needs. This would be what I call a "theme" in the chart, for that person would then experience this pressure to face relationship feelings and activities more realistically as a major theme in his or her life for many months and possibly even for over two years. But, in any case, Saturn's house position invariably shows what field of personal experience one is (or should be) trying to structure and define more clearly and in what area of life activity one should be trying to build a solid, lasting understanding and approach.

Considering Saturn's cycle through all the twelve houses as a complete circle of life-experience and maturation is necessary in order to put into perspective the meaning of Saturn in any *particular* house. But it is equally important to know why one is emphasizing a certain starting point or focus during this cycle. The natal position of Saturn is naturally one focal point in this entire cycle and in the growth process which it symbolizes. Although Grant Lewi's early work with the Saturn cycle was a great breakthrough in practically applying astrological knowledge and contains a great many valuable insights, I do feel that he over-emphasized only one approach to the Saturn cycle: namely, its meaning in relation to worldly achievement and career goals. If, like Lewi, one is using the transits of Saturn through the houses as an index of only this area of life experience, then—like him—one should emphasize the 4th house as a focus of new beginnings which can lead to achievements as Saturn crosses the 10th house area. In that approach, Saturn's transit through the 1st, 2nd, and 3rd houses—called by Lewi a "period of obscurity"—is not emphasized as important except in so far as it is a period of preparation for the ambitions which come into clearer focus at a later time. If one is using astrology as a tool for *vocational* guidance alone or perhaps for personnel work for a large company or for a government agency, Lewi's approach and concepts should be sufficient and usually fairly accurate. But if one is involved in counseling human beings at a more intimate and subtle level, wherein their more personal feelings and needs are being taken into account, it will be of little value to tell someone that he or she is entering a period of "obscurity" for the next seven years and that all the person can do at this time is to wait patiently for some ill-defined (but of course absolutely wonderful!) future work or vocation which will eventually give the individual's life a profound excitement and significance.

The kind of astrological counseling which always uses future promises as the primary area about which one can say something positive and hopeful is also the kind of astrology which usually proves to be empty and to be useful mainly for avoiding the counselor's admission of faulty understanding or plain ignorance. To hold out such illusory hopes to a client is indeed not *counseling* at all; it is merely encouraging the person to focus on fantasy rather than on immediate facts and feelings, a type of astrological practice which bears great resemblance to the methods of the fortune-tellers with whom most astrologers claim vociferously that they don't want to be associated! Of all the planetary symbols used in astrology, there is none which calls to our attention more strongly the need to face reality in the here and now than Saturn. Hence, I think we can outline here a more constructive way of explaining Saturn's cycle to clients or friends, or for our own use in trying to understand our experiences.

The best way of viewing the Saturn cycle is to focus on the wholeness of the entire circle, the entire, unending process of development that is thereby symbolized, with particular emphasis on the *first* house position of transiting Saturn since the first house represents the most personal and individual area of the birth-chart. By viewing the first house as the most important phase of the entire cycle, rather than as simply the beginning of a "period of obscurity," one can take into account the importance of Saturn's cycle as an indicator of not only career and vocational changes, but also of personal inner development on the psychological and spiritual levels. It is in this way that we will discuss Saturn's transits of the various natal houses; but, before getting into the details of each house, we should provide an alternative way of looking at Saturn's transit of the quadrants of the chart that is broader and more psychologically-oriented than the meanings given by Lewi. Similar explanations have been provided by Marc Robertson in his book *The Transit of Saturn* and are based on concepts initially developed by Dane Rudhyar. These ideas can be outlined as follows:

In Quadrant I (Houses I, II, & III): Saturn reveals our ability to grow in *essential being* and in *self-awareness.*

In Quadrant II (Houses IV, V, & VI): Saturn reveals our ability to grow in our *capacity for understanding* and in our *mode of self-expression.*

In Quadrant III (Houses VII, VIII, & IX): Saturn reveals our ability to grow in our *method of functioning with other people* and in our *awareness of others as individuals.*

In Quadrant IV (Houses X, XI, & XII): Saturn reveals our ability to grow in our capacity for and in the expression of our *influence on others or on society at large.*

It should be noted that the above concepts are general in nature and are for the purpose of giving the astrologer an overall sense of the meaning of the Saturn cycle; in most cases, the most accurate approach is to keep this general outline in mind as a background for understanding the specific experiences shown by transiting Saturn's exact house position.

Another point worth mentioning is that the meaning of a Saturn transit through a particular house may change noticeably as Saturn proceeds further and further into the house. As Saturn begins to enter a house (which is often felt by the individual when Saturn comes within 6° or so of that house's cusp*, although the planet may technically still be in the

---

*I use the Koch Birthplace House System in all my work; after having experimented with Placidus, Campanus, and Equal Houses systems, I have found that the Koch cusps give the most accurate timing of important changes shown by a transiting planet changing houses. An approximate orb of within 6° of the cusp is used not only in work with transits but also in the analysis of natal charts. In other words, in a particular natal chart, if a planet is technically in the 5th house, for example, but within 6° of the 6th house cusp, it will often make more sense to interpret that planet as a 6th house planet rather than as a 5th house planet. In some cases, however, both interpretations seem to make sense.

previous house), one often feels a more *intense* urge to do something about the area of life indicated than will be felt later. The problematical side of Saturn's position in a given house usually seems to be more apparent during the first year or so when Saturn is in that house. After that, in many cases, it seems that the person has been pressured to learn enough about how to cope more realistically with this area of life to enable him to take the further lessons in his stride. Naturally, how quickly one learns the Saturnian lessons depends on the individual, and this guideline cannot be made into a dogma. But it is often the case that a person will feel the weight of a Saturn transit most heavily when the planet is in the first half or so of a certain house. The frustration and pressure to act or to work in some way is likely to be strongest at that time. Then, as the person achieves more stability and understanding in that field of experience, the pressure still remains but it is not felt to be as oppressive or as intense. This guideline is especially true of houses where there are no natal planets situated, for—when one does have planets in a certain house—Saturn's exact conjunction of those planets is often the period of peak intensity. If one has taken the proper approach to dealing with the inner and outer pressures that are felt during the first phase of such a transit period, then the second phase may be seen as a time to assimilate more deeply the important realizations involved.

As transiting Saturn gets toward the end of a house and is about to enter the next house (in other words, when it gets to within 6° or so of the next house cusp), there is often some sort of event, experience, or realization that is clearly related to the entire period just ending and to the basic meaning of the house that Saturn is leaving. Often something will occur that clearly symbolizes a consolidation of the previous two or three years' efforts, and the occurrence in many cases—although it is often quite important—will not coincide with any other major transit or progression. In other words, in very many cases, no major astrological factor other than simply Saturn's leaving a particular house can be found to symbolize whatever is happening. Whatever does occur is often accompanied by a sense of relief, or by a sense of catharsis or satisfaction, a kind of clearing the decks prior to launching out on the Saturn transit of the following house. I mention this phenomenon at such length because I have repeatedly seen it occur with great regularity, and often an astrologer will frantically look for some specific transit, progression, or direction to "account for" such an experience. In fact, the same phenomenon happens also with the progressed Moon, as it is about to leave a certain house and enter the next. An entire book could be filled with my case histories related to these common occurrences, but we must get on to discuss the specific meanings of transiting Saturn in the various houses.

House I: As Saturn transits this house, a new order is being created after the old order was dissolved while Saturn was in House XII. As Saturn approaches and then conjuncts the Ascendant, you often experience something that brings you down to earth, that makes you realize the results of your actions and past behavior patterns, and hence that can prompt you to take more responsibility for yourself and your actions than has been the case in the past. Usually, some outer circumstance compels you to face up to important immediate facts or situations that have perhaps been neglected or taken for granted in the past. This sort of experience is the beginning of a long phase of coming to realize some practical truths about yourself. Since most people are more aware of their faults and needs for future development at this time, it is often a period when one actively seeks feedback from others in order to get a clearer picture of what and who one truly is. One may seek this feedback from friends, but it often takes the form of going to a counselor, psychiatrist, astrologer, or other kind of therapist. In short, it is a period of becoming more realistic about yourself, of trying to get a perspective on what kind of *You* you want to create, and of beginning to *build* this new You through concentrated effort and honest self-appraisal. It is a period of paying attention to yourself with considerable seriousness, a time when you can begin to know yourself more deeply than ever before, and a time to learn more about your individual capabilities. Saturn's transit through both the 12th and the 1st houses is often a period of personal crisis, a rebirth process which can last over five years. During that entire period, the old personality structure is irretrievably left behind, but the kind of new structure and the new way that you will approach life and express yourself is largely dependent upon the level of honesty with which you confront yourself at this time. It is my feeling that the entire period when Saturn is in the 12th and the 1st houses should be viewed as comprising one of the major transition phases in anyone's life, and therefore it is advisable to relate the meaning of Saturn in the 1st house to Saturn's transit of the 12th house rather than seeing each phase as an isolated time period.

The expression "getting it together" is an apt one for describing Saturn in the 1st house, for—as Saturn leaves the 12th house—the individual often feels like a new-born child, open to everything, endlessly curious, but also without much discipline or definite structure in the personality. The new potentials that appeared during the 12th house phase are not as yet integrated into a coherent, functional whole. As Saturn enters the 1st house, you often feel the need to become something, to work actively at developing yourself rather than remaining in the open—but passive— state of being symbolized by the 12th house. One then often puts in considerable effort to mould a new sense of identity, a new, deeper level of confidence; and often, as Saturn gets toward the end of the 1st house, one will have an experience or will meet someone who leads one toward the experience of realizing one's wholeness with heightened clarity. This new feeling of being *integrated* and inwardly strong is based on a deeper sense of enduring values and on a greater sense of one's personal responsibilities and essential individuality.

While Saturn crosses the Ascendant and remains in the 1st house, often there are also marked physical changes. Losing weight effortlessly is common, occasionally even to the point of looking emaciated. The physical energy is often quite low, manifesting as tiredness, poor digestion, and at times feelings of depression. However, one should realize that this is *the* period of maximum opportunity for building a new body as well as a new personality; but that building takes discipline, perserverance, and lots of work. I have seen robust and healthy people waste away to nothingness during this transit, if they took no steps toward improving their health habits and disciplining their living and eating patterns. But I have also witnessed weak and sickly people begin a health regimen during this period which resulted in their achieving a state of excellent health and abundant energy even before Saturn left the 1st house!

In other words, Saturn's transit of the 1st house can be considered to be the key phase of the Saturn cycle, for it is during this period of life that we are, in effect, creating the kind of person that we want to be and realizing what kind of person our karma demands that we be. Therefore, all of one's activities and involvements in the outer world during the rest of the 29-year cycle will grow directly from the values that one commits oneself to and from the sort of character that is built during this period. Saturn's transit of the 1st house can indeed be considered a "period of obscurity" in the sense that one is paying attention primarily to oneself during this time rather than actively engaging in major involvements and ambitions that would be readily noticed by the public (though there are some exceptions to this!). But it is of course almost always necessary that one turn within oneself and withdraw to some extent from involvements in the outer world during any period of marked personal transformation and quickened growth. It should also be pointed out that it is fairly common for the person to begin working at some study, interest, or long-term goal at this time which will eventually grow into a full-time vocation or major ambition, for the planet of ambition and career (Saturn) is in the house of new beginnings (1st house). What once were the person's major ambitions and long-term goals usually collapse or are seen to be empty while Saturn is in the 12th house, whereas new goals and vocational interests begin to take form as Saturn transits the 1st house. The person often does not realize that these new interests will have such an important part to play in the major activities of later years, yet the individual often seems to be guided toward specific types of work at this time, even if he or she feels a definite resistance to pursuing such activities. After all, Saturn is often felt as the "hand of destiny" reaching into our lives, and this is just one more instance of it playing that role in defining our future orientation.

House II: As Saturn enters the 2nd house, the period of being concerned about your own identity phases out, and there is often a marked sense of relief as well as a stronger feeling that you now have to get down to work in order to be productive. Many people express this shift in emphasis something like this: "I'm tired of just thinking about myself and all my problems. I feel that I now have a pretty good idea who I am, and dwelling further on such a question will only be self-indulgence. What I want to do now is to get something going in the real world, accomplish something definite, and make some money." Hence, the person who has Saturn transiting through the 2nd house usually has a strong urge to structure his or her financial situation, to put some hard work into setting up or furthering some means of income, savings, investment, or livelihood. It is commonly a time when a person will begin to build a new business from scratch, to engage in some kind of apprenticeship (whether formally or informally), or to acquire some kind of practical training which will eventually enable the individual to make more money. It is, in other words, a period for laying the groundwork of one's security and stability in the material world; and, although one's income may not be very great while engaging in such preparatory efforts and although one may feel strong anxiety about money or other security factors, the commonly heard statements about this Saturn position referring to indebtedness, poverty, and great tribulation are in my experience considerably exaggerated. Most people do indeed feel the Saturnian pressure in this area of their lives, but the majority of clients I have seen have dealt with these concerns in a very practical way and have not experienced particularly great financial calamities. In fact, one client won $15,000 in a contest while Saturn was in her 2nd house; and a number of other clients started businesses or new training during this time which eventually prospered on a large scale.

What often does happen during this time is that financial necessities are made more real to the person, and some practical lessons about survival are driven home through the pressure of necessity. How attuned you are to taking care of your material needs at the beginning of this phase will have a great impact on what kinds of things you experience during this period. The primary thing to keep in mind is that Saturn is slow but sure, and that material benefits can eventually result from taking a patient, exacting approach to practical affairs during this time. The benefits may not be immediately apparent; but, if you do face up to the need to build a financial and security structure without ignoring the true personal costs, what is built now may serve you quite well for many years. Saturn's transit through the 2nd house is not limited in its meaning to material things alone, but—since this is the area of life where most people feel it most immediately—I have concentrated on that dimension of this transit. One can say, however, that it is a time of slow but sure accumulation of *all* kinds of resources, both material and psychological, all of which can contribute toward self-confidence based on knowing what support and momentum you have going for yourself and what deeper understandings and resources at your disposal may be drawn upon as you go through life. It is also a time of taking stock of how you have used specific skills and ideas in the past (the 2nd is the 12th from the 3rd house) and whether they have served you well and enabled you to produce something, or whether they have merely proven to be useless and impractical. If they have proven to be valuable and if one applies oneself to the tasks at hand, one often experiences some kind of consolidation of one's financial situation as Saturn begins to leave this house.

House III: As Saturn begins to transit the 3rd house, the feeling that many of the practical matters that have long preoccupied attention are now settled enables one to begin putting energy into new learning that will enhance the depth of one's professional background and the value of one's ideas. This period is not usually felt to be as heavy as Saturn's transit of the preceding earth house, although the relative importance of the third-house phase depends upon whether the person is intellectually oriented or engaged in work that involves communication or travel. There is often a tendency toward pointless worry during this period, and any insecurity about one's opinions or the depth of one's knowledge usually becomes apparent. It is a time when one should concentrate on learning new facts, new ideas, and new skills which will lend depth and practicality to the expression of one's intelligence. It is an excellent period for research or any kind of deep thought; and more effort is often put into structuring one's educational plans, teaching or writing methods, or the mode of expressing one's ideas. There is increased emphasis on serious analysis, practical thinking, and the capacity to express ideas more definitely. Many people find that they stay up late reading more during this period, and a few people find that not only their method of communication but even the tone of their voice changes. Such developments are brought about by the person's feeling that he or she needs to build a more solid structure upon which to base ideas and opinions. Hence, the individual often takes on more educational activities or pursues private research which can serve this purpose; for, even though many of the ideas, facts, and skills learned during this time may not be used a great deal in the future, the person's acquaintance with such a variety of techniques and points of view provides a broad background of knowledge that can enable him to compare and judge theories, concepts, and methods on the basis of his own personal experience.

Broader learning or research is also necessary at this time in order to deepen one's sense of security about one's intelligence; for, heretofore, the person may have been merely expressing opinions or ideas in the abstract without having the immediate experience which lends them credence. In many cases, this is also a period of increased travel activity resulting from the demands of one's profesison, familial duties, or other responsibilities. It is also a period of "tying up loose ends" in not only the intellectual areas of life but also in one's relationships with other people. One tends to define exactly what the limits are of various relationships with friends and acquaintances during this period.

House IV: Saturn's transit of the 4th house is a time to get down to the basics of security and survival, a time for tuning in to your basic needs for a feeling of belonging and tranquility. You tend to look at your place in the community more seriously, and you often try to establish a sense of solidity and order in the home environment. This can naturally mean many different things to different people, but there are usually two areas of attention in regard to the home: 1) the physical condition and design of the home may seem inappropriate for your purposes, in which case you often take steps to change the home situation in some way, often building something onto the house itself or in the yard, or at times even moving into an entirely new residence; and 2) your obligations to your family become more real and pressing. You could feel cramped in your surroundings, which may be a hint that you need to define further the boundaries of not only your home life but also your life ambitions (10th house—polar opposite of the 4th). In fact, Saturn's transit of the 4th house is a time when you *should* lay the foundations for any long-term ambitions you may have and determine what base of operations is needed in your career. This may lead to relocating your business or profession, or at least to restructuring the environment in which you work. One last note about the 4th house is that people often seem to experience direct karma during this time that is related to their past creative efforts and/or love affairs. This can be explained by seeing that the 4th house is the 12th house from the 5th.

House V: Saturn's transit of the 5th house is somewhat similar to its transit of the previous fire house—House I—in that it is a time of greater seriousness about oneself and often of reduced vitality and buoyancy. Since the 5th house is associated with Leo and the Sun, this transit markedly affects one's sense of joy, spontaneity, and well-being. Some people complain that they never have much fun during this period and that they feel unloved and unappreciated. Such feelings are understandable when we realize that this transit's essential meaning is to make us aware of how we are using our vitality in every area of life: our physical and sexual energy, our emotional love energy, and all other forms of creative power. It is not that we suddenly experience all sorts of blockages and inhibitions that we never felt before; it is rather that we come to realize during this period what blockages and fears have *habitually* been depleting our energies or interfering with the expression of our creative forces and love nature. It is, in short, a time to confront whatever fears or habits have been causing us to feel devitalized, creatively frustrated, or unlovable and unloving. It is a time of putting more depth into our mode of self-expression and a period when we should be working to make a *deep* impression on others through responsible and disciplined action rather than merely through dramatic displays or empty show.

The pressure of Saturn during this period throws you back on yourself, having the effect of tuning you in to developing your own inner sources of love and creativity rather than looking toward the outer world to satisfy these needs. The feeling of being lonely or unloved, however, may prompt you unconsciously to look for more attention from spouse, children, lovers, or others; but you may become too demanding— usually without realizing it—and so you may put off the very people whom you want to get closer to, thus leading to a feeling of rejection. However, if one can express one's deepest affection and loyalty at this time through responsible honesty, duty, and effort, it can be a period of deep satisfaction; for one can realize that there is no real love in this world without an accompanying sense of responsibility. One's expression of love to others can become more paternal and protective, and such feelings can become especially strong in attitudes toward children since this is a time of getting in touch with one's children's real needs and with one's deeper duties toward them. One is often attracted to Saturnian types of people as possible lovers during this period, for one senses in these people a kind of emotional stability that one currently lacks. This can take the form of being attracted to an older person or simply to someone who has a strong attunement to Saturn or Capricorn. The detachment, aloofness, and matter-of-fact ways of a Saturnian person can be appealing during this time, for one is slowly learning how to be more detached and objective oneself in attempting to fulfill emotional needs. In some cases, a person with Saturn transiting the 5th house will be inclined toward using others (often unconsciously, hoping that he or she is "in love") in order to try to alleviate the feeling of loneliness and to try to escape from confronting one's own lack of deep, responsible lovingness.

A compelling inner pressure to create something at this time can challenge you to discipline your creative work habits and to put in more effort to open a channel so that your creative energy can flow. If you have ambitions in the area of the creative arts, for example, this is *the* time to commit yourself to a regular work schedule and to begin to rely more on consistent effort and organization than on transitory flights of "inspiration." It is a time of realizing that any creative acts that you might achieve actually come *through* you rather than emanate directly from you. In other words, we can realize that—if it is our karma to create something—we should merely put forth the effort regularly to allow the creative forces to express themselves through us. This is difficult to achieve, however, since we usually have very little faith and confidence during this period, and thus we tend to close off or to become fearful of failure. We tend to take life in all its dimensions much too seriously at this time because we tend to take ourselves too seriously. And hence, this is often a time of creative blockage, when even accomplished writers, artists, and others experience considerable discouragement in their work. But this period can be one of solidifying our self-confidence and our methods of creative expression if we realize that inspiration is common but work is not, that 95% of creativity is just plain hard work. As the writer Henry Miller wrote in his journal, "When you can't create, work!" Also, the writer William Faulkner was once asked when he did his writing, to which he replied, "I only write when I feel like it...and I feel like it every morning!"

Since the 5th house is also the house of play, hobbies, and recreation, Saturn's transit through this house also has an impact on these areas of life. Overwork is common at this time since it is so difficult for the person to take time off to enjoy himself. Even if the person takes a "vacation," he may find that he can't relax because his mind keeps dwelling on such serious thoughts. In other cases, what used to be a hobby becomes more productive and often even becomes a regular and structured business. Another insight into this period appears when we consider the 5th house as the 12th from the 6th house; hence, the results of one's previous work and of how effectively one has performed one's duties become manifest, either as pleasure at a deep level of satisfaction and as a steady flow of creative energy or as dissipation and gambling in a futile attempt to make up for what one never really earned through applied effort.

House VI: Saturn's transit of the 6th house is a period of self-adjustment and change in one's thinking, work, and health habits. The person is usually either urged from within or pressured by circumstances to become more organized and disciplined in many practical areas of life, but particularly in work and health. Job changes or changes in work structure are common, as are annoying chronic health problems. I have even seen one person who was notably disorganized and inefficient become so much more disciplined in his work methods during this time that he exclaimed, "I can't believe how much I'm getting done these days. I'm getting so efficient!" Saturn here pressures us to determine for ourselves what it is we are trying to do and to *discriminate* between the important and the tangential. In fact, the faculty of discrimination sometimes is so active during this period that the individual suffers from depression or psychosomatic ailments stemming from *excessive* self-criticism. This self-criticism is further motivated by our beginning to see at this time how people with whom we live and work really feel about us. We see whether we are really useful or whether we are considered burdensome. In other words, since the 6th house is the 12th from the 7th, we become more aware of the *results* of the various relationships in our lives.

The sixth-house phase of Saturn's cycle deals essentially with self-purification at every level. Many of the health problems that arise during this period can be directly related to the person's dietary habits and thus to a high level of toxemia. It seems that the body is trying to throw off impurities during this time; and, if you don't cooperate with that purification process, physical symptoms often manifest. Saturn's transit through the 6th house is an excellent period for adjusting one's diet, exercise routines, and other health habits, or for engaging in a prolonged fast or purifying diet. The main thing to be aware of at this time is that any health problems (or problems with one's work situation) are specific lessons showing you what changes are being required of you in the habit patterns of everyday life and preparing you for another phase of living which begins as Saturn rises over the natal descendant into the 7th house.

House VII: Like Saturn's transit of any other house, this position can manifest at a number of different levels simultaneously. A few of my clients began to establish business partnerships at this time, which were usually consolidated financially when Saturn entered the 8th house. All relationships are taken more seriously at this time, and the person often begins to take more responsibility to uphold his or her side of a specific relationship. The focus of attention in most cases, however, seems to be on the individual's primary personal relationship or marriage. As Saturn crosses the descendant and begins its above-the-horizon semi-cycle, there are often realizations about one's relationship needs, limitations, and duties; and this time also marks the entrance of the person onto a wider stage of public and social participation. If one has been taking any important relationship for granted or has been feeling that a particular relationship is not meeting his or her needs, this will be the time to deal with it realistically. (Saturn's transit of natal Venus is similar.) Saturn brings you down to earth in whatever area of life is indicated by its transiting house position, and here you should try to establish a solid, well-defined approach to those relationships which have a strong impact on your overall lifestyle and your identity. (Note that, as Saturn transits in conjunction to the descendant, it is simultaneously in opposition to the ascendant!) If you are expecting too much from a relationship or marriage, or if you sense that it is unworkable in ways that are important to you, this is the time to face those facts with objectivity and detachment. A certain coldness and reserve in attitudes and behavior in close relationships often develops at this time, and your partner may wonder why you seem to have withdrawn from your usual ways of dealing with him or her. If it can be explained that you are simply detaching yourself from the other person for a while in order to get a clearer perspective on the relationship and on the extent to which you want to participate in it, at least the partner won't tend to imagine things that are worse than the actual situation. There is no doubt that this can be a trying time for many people's marriages and intimate relationships, but the amount of stress experienced during this period depends upon the quality and level of authenticity that has characterized your relationship for many years.

In my experience, in contrast to some traditional astrological assertions, divorce is no more common at this time than during the period when Jupiter transits the 7th house—in fact, it seems less common than the Jupiter transit period, for the Jupiter period is the time when one seeks to branch out and expand the boundaries of his or her relationships *beyond* their present limits. But Saturn's transit through the 7th is a time of relationship decisions and commitments (or re-commitments), and perhaps the most important thing about this period is that it gives you the ability to see your partner more objectively—as an individual person totally distinct from you, rather than as an appendage or merely as an object onto which you cast your projections. In short, if a particular relationship is sufficiently healthy and flexible that it allows you to experience your own self fully and to relate to others and to society with full awareness, then it is likely quite workable; and that is what you will realize during this period, although that realization may come only after some severe tests of the relationship's quality. Otherwise, however, the relationship itself and your approach to it need to be redefined at this time, and decisions have to be made about how much energy you are going to put into it to make it workable.

House VIII: This period can emphasize any or all of the following dimensions of life: financial, sexual-emotional, psychological, or spiritual. Since the 8th house is associated with Pluto and Scorpio, this period is particularly important as a time of terminating many old life-patterns and—through letting go of some intense desire or attachment—experiencing a kind of rebirth once this phase is completed. The need to discipline one's desires and to structure one's emotional attachments is usually made clear either by circumstances compelling you to face certain facts through the pressure of frustration or by your realizing within yourself the ultimate ramifications of your desires and how you have been using all forms of power: financial, sexual, emotional, occult, and spiritual. Many people experience this period as a time of deep suffering, the cause of which is difficult to pinpoint. Some people even describe it as feeling as though they were going through a hell or purgatory, in which their desires and attachments are being refined and their awareness of the deeper energies of life is being awakened. It is, in short, a time to face the ultimates of life, the core experiences which are so often ignored or neglected. Many people seem preoccupied with the essential realities of soul life, afterlife, and death itself during this period. It is a time to face the inexorable fact of death more realistically, and the awareness of the inevitability of death often prompts people to put energy into organizing their estates, joint assets, and wills. Other major financial dealings are also frequent at this time, but the common factor is that the individual is seeking to protect himself and often to establish some kind of "soul security" at the deepest level possible.

It is also a period of realizing the importance of one's sexual life and the implications of how one has been channeling sexual energies. In some cases, it is a period of sexual frustration which seems to happen to the person, thus forcing him or her to become more self-contained and disciplined. In other cases, the person will consciously act to cut off certain sexual outlets or activities that had previously been major involvements, realizing the value of retaining the sex force within oneself unless it is being used for a healing and constructive purpose. It is also a time when a great many people become heavily engaged in occult studies, spiritual practices, or various kinds of research. It seems to me that one of the keys to this period of time can be inferred from realizing that the 8th house is the 12th from the 9th: in other words, Saturn's transit of this house brings to the surface the results of your attempts to live your ideals and beliefs. This then manifests as your experiencing transformation—either joyously or through the suffering required to further redefine your life ideals.

House IX: Saturn's transit of the 9th house is primarily a period of assimilating many years' experiences and relating them to some meaningful ideal, philosophy, or regimen of self-improvement. It is common for people to embark upon a rather structured journey toward gaining greater breadth of understanding at this time, whether through actual physical travel, academic training, attending lectures or church services, or solely through concentrated individual study. I have seen cases where the person actually combined more than one of these possibilities, e.g., by going to school in a foreign country. Basically, this is a time to investigate and define your ultimate beliefs, whether those leanings take you into a philosophy, a religion, metaphysical studies, or legal or social theories. Your beliefs need to be defined during this time because they will hereafter serve as ideals which guide your life and illuminate your self-direction.

It is, in short, a time when most people have a strong urge toward self-improvement. For some, this means that they should bring their lives into alignment with a higher ideal. For others, it means that they feel the need to travel about the world or to study diverse subjects in order to achieve a wider perspective on their lives. And for still others, particularly those who tend to accept socially-defined notions of what it means to improve oneself, it is a time when they begin or at least commit themselves more deeply to an academic training program. It is an excellent period for the serious application of one's mental energies, and it is commonly a time when one's ambitions related to influencing others through teaching, lecturing, or publications are consolidated in some definite way. It should also be noted that the 9th house is the 12th from the 10th; hence, it represents the results of how you've worked toward gaining your ambitions, manifesting either as restlessness and dissatisfaction or as simply realizing that you need to work harder now at expressing the knowledge that has been gained from past accomplishments or vocational activities. This transit period is also a preparation for the ensuing 10th house phase in the sense that what ambitions you seek to accomplish then will depend greatly on the ideals to which you commit yourself now.

House X: Saturn's crossing the Midheaven and going into the 10th house will usually bring to the fore a serious concern with your ambitions, your hopes for achieving something in your career, your role in society and the amount of authority you have, and the specific work structure through which you're trying to attain your goals. At times, it can be felt as a period of frustration in these areas of life or as a time of anxiety when you are burdened with distasteful duties, but this is the case primarily when the career or vocational structure you have built is too oppressive or not realistic enough to suit your true nature. Contrary to what some astrological traditions would lead us to believe, this phase does not necessarily indicate that your ambitions are going to be thwarted. It simply shows that this is *the* time for working extra hard at defining the range and meaning of your ambitions. In fact, some people experience a very positive culmination of their career goals at this time, with considerable recognition and fulfillment. This, however, does not seem from my experience to happen with as great a regularity as Grant Lewi's theories seem to predict, although it is common. It is also a time of gaining a detached perspective on what you have *really* achieved, as differentiated from your reputation (which is often inaccurate) or what you'd like to think you have accomplished. If we see the 10th house as the 12th from the 11th, we can further deduce that this phase shows the results (12th house) of your associations, objectives, and sense of individual purpose (11th house). If your career or vocational structure seems frustrating at this time, it often stems from the fact that you haven't sufficiently incorporated your true *personal* goals and socially-valuable ideals into it. But you can begin to do so as Saturn enters the 11th house.

House XI: The meaning of the 11th house is rarely clarified in most astrological texts, and the key words given for the 11th house are often vague and confusing. It seems to me that, more than anything else, this house symbolizes your sense of individual *purpose*, i.e., how you see your function in society and how you want to develop in the future on a personal level. This house is probably the most future-oriented of all the houses, and people with the Sun or other important planets in this house tend to be particularly attuned to the future, both in the sense of what they want to become and in the sense of how society is developing and where that will lead.

Hence, Saturn's transit of this house indicates a time when you realize what you've done, what you didn't do, and what you should do in the future, especially in relation to other people or to society as a whole. It is a time of finding out what you should be giving to other people now that you have established yourself in some position within society (10th house phase). It is a time when it is important to think through your own objectives: not so much career objectives as your own *personal* objectives, what you want to be and become and what role you feel you are cut out to play in the community of fellow human beings. It is a period to define your own intimate hopes and wishes and sense of purpose for yourself *in relation to* the needs of fellow beings. It is therefore a period of taking more responsibility for the way you relate to all people, and this increased concern leads to a more sober attitude toward not only individual friendships and alliances but also to one's involvements with large groups of people. In some cases, you may need to cut off various friendships or group associations; but in other cases, you may find that you have the urge to take on *more* responsibility in the way you deal with them. For example, one lady took on the job of organizing (Saturn!) excursions for a large singles group as Saturn transited through her 11th house. As can be seen in this house's association with the sign Aquarius, it is a time of distributing and dispensing to others what you have learned and acquired during Saturn's transit of the previous ten houses.

House XII: As stated at the beginning of this section, Saturn's transit of this house, together with its transit of the 1st house, coincides with an important transition phase in everyone's life. Saturn's 12th house phase is a period when you meet the results of all the thoughts, actions, desires, and activities that you have engaged in during the last Saturn cycle through the other houses. The way you have been expressing yourself in the world (1st house) for some time now has inevitably led you to confront this particular kind of karma. If this is Saturn's first transit of the twelfth house during this lifetime, then the phase of life coming to an end during this period may be one which began in a past life. But, in any case, it is the end of an old cycle; and hence, one often experiences discontent, confusion, disorientation, and a feeling of emotional-mental confinement as the old life structures begin to collapse. In other words, those ambitions, values, priorities, activities, and beliefs that once gave meaning and direction to your life are beginning to dissolve as Saturn enters this house; and the prevailing feelings of being spaced out or lost are usually strongest during the first year or so of this phase, until one has consolidated new values and new, more refined attitudes towards life itself. It is therefore a time for defining one's ideals and ultimate spiritual orientation, and many people spend this period experimenting with various new approaches to life after having shed the old attachments which have now proven to be quite empty and lifeless. It is, in short, a period of working at clarifying those transcendent and subtle dimensions of life which, although they are often difficult to verbalize, constitute the innermost source of strength which aids us in carrying on our struggles toward growth in the midst of life's battles and obstacles.

The 12th house has been called the house of isolation, and some sort of physical isolation is fairly common during this time. But what is much more common is that the person, at least during the first half of this period, feels like he is in an emotional prison, isolated from the outer world which seems distant and unreal. It is a time when we should turn inward, in order to tap inner sources of emotional and spiritual strength; and it often seems that, if we do not consciously choose to go within at this time, circumstances arise which compel us to experience some form of personal isolation which will leave us no choice but to reflect on our lives from a detached perspective. But, in most cases that I have seen, the person craves isolation and a means of retreating from the concerns of the outer world, whether this takes the form of running off to a monastery or merely retiring from many of the worldly associations and activities that used to be meaningful. It is an excellent time for the study of spiritual, mystical, or occult subjects, and many people also feel particularly drawn toward musical, poetic, or visionary expression during this time since what they are feeling cannot be expressed in logical or rationalistic terms but only through images, vibrations, and intuitions. There is also often a pull toward humanitarian activities and service work as a means of finding value in one's own life.

Health problems are not uncommon at this time, and they usually are psychosomatic, hard-to-diagnose ailments which only psychological/ spiritual therapy will affect. One's physical energy at this time is often low due to the emotional drain of experiencing the utter dissolution of one's entire old personality structure. The old is being dissolved at this time in order to make room for the birth of the new life-orientation and life structure. However, what is so disorienting about this time period is that it is a period of waiting, dreaming, and inner exploration during which the individual has no firm boundaries or solid anchors to hold to. One is awaiting and preparing for the birth of the new structure, but that won't even begin to be built until Saturn has crossed the Ascendant into the 1st house. But if one can gain inner strength from realizing that a whole new YOU is being created, freed of many useless encumbrances, then—as Saturn moves through the 12th house and approaches the Ascendant— we can become lighter and lighter, happier and happier.

Virgo

6

Aspects of Transformation in the Natal Chart

For a tree's branches to reach to heaven,
Its roots must reach to hell.
—Medieval alchemical dictum

The individual may strive after perfection but
must suffer from the opposite of his intentions
for the sake of his completeness.
—C.G. Jung

Each of the above quotations makes the same essential point, one that should always be remembered in any effort to understand astrological aspects: namely, that life itself requires us to encounter all manner of experience, the high and low, the light and dark, the good and bad, the easy and difficult in order that we may grow in awareness and become more whole. Many of us are familiar with the fact that an experience which seems particularly difficult or traumatic at the time is often the very experience which gives us the increased understanding which illuminates our life and motivates rapid growth for years to come. Due to the particular type of consciousness which prevailed in England and the United States during the early part of the twentieth century, however, the great majority of astrological writings neglected to take this fact into account. In astrology books produced during that period, almost every factor in an individual's chart was regarded automatically to be good or bad depending upon how "easy" or "difficult" it might be for the person to express, satisfy, or integrate that part of his or her nature. A particularly narrow and distorted view of life thus developed in the minds of people who digested these early astrological writings, and—unfortunately—this narrow view still predominates today among many people active in the astrological field.

In recent years, a reaction to this negative, distorted outlook has taken place, as many writers and lecturers have reformulated astrology in the light of the subtler, more psychological perspective that was initiated by Dane Rudhyar and Marc Edmund Jones. As so often happens in any field when a reaction to an extreme approach sets in, many of the pioneers of a more positive, growth-oriented approach to astrology have tried to compensate for the faults of traditional astrology by going to the other extreme: i.e., by over-emphasizing the light side of life and neglecting to confront the darkness. What used to be regarded as "difficult" aspects in a chart are then sugar-coated with all sorts of idealized and flowery language, and the fact that some of these aspects indicate not only real problems for the person but also major defects or negative qualities in the character is ignored. It seems to me that it is time to be realistic about astrology, which means that we must become more realistic about ourselves and our view of life. Life *is* full of difficulties and problems. That is what makes it such a profound learning experience for the soul. If we view the birthchart as a comprehensive symbol of an individual's life potentials and life pattern, then that symbol must include indications of these crucial life problems, these areas of life wherein we can learn major lessons which further our growth. What is not shown in the chart, however, is the *attitude* toward our cosmic inheritance and karma which we can consciously build and cultivate. Because the inner attitude cannot be determined from the birth-chart alone, the astrologer must be careful in any evaluation of a planetary configuration since it shows primarily the energy *potential* within that person, but not the specific manifestation of that energy as a predetermined fact. Such a realization calls for a period of exploratory questioning and dialogue in any astrological counseling session, in order that the counselor can get a feel for the specific attitudes and ideals which may be guiding the individual's use of his or her energies.

Since some people take difficulties and problems in stride, accepting them as a part of life, and since such people are sustained by an inner optimism and faith, what is shown in the chart as potentially troublesome is not always viewed by every person as a major problem. It may simply be seen as a fact of life, as an accepted part of the person's nature. If the counselor tries to over-emphasize the problematical side of such a symbolic configuration, it may seem to the person that the counselor is just stirring up all kinds of troublesome questions for no constructive purpose. In fact, this often happens in an astrological "reading" that is merely a one-sided performance by the astrologer. If, on the other hand, the counselor views and explains the "difficult" aspects as *challenges* that the person will encounter in this lifetime, an energetic, positive-thinking person will be interested in knowing about such tests of his or her character, strength, and knowledge. And the more fearful, self-conscious person may then begin to view these major life questions in a new light. The main thing we should realize not only intellectually but also spiritually is that such challenges, difficulties, problems (call them what you will!) are necessary for health and should be welcomed as opportunities to learn what we need to know. As Jung writes:

> Fear of fate is a very understandable phenomenon, for it is incalculable, immeasurable, full of unknown dangers. The perpetual hesitation of the neurotic to launch out into life is readily explained by this desire to stand aside so as not to get involved in the dangerous struggle for existence. But anyone who refuses to experience life must stifle his desire to live—in other words, he must commit partial suicide. (from *Symbols of Transformation*, CW Vol. 5, par. 165)

Surely no astrologer would want to believe that he or she is actually encouraging "neurotic" behavior in clients; and yet, the form of astrological practice that prompts the client to fear his destiny, to hesitate to act until the planets are in the right places, or to do anything possible to avoid "dangerous" or challenging situations is actually encouraging neurotic dependency on the astrologer and inhibiting the development of faith and self-confidence in the client. Perhaps in essence the traditional "difficult" aspects indicate areas of maximum stress and tension in the person's *inner* life, and this tension can also be welcomed with an open attitude. Again to quote Jung:

> The greater the tension, the greater is the potential. Great energy springs from a correspondingly great tension between opposites.

In the remainder of this book, I therefore prefer to use the following terms in categorizing aspects, rather than the traditional easy-hard, good-bad classifications:

> **DYNAMIC** or **CHALLENGING** aspects: This term refers to those angles between planets that are usually called "stressful" or "inharmonious," including the square, opposition, quincunx (or inconjunct), some of the conjunctions (depending on the planets involved), and some of the semisquares, sesquiquadrates, and other minor aspects (depending on the harmony of the elements and signs involved). These angles correspond with the experience of inner tension and usually prompt some sort of definite action or at least the development of greater awareness in the areas indicated. Although the term "inharmonious" *does* apply to many of these aspects, this term is often misleading since it is possible for the individual to develop a relatively harmonious mode of expression for these energies by taking on responsibilities, work, or other challenges which are capable of absorbing the full intensity of the energy being released.

> **HARMONIOUS** or **FLOWING** aspects: This term refers to those angles between planets that are usually called "easy" or "good," primarily including the sextile, trine, some of the conjunctions (depending on the planets involved), and some of the minor aspects (primarily depending on the harmony of the elements of the signs involved). These angles correspond with spontaneous abilities, talents, and modes of understanding and expression which the individual is able to utilize and develop with relative ease and consistency. These abilities constitute a set of steady and reliable psychological assets upon which the person may draw at any time. Although the individual may prefer to concentrate his or her energy and attention on the more challenging, dynamic aspects of life, these flowing aspects do represent the *potential* for developing extraordinary talents. But they contrast with the dynamic aspects in that they are more indicative of *states of being* and spontaneous attunements to established channels of expression; whereas the dynamic aspects indicate the need for adjustment through effort, definite action, and the development of new channels of self-expression.

Before getting into the subject of aspects in more detail, we might examine the question of why the dynamic angles in a chart seem to receive more attention in astrological studies than do the flowing aspects. Is it just a case of negative thinking wherein astrologers find masochistic pleasure in dwelling upon the more problematical side of life? Or is there some other explanation for this phenomenon? I think that C.E.O. Carter clarifies this point when he writes in *Astrological*

Aspects that the "inharmonious" aspects are easier to talk about due to the fact that these "have affinity with materiality and therefore manifest themselves more clearly and perceptibly." Carter's statement is supported by the fact that, until recently, the school of astrology known as Cosmobiology has almost totally ignored the harmonious aspects, preferring to use the dynamic aspects in their work; and anyone familiar with the underlying assumptions and orientation of most Cosmobiologists' work knows that they are *primarily* interested in events, major changes, obvious traumas, and, in general, the happenings of the material world rather than the individual's psychological attitude toward experience or its spiritual significance. I myself greatly emphasize the dynamic aspects, not because my orientation is the same as that of the Cosmobiologists, but because these angles reveal where one is being challenged to adjust oneself markedly and to grow through concentrated experience. And, since the majority of my astrological experience has come from interpersonal dialogues with clients (rather than solely from personal research, study, and working with my own chart), I have been drawn to the study of the positive potentials which are implicit in my clients' various life crises, and which are so often symbolized by the challenging aspects. Therefore, in this chapter I will primarily emphasize the dynamic aspects, in an effort to clarify in a positive light what is interpreted negatively in most astrological texts. And I will especially focus on those aspects involving the trans-Saturnian planets since they represent particularly definite forms of personal transformation.

Aspects in Modern Times

During the latter part of the twentieth century, as modern astrology has exploded with new techniques, theoretical speculation, and levels of application which boggle the mind and make it impossible for any one person to assimilate and understand all the new developments, it is especially difficult to treat the subject of aspects in any comprehensive way without writing a huge and exhaustive treatise on the subject. Modern research and clinical experience has conclusively shown that such factors as midpoints, planetary pictures (configurations involving numerous planets and midpoints), and harmonics can provide the practicing astrologer with additional tools with which to understand human beings and which often contribute insights which traditional methods do not provide as specifically. We are seeing more and more that the relationship between the various planets (and hence, between the various dimensions of a human being's psycho-somatic-energetic structure) is not limited merely to isolated aspects between two planets or to the specific angular distances between planets that traditional astrology has emphasized for centuries. As mentioned in the Introduction to this book, it is becoming common to hear astrologers speak of planetary dialogues or interchanges, that is, planetary relationships that can manifest strongly even if no close traditional aspect is present. It is also becoming increasingly evident that the *planets* involved in any particular configuration (rather than just the type of configuration or aspect) primarily determine the nature of the psychological factors at work and the tone of the energy release. These facts make it difficult to establish reliable rules of interpretation for specific aspects when, in empirical experience, one finds so many diverse manifestations of the same basic aspect.

Therefore, for those who keep up with the latest research findings and feel the need to integrate those new insights into their practice, and for those whose integrity compels them to evaluate the validity of traditional astrological tenets realistically, astrology has become more difficult and complex than its usual simplistic presentation implies. This realization of the complexity inherent in astrology has been bemoaned by some people in the field, but the overwhelming proliferation of new techniques and concepts in recent years can have two very positive effects. First of all, it can motivate us to search for unifying and synthesizing principles with greater effort, as I am trying to do in my various writings. Those underlying principles are already present within the framework of astrology; they do not have to be invented or discovered through computer analysis. They merely have to be more clearly recognized and more deeply understood if they are to be fully relevant to the practical application of astrology in human lives. And secondly, this explosion of new ideas can more immediately reveal to the astrological student or practitioner the impossibility of obtaining easy, rigid, simplistic information from a birth chart and thus force us to rely on our own insights, experience, counseling ability, and our capacity for developing a totally individualized form of astrological practice which specifically suits each of us.

In addition, when considering this seemingly unending growth of complexity in the astrological field, certain other facts stand out. One obvious fact is that the astrological counselor who has a fairly large practice, and particularly one who has to earn his or her entire livelihood from counseling work, simply does not have the time to use even a small proportion of the techniques available in traditional astrology in any given consultation, let alone introduce possible insights found by newer methods. For such a professional counselor, the demands of financial survival plus the immediate needs of the client take precedence over one's intellectual curiosities. If one focuses mainly on the client's need for *counseling* rather than on the birthchart's endless multitude of *data*, there will rarely be any need or desire for more insight than certain basic astrological procedures can provide—assuming one really *understands* the symbols that are immediately apparent. For example, I have found the Key Cycle system developed by Wynn* to be an extremely accurate and psychologically penetrating technique. I have often found it to symbolize clearly certain developments or orientations in a more specific way than do commonly used transits and progressions. However,

---

*Cf. *The Key Cycle* by Wynn; originally published as a series of articles in the *AFA Bulletin* in 1970, it is now available in pamphlet form from the American Federation of Astrologers.

I rarely have the time to use it even for myself, let alone for dozens of clients. But I rarely miss it, although I realize that it would often give me additional and reliable data to work with. But my main orientation is *counseling with the person,* establishing a dialogue on a personal level while using astrology primarily as a structural map and guidance system. Ignoring a few bits of comparatively trivial data should not inhibit a good counselor from helping clients to gain a clearer and more positive perspective on their lives!

Another point to keep in mind is that, if one sees a birth-chart as similar to a piece of music, various themes will stand out. Those themes may be discovered through any number of astrological methods, and most of the time the use of complex new techniques will not reveal any major new theme but will only further emphasize and perhaps give a bit more detail about those themes shown clearly by fairly simple and traditional methods. In other words, the use of many of the recently popularized methods rarely gives more insight into the psychological essence of the individual person in any way that can be *immediately and practically utilized.* Many of these new ideas are interesting, challenging, and hold out the promise of eventually being utilized in such a way that statistical studies and prediction attempts will produce significantly better results. But what about the individual person having troubles? What is the application of these methods in the counseling situation? And how can they aid the astrologer who is using astrology not to convince "scientists" or to predict events but to aid others in self-understanding? It seems to me that this is one more instance which points to the fact that astrology has become a highly specialized field and that some astrologers are primarily counselors, while others are primarily researchers or theoreticians. The important thing is that the individual practitioner be aware of his or her particular role, underlying philosophy and—most of all—the *purpose* each hopes to accomplish with the aid of astrology. If one's role is that of "counselor," whether formally through an established professional practice or informally through dealing chiefly with friends and relatives, one should be careful not to unnecessarily complicate the situations with which one is confronted day in and day out. For the archetypal human stories and problems are actually very few, and they go on repeating themselves in all our lives as intensely as if they had never happened before. Counseling others in order to help them to deal with these archetypal problems is a highly demanding art, and our purpose should be that of aiding others to gain the perspective on their individual situations that will enable them to live life more fully through greater understanding.

The Nature of Specific Aspects

Many writers have spoken of aspects as relating to "lines of force" between the various energy centers (planets) in the individual's energy field. Some of the most practical insights into the physical and psychological manifestations of these forces can be found in Dr. William

Davidson's *Lectures on Medical Astrology,* in which he discusses with great originality the various "diseases" and basic principles associated with the various aspects. Naturally, a configuration of energy potential, such as an aspect symbolizes, is neither good nor bad in itself. It is merely a *potential* with an inherent *tendency* toward harmonious and pleasurable *or* destructive and painful expression. Dr. Davidson's experience with astrological symbolism in the medical field leaves little doubt that the dynamic aspects *do* symbolize a greater tendency toward physical disease than harmonious, flowing aspects; for the dynamic aspects generate an inner tension and put stress on the physical body. But how the individual deals with that stress and how he or she channels that energy and tries to relieve that tension is the key to whether a particular configuration will eventually manifest as a serious physical problem or whether it shows a reservoir of energy which can be tapped for creative purposes. We should not underestimate the power of the mind and will; for our very thoughts, ideals, and desires can subtly alter the lines of force within our total energy field. An example of this process in its simplest form can be found in the considerable amount of research that has proven—even to skeptical scientists—that meditation techniques such as Transcendental Meditation markedly alter certain physical rhythms and constitute an effective technique for releasing stress.

Another point worth repeating is that each aspect must be evaluated according to the nature of the planets involved. There is considerable evidence that some of the trine aspects correspond with wasteful or problematical conditions in far more cases than traditional teachings about the "beneficial" effects of trines would indicate. For example, the trine of Neptune is often found in charts of people who exhibit rather negative Neptunian tendencies: drug problems, escapism, impractical or hypocritical "spiritual" interests, and even major psychological dissociations described as psychosis, uncontrollable hallucinations, delusions of grandeur, or simply inability to deal effectively with the material world. Uranus trines are almost as common as the more dynamic Uranus aspects in charts of people who are particularly self-centered, unable to cooperate, given to the "I know it all" syndrome, and so speeded up with excitement about their own interests that they are extremely impatient with others. Jupiter trines often seem to indicate little more than a tendency toward lazy self-indulgence and a preference for relying on anything other than one's own hard work. By contrast, the dynamic aspects involving these planets, as we will examine in detail shortly, are often found to symbolize energy that can be expressed with great concentration, power, and creativity, although admittedly they do often show conflicts and problems (sometimes simultaneously). If we can thus attain the level of understanding wherein we begin to see the value inherent in effort and even in pain, rather than seeing astrology as a phenomenon isolated from life itself, we can then begin to understand the aspects in an accurate, deep, and practical way. My favorite law for interpreting aspects is:

The planets in the signs represent the basic *urges toward expression* and *needs for fulfillment,* but the aspects reveal the actual state of the energy flow and how much personal *effort* is needed in order to express a particular urge or to fulfill a particular need.

In other words, a particular aspect does not tell us: this person will or will not do such-and-such; nor does it tell us whether a person *can* experience or achieve something. But it does tell us how much effort will be required, in a relative sense, to achieve a given result. We might add, however, that the entire chart, as well as the individual's background, environment, and specific training, must be evaluated in order to give us an idea of whether the person's actual abilities and karmic pattern will enable him or her to satisfy these urges and needs.

Keeping in mind the limitations of applying general principles to individual cases, we can now begin to analyze an energy flow theory of aspects. But we must remember that the following concepts are an attempt to describe specific kinds of energy flow at a very subtle level of operation. This energy can manifest as innumerable kinds of behavior and as an infinite variety of personality traits. For the sake of simplicity, we can categorize aspects into the two groups mentioned earlier: *dynamic* or *challenging* aspects, and *harmonious* or *flowing* aspects. The harmonious aspects show that the two energies involved (and thus the two dimensions of the individual's being) vibrate in harmony and *reinforce* each other within the person's energy field, similar to two waves harmonizing and blending into a unified expression of complex energies. For example, if Mercury and Mars are in harmony with each other, there is a blending of the two energies which can produce mental strength, the power to assert one's ideas, a strong nervous system, and the ability to project one's ideas into definite action. It is as if Mercury lends its intelligence to guide the Mars self-assertion, while simultaneously Mars energizes the Mercurian perception and verbal expression. Such a planetary interrelationship might be visually expressed like this:

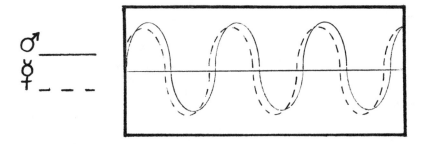

In other words, the harmonious aspects indicate a state of being and attunement that is inwardly stable and strong, a way of using our energy to stay flowing and relaxed. (This of course is not to say that the energies cannot be misused in a given person or situation. It simply shows that the energy does flow rather easily).

The challenging aspects show that the energies involved (and thus the life-dimensions of the individual whose chart has such an aspect) do not vibrate in harmony. Rather than reinforcing each other, they tend to interfere with each other's expression and to create stress within the energy field, as if two waves were in a discordant relationship to each other, setting up what one might call an unstable or irritating tone. This irritation or instability can, however, prompt the individual toward some sort of definite action in order to resolve the tension. To use again the example of Mercury and Mars, a dynamic aspect between these two planets can manifest as an impatience (Mars) to communicate (Mercury), a strong drive (Mars) to learn (Mercury), the tendency to assert too forcefully (Mars) one's ideas and opinions (Mercury), an irritable nervous system, an overly critical nature, etc. If the irritability and inner tension is successfully controlled and directed, however, such an individual may well be able to focus the tremendous drive toward learning into the development of exceptional skills which require keen intelligence. Such a planetary relationship may be expressed like so:

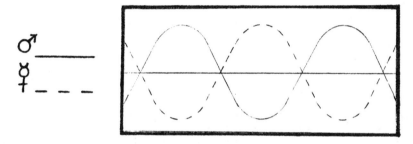

The above diagrams of energy flow become even more instructive if we compare this theory of aspects with electrical theory. In electrical wiring, a 3-phase current at 60° spacing is the *least stressful way of conducting energy* through wires. This corresponds with the sextile (60°) and trine (2x60°) aspects in astrology. 90° or 180° wiring is very stressful and heats up the wire since there are *peaks of too much voltage at times and none at other times*. This type of wiring naturally corresponds with the square and opposition aspects, where we find that the energies within the individual flow erratically, sometimes operating in unison and sometimes creating mutual interference and static. This sort of alternation in energy flow has been characterized by C.E.O. Carter as a "fitful" expression of energy; for sometimes the person has lots of the energy at his disposal, while other times he seems utterly depleted. Note that, in the above diagram, the lines of force alternately join and separate). When the stress reaches its peak, even more energy (heat in the case of wiring) is released; and this additional energy can be consciously directed toward some constructive goal, or it can simply explode and cause problems in the individual's life (in our electrical analogy, the excess heat could start a fire).

An excellent summary of aspects, both their theory and traditional meanings, appears in Nicholas DeVore's *Encyclopedia of Astrology*, a book which I feel is a true classic in the field and exemplifies an amazing range of enlightened scholarship combined with common sense. DeVore's *Encyclopedia* points out that all organic structures are built of cells which in their simplest form are hexagonal, similar to those of the honeycomb, and it goes on to say that the hexagon is the primary structural pattern of harmony. This idea is supported by the fact that engineers have recently "discovered" that the hexagon is the strongest and most economical storage bin, something that bees have been building for millions of years. The section on aspects continues:

> When light enters at the external angle of 60°, and the internal angle of 120°, it necessarily illuminates all parts of the structure in equal lines of influence. The light that pours in at either of these angles imparts . . . harmonious vibrations which stimulate growth. Opposed to this is the process of crystallization, recognized in magnetism and electricity, wherein two forces operate at right angles to each other—a geometrical relationship that is destructive to organic form. As a result, side by side through Nature two mutually antagonistic forces exist, which, despite their antipathy toward each other, work together toward the ordered disposition of the whole; one based upon the quadrature, the other upon the hexagon—the square and the trine.
>
> Astrology postulates: that the quadrature relationship between energy sources is destructive to form, through releasing the energy that is locked up in the various structures Nature has built; and that the trine aspects constitute the constructive side of Nature, whereby organic forms are created, nourished and perpetuated, to be released when subsequent destructive configurations are encountered. (p. 26)

From the above quotation we can deduce another way of classifying the aspects: *energy-releasing* and *form-maintaining*. The "energy-releasing" aspects are, of course, primarily the square and opposition, although some of the conjunctions and minor aspects (depending on the planets, signs, and elements involved) also symbolize particularly dynamic modes of energy release. The "form-maintaining" angles are primarily the sextile and trine, although again some of the conjuctions and occasional minor aspects also fall into this category. The relative dynamism or harmony of any particular interchange depends not only on the specific angle between planets but also on the elements involved. The meaning of the term "form-maintaining" can best be illustrated by seeing these types of energy flow as especially stable. The hexagon was explained above as a particularly stable and life-enhancing structure. The triangle likewise is a stable, self-perpetuating form; and this is most readily seen in the pyramids which have long outlasted structures built thousands of years later. The forms indicated by the "energy-releasing" aspects (such as the square) *seem* at first glance to be extremely stable; but when one views structures from the vantage-point of *energy-flow*, such forms are seen to be more unstable and prone to decay than hexagonal and triangular structures. The ideal in an individual birthchart is to find a balance of form-maintaining and energy-releasing aspects, for there can then be a synthesis of these complementary energy functions within the person's total energy field.

How the energy actually flows through the "form-maintaining" aspects should be fairly obvious since most of those aspects involve combinations of harmonious elements. But it would be worthwhile to mention how the energy is actually released through the more dynamic aspects. If the dynamic aspects involve planets in the cardinal signs, the energy released manifests as restlessness, tremendous urges toward action, starting new activities and projects, and facing crises. The person is usually a "go-getter" who has lots of plans and is pursuing a fairly definite direction. If fixed signs are involved, deeply ingrained habit patterns are indicated which generate extremely concentrated power and manifest as subborn willfulness. However, once this energy gets flowing, wide ranging capabilities and uncommon determination to bring things to a conclusion are evident. With mutable signs involved, the energy released seems to flow primarily through mental channels, manifesting as a wide range of interests and as an intense need for a broad variety of experience to satisfy the individual's craving for new learning.

Some key concepts for the major aspects should be outlined here:

CONJUNCTION: *Any* conjunction between two planets (or between a planet and the Ascendant) in an individual chart should be regarded as important since it indicates an intense merging and interaction of two life energies. The conjunction is the most powerful aspect in astrology, and the most important and powerful of all conjunctions are those involving one of the "personal planets" (Sun, Moon, Mercury, Venus, & Mars) or the Ascendant. Such conjunctions almost always characterize dominant dimensions of the person's life, over-riding motives and needs, and particularly strong modes of energy flow and personal expression. The keynote of the conjunction is *action* and *self-projection*, and thus one often finds that a conjunction with a personal planet or Ascendant characterizes a dimension of the individual's life that is much more consistently and significantly expressed than any other aspect of the person's nature.

SEXTILE: The meaning of the sextile aspect was unclear to me for years until it was pointed out to me that a sextile from the Ascendant in a natural chart connects with either the 3rd or the 11th house cusps, both of which are "air" houses and both of which are related to friends, intellectual pursuits, and experimentation with new varieties of experience. Hence, it seems to me that the sextile is an aspect of *openness* to the new: new people, new ideas, new attitudes; and it symbolizes the potential for making new connections with either people or ideas which can ultimately lead to new learning. The sextile is chiefly an aspect of flexibility and potential understanding, and it tends to be a mental aspect, although the planets involved in such an angle have to be taken into consideration. Perhaps most importantly, the sextile shows an area of life where one can cultivate not only a new level of understanding but also a greater degree of objectivity which can lead to a feeling of great freedom.

TRINE: A trine aspect represents an easy (but depending on the planets involved, sometimes undisciplined) flow of energy into established channels of expression. One does not need to build a new structure or to make marked adjustments in qne's life in order to utilize this energy creatively. The planets involved in the trine aspect reveal dimensions of life and specific energies which are naturally integrated and which flow together harmoniously. Such an aspect often shows a way of *being*, however, rather than a way of *doing;* for one often takes for granted the abilities and talents shown by the trine and thus does not feel challenged to make the effort required to use the energy constructively. In fact, in many cases, the natural abilities are taken so much for granted that the person may remain totally unaware that he or she has such talents, unless encouraged to use these energies by supportive feedback from others. Because trines show areas of life wherein we can experience an easy flow of complex energies, they often give indications of what an individual does in order to relax and enjoy himself; and—in terms of karma—one might assume that these aspects often show abilities which we have developed through many lifetimes, thus explaining why they manifest so easily in the present.

QUINCUNX (or INCONJUNCT): Planets in a 150° angle to each other often indicate a strong flow of energy between those dimensions of life symbolized, but the individual may feel that the experience of those energies is too compulsive or consistently annoying. Almost invariably, there is a need for acute discrimination as a way of gaining freedom from such compulsions and for some form of discipline to give the person a gentle push toward transformation in this area. It often seems that the expression of each of the two factors involved is mutually dependent on the other and thus that the person finds it difficult to express one of the urges or to satisfy one of the needs without also dealing with the other energy. Hence, the discrimination required should be more in the form of subtly adjusting one's approach to those areas of life rather than trying to force a radical inner division and total severance from the past patterns.

SQUARES & OPPOSITIONS: Enough has been said already in earlier sections of this book to give the reader a good feel for the potentials indicted by these challenging aspects. Of these two aspects, the square is the more problematical since it usually involves planets in inharmonious elements and thus calls forth more effort in order to integrate such divergent energies. A square aspect shows where energy must be *released,* usually through action of a definite sort, in order that a new structure may be built. The opposition, on the other hand, particularly since it usually involves planets in harmonious elements, often indicates a degree of *over-stimulation* in the person's energy field which manifests most intensely as a life challenge in the area of personal relationships. There is often a marked lack of objectivity since the individual tends to engage in "projection" of different sides of his nature onto others; and thus there is often some difficulty in distinguishing what is your's and what is somebody else's. The squares and oppositions are necessary both in our individual charts and between two charts in synastry in order that we can become *aware* of our own energies and desires. One might say that we need the squares and oppositions for challenges, but that we also need the flowing aspects for resources with which to meet those challenges. The tension involved in the challenging aspects forces us to act in order to change unsatisfactory conditions both within and without; for, if we don't act and confront the challenges, we then live in a state of inner frustration and turmoil.

Planets in challenging aspects are more energized than those in harmonious aspects; hence, one often *strives* more in those areas of life because of the added challenge and in order to relieve the tension. And also, once one has dealt effectively with the indicated challenges, one often gains a greater sense of satisfaction than would come from using the harmonious energies alone. One might say that squares show what you *have to* deal with through immediate experience, whereas trines indicate what you'll probably flow into naturally. But one cannot know from the chart alone whether you will prefer the challenge of the dynamic aspects or whether you'll prefer the ease of the flowing angles.

Many astrologers have written that the square aspect has the nature of Saturn: thus, what you *have to* deal with. Another Saturnian quality related to the square is *fear*, for we are often afraid of dealing with whatever is symbolized by the squares in our charts. In trying to deal with the indicated opportunities, we should remember that *fear is the enemy!* Fearing challenge restricts the energy available to deal effectively with whatever problem is at hand. One occasionally comes across a chart that lacks squares *and* challenging conjunctions, and it has occurred to me that many such people have never learned to face problems or challenges. They often live in their own world (usually a world of delusion); and many of their problems seem to be self-created in this very life rather than arising from difficult karma from the past.

Aspects & Karma

Planets involved in the challenging aspects give us sharp insight into what sort of karma has to be dealt with in this lifetime, especially in the sense that planets in such configurations show what our deepest attachments and most imbalanced mental-emotional patterns are. It often seems that a particular planetary function and energy is blocked or inhibited to some extent in order that we can—through immediate experience—realize the *implications* of our actions, emotions, thoughts, and desires. If this particular pattern of thought or action could be expressed with no difficulty (a difficulty that forces us to reconsider what we are doing), how could we learn anything? We would just continue to act out our old habits without reflection or self-analysis. In fact it often seems that a planet in a challenging aspect reflects a previous mis-use of that particular energy in the past; thus, the negative habit carries over into the present. In this life, however, we can *work out* those imbalances or blockages in our nature. Trines, sextiles, and harmonious conjunctions may also indicate attachments, but it seems to me that such attachments are not so negative or spiritually destructive that they pull us down or block our life energy in a major way. Naturally, what a particular aspect shows in an individual chart must be considered in relation to the other chart factors and in relation to the person's current lifestyle, ideals, and accomplishments; but the following may give readers some guidelines for this type of approach to aspects. The following planets in *challenging* aspects might be considered to indicate these sorts of attachments:

SUN: too much attachment to being someone special.

MOON: too much attachment to the past, to family and racial background, and to earthly peace (in the sense of expecting the outer world to be perfect).

MERCURY: too much attachment to intellect & mental pride.

VENUS: too much attachment to physical comfort, emotional satisfaction, and to other people in general.

MARS: too much attachment to action, achievement, winning over another person, and attainment of one's end desires.

JUPITER: too much attachment to doing things in a big way (and thus a lack of humility).

SATURN: too much attachment to social approval, power, authority, and reputation.

In the remainder of this chapter, I primarily want to focus upon the aspects involving Uranus, Neptune, and Pluto. Saturn aspects have already been dealt with in Chapter 5; and, except for Saturn's aspects, it is those which involve the trans-Saturnian planets which can truly be called "aspects of transformation." (We will deal with the important aspects involving the Ascendant in Chapter 10.) In addition, I will emphasize the aspects with the trans-Saturnians which involve one of the personal planets, for these aspects are by far the most important since they indicate inner dynamics which are unusually immediate and compelling.

Aspects with Uranus

Whereas Saturn's aspects show where we have little freedom and where we have to discipline or tone down a particular channel of expression, the aspects involving Uranus show where we have to open things up, experiment with the new and different, and become more receptive to truth with complete objectivity. All aspects of Uranus to personal planets indicate areas of our lives wherein we have a strong urge to attain freedom of expression without restraint and where we feel the need for constant excitement and experimentation. It is in those areas of life where we want to be different from everyone else, where we want a broad scope of independence from binding traditions and past conditioning, and where there is often a marked capacity for originality, inventiveness, and broad-minded objectivity. However, although there is the capacity for such positive modes of expression in any person who has the Uranian vibration touching some dimension of his or her life (in other words, who has Uranus in *any* close major aspect with *any* personal planet or the Ascendant), we should remember that Uranus represents a high-strung, temperamental, and rapidly changeable vibration. In a split-second, there can be a change (or "re-polarization") from one extreme to another, and the constant need for excitement and often-purposeless change can lead to willfulness, impatience, and fanaticism. In considering aspects with Uranus, as with the aspects of the other trans-Saturnian planets, it is misleading to evaluate a particular configuration as a *priori* likely to be expressed constructively or destructively; for, more than any other planet, Uranus represents the level of consciousness where one thinks and acts in a *both/and* way rather than in an *either/or* fashion. In other words, a Uranian person usually expresses some of both polarities: positive *and* negative; and he may express both simultaneously!

To concentrate on the essence of Uranus aspects, we can establish certain principles:

a) Uranus aspects reveal a *spasmodic* rhythm of activity and energy flow; it can change in a moment and is totally unpredictable. And the creative manifestations of Uranus energy are usually accompanied by some of the less-desirable Uranian qualities.

b) The correlation of Uranus with spasmodic activity explains many physical ailments whose root cause, according to Dr. William Davidson, is spasm.* Hence, the Uranus energy is very hard on the physical body; and anyone who is particularly attuned to Uranus should cultivate specific ways of dealing with the constant stress that Uranus energy puts upon the nervous system.

c) Uranus *electrifies* everything it touches. Hence, any personal planet in *any* close aspect with Uranus is electrified, speeded up, and subject to both high-voltage flashes of insight and shocking impulses and experiences. (The correlation of Uranus with electricity seems to be valid not only literally but metaphorically; for the discovery of Uranus heralded the era of global communication utilizing electronic technology, and Uranian people are known for their delight in doing things that *shock* others out of the lethargy of tradition.)

d) The objectivity and impersonal freedom for which Uranus is noted is in certain situations a positive quality. However, this orientation is often accompanied by a lack of personal warmth and even by an icy detachment from both others' and one's own deeper feelings. This depends especially on the signs involved.

e) Uranus ultimately is impossible to pin down or to classify rigidly; for it breaks all the rules and is intensely ego-involved with the delight of shattering all conventions.

f) The transformative meaning of Uranus aspects may be summed up by saying that Uranus serves the purpose of radically re-polarizing an individual's approach in a particular area of life and rapidly cutting away all traces of past life patterns. It opens one up to new areas of experience either through enjoyable excitement or through shocking, traumatic crises; but, one way or another, whether one likes it or not, one is confronted with the freedom to experiment with new ways of living.

As we consider the following planetary interchanges, I primarily want to focus on the quality of energy and experience symbolized by each combination. However, some special emphasis will be placed on how the energy manifests when the combinations form the dynamic aspects. I do not want to waste your time and mine by reiterating what other authors have already explained clearly, for example in Carter's *The Astrological Aspects* and Oken's *The Horoscope, the Road, and Its Travellers,* both of which include excellent treatments of specific aspects.† Therefore, I will mainly point out qualities of these aspects which seem to me particularly interesting, unusual, important, or poorly understood.

---

*Cf.*Lectures on Medical Astrology* by Dr. William Davidson; published by The Astrological Bureau; Monroe, N.Y. (Available from CRCS Publications.)

† Carter's book must be studied carefully in order to penetrate to its deeper insights. Certain of his evaluations must be taken with reservations, since he does occasionally make rigid or biased statements and lapse into using the categories of good/bad configurations. But one must keep in mind that this book was written in 1930 when this type of astrological language was common. The book still remains a mine of insight and well-reasoned observations, and it is one of the very few astrological works which gives me new insights with each reading.

Sun-Uranus Aspects

The individuality is toned by the excitable, unpredictable, and self-centered Uranian vibration. This individual is often unusually creative in a variety of activities, but he or she often finds it difficult to settle down into any one field of specialization since there is such a strong need for constant new stimulation and a dislike of routine. Hence, these people often go through many lifestyles, types of work, relationships, and interests during the course of their lives. They usually feel the need to join forces with some larger purpose or group effort, although they often find that the cooperation required in such efforts markedly tests their patience. There is almost always a powerful streak of independence in their nature, and these people often act on the assumption that they have the right to do whatever they want, regardless of various responsibilities or duties they might have assumed. One finds willfulness and the "I-know-it-all" attitude in many of these people, although those with the challenging aspects tend to exemplify this trait more than the others.

At best, these people are truly scientific in the literal sense of the word; that is, they are open to trying anything at least once in order that they can *know* from their own experience what is true and what is not. Those with Uranus in a close aspect to the Sun often exhibit qualities and energies that are commonly associated with Sun in Aquarius. These people also tend to experience periodic *radical* changes in their life structures and in their mode of self-expression since, when any important transit or progression activates the Sun, it will also activate Uranus.

The primary difference between the flowing and the challenging aspects of this type can be viewed this way: those with the flowing aspects are usually able to integrate their new insights, impulses, and experiments within the life structure that they have already established; whereas those with the challenging aspects often experience a tension which urges them to step beyond their current way of life into the unknown in a much more radical way. With the flowing aspects, the person's consciousness may be transformed and the lifestyle severely altered periodically, but he or she usually has the ability to build the new attitudes and orientations upon the foundations of the old; whereas those with the more dynamic aspects often feel that they have to cut away all remnants of the old in order to be totally free to experience the potentials inherent in the new seeds being sown. Both get sudden flashes of insight, but—although these flashes *can* at times be markedly inaccurate and unreliable in both cases—those with the dynamic aspects have a stronger tendency to go to extremes of opinion without regard for accuracy.

With both the flowing and the challenging aspects, the individual has the ability to delve into new frontiers of thought and action; but the difference seems to be that those with the challenging aspects often cannot handle the urge for change and find it hard to endure the tension that develops. They often therefore seem pushed into making radical departures from the norm or from their old way of life simply as a release of tension. Those with the challenging aspects, therefore, often toss aside that which other people might retain. In their excitement about the possibilities of new and freer horizons of life, they seem to feel that the quickest way to get on to the new is to simply dump the old without reservation or any trace of sentimentality. And, because they believe in what they do and in their right to do almost anything, they are not secretive about their plans; they tend to be uncompromisingly sincere and honest, although often quite tactless and insensitive to others' feelings. As my editor with Sun conjunct Uranus says, whatever the aspect, Sun-Uranus people have the task of fully expressing their individuality as a *testimony* to the uniqueness and value of *every* person. By going beyond mere egocentricity, these people can be channels for the truly humanitarian vibration of Uranus.

Moon-Uranus Aspects

Some of the same qualities and principles described in the above section on Sun-Uranus aspects also apply to these aspects. However, as Carter has pointed out, there is often an inflexibility and difficulty with adjusting to life changes in these aspects that seems as common in the flowing aspects as in the challenging ones. This can be explained by realizing that the flowing aspects are often rather lazy; hence, the individual does not want to adapt himself to any outside influence and prefers just to maintain his current momentum of self-initiated action. The challenging aspects may also manifest in a similar, inflexible way in some cases, but in other cases there is a strong urge toward change and excitement which makes the person welcome outside stimuli toward revising his lifestyle. Seemingly, those whose charts contain the dynamic aspects of Uranus with the Moon have little choice but to accustom themselves to the need for periodic radical changes in their lives, starting with their early youth. Both types of aspects may be better understood by relating them to the essential meaning of the Moon in Aquarius, where one finds a strong need for variety and change together with a forceful urge to have control, and thus a resistance to changing one's mind. (Aquarius is a *fixed* sign!) Aquarius is a complex mixture of experimental openness to anything new and different *and* a tendency toward an inflexible, even fanatical adherence to one idea or attitude. Such complexity is especially strong if the Moon is in Aquarius, and similar qualities are evident in those whose charts contain Moon-Uranus aspects.

The intuition is particularly incisive in those who have these aspects (although it may be argued that the flowing aspects indicate a more reliable and steady type of intuition), since the Moon is a receptive, intuitive planet itself. Those with the challenging aspects often have a conscious desire or an inner urge to change their identity in a *radical* way and to rid self of the past conditioning upon which their old sense of self is based. This is reflected in the fact that many of these people experience one or more name changes during this lifetime (other than the usual name change which women traditionally accept in a marriage). Sometimes, this happens to the person when they are young and have, for example, a change of fathers; and other times, they seem to choose the new name because of its transformative symbolism.

Carl Payne Tobey, who has written some particularly incisive material on aspects, points out that those with the challenging aspects of Uranus experience decisions that "come like the flood that bursts the dam." There is usually a lot of moving around and restlessness, and men with these aspects (of any type) often find traditional marriage and monogamy to be severely restrictive to their need to experiment with many modes of emotional expression. Tobey also points out that the flowing aspects of Uranus with the Moon often produce extremely unique and useful qualities, such as a marked efficiency of method in many areas of activity. He writes that "excellent reflexes enable one to react well to almost any given situation," and he states that these people can depend on the right insight at the right time; they react with an appropriate course of action instantaneously. This idea points to the fact that those with Uranus in close aspect to personal planets (especially to Sun, Moon, and Mercury) have the ability to draw forth information and knowledge from other dimensions in a split-second to deal with any problem. The only thing needed in order to utilize this information is a keen ability to discriminate between true, objective knowledge and mere fanatical, emotion-charged opinions.

Mercury-Uranus Aspects

All aspects of Mercury with Uranus denote an attunement of the conscious, logical mind to the Universal Mind in some way; but the harmony of the attunement should be noted. All of these aspects indicate that the nervous system and the perceptions are speeded up to the point where the person can exhibit great insight, ingenuity, originality, and memory; but the functioning of the mind tends to be erratic and undependable, especially where the aspects are challenging ones. These aspects symbolize an unusual association of ideas, and a rapid connection of and insight into apparently unrelated ideas. The mind operates so fast that other people may think that such correlations are illogical or even ridiculous, while the person whose chart has such an aspect is often impatient with the slowness of other people's thoughts. However, if the person's mind is clearly attuned to Uranus, the ideas thus produced are seen in retrospect to be quite logical, although the individual seemed to skip over a few analytical steps in arriving at his or her deductions. A person with these aspects is also usually impatient with the traditional system of formal education, which allows so little room for creative and original thinking and which limits one's thought by imposing rigid boundaries on the scope of truth that one is allowed to perceive.

Hence, although such a person's mind often seems to function more through intuition than logic, there is usually a logical process at work when the attunement is sharp. But these people are almost always high-strung, somewhat eccentric thinkers, whose scope of original ideas is broad, though not at all consistent in quality. In extreme cases, the person seems to worship intellectual knowledge and be prone to the "know-it-all" syndrome. And in almost all people whose charts contain these aspects, the tendency to be overwhelmed by jolting flashes of insight or new tangents of thought leads them to appear inconsistent and mentally undisciplined. One of the key factors in this type of person is that he gets so excited about his own ideas and so infatuated with his own mind's operation that he rarely slows down long enough to listen to anyone else or to absorb the kind of feedback that he needs in order to refine his original mental impressions. This impatience, especially when the aspect is one of the challenging ones, is thus often a detriment to the person's capacity to relate easily to others; for how can we relate if we can't sit still long enough to hear another person's point of view? The opposition of Uranus and Mercury particularly manifests as erratic mental functioning. This person can be alternately brilliant—with a photographic memory and rapid understanding of new ideas—and at other times absent minded and fanatically opinionated. Although the mental impulses are erratic, it seems that the person who has any aspect of these two planets has the ability to tap into his reservoir of knowledge and insight whenever it is truly important to do so. When the chips are down, the mental abilities come into play full force. For example, I know of a doctor with Mercury opposite Uranus who never studied during his years at medical school except immediately before tests. At that time, he would simply race through the required material, mentally "photograph-ing" it, and he would inevitably get high grades. He eventually graduated third in his class. On the personal level, he has no close friends since he is unable to communicate harmoniously with others and since he is so impatient with everyone else that no one feels comfortable being around him. He is fanatically opinionated and has little of the open-mindedness usually associated with these aspects. He is also an example of the type of person with this opposition aspect whose main troubles in life stem from the inability to communicate effectively.

Venus-Uranus Aspects

Aspects involving Venus are poorly explained in most astrological textbooks; hence, before dealing with these specific aspects, we should clarify an important point about all Venus aspects. Venus aspects in the chart (as well as its sign position) show the *capacity* for conscious relationship with another human being. The challenging aspects with Venus do not necessarily mean that one is not loved or that one doesn't feel any love within himself or herself; they simply mean that one may tend to block the *expression* of love feelings and that one may likewise inhibit oneself from receiving affection from others.

All aspects between Venus and Uranus have been poorly explained in traditional books, particularly the challenging aspects. The dynamic aspects between these two planets have been called "divorce aspects" and have often been correlated with sexual promiscuity and perversion. There is of course some truth to the connection of such aspects with these types of experience; but, as Carter writes, these aspects "do not incline to promiscuity or vulgar vice, and its connection with sexual perversion has probably been extremely exaggerated." Granted that there are cases where such aspects seem to correlate with this type of behavior, the majority of people whose charts have such aspects express these energies in subtler ways. There is usually a strong need for emotional excitement and romantic adventures, but the degree of sensuality and sexuality involved will depend primarily on the *sign* placement of Venus, along with other factors in the chart. If Venus is in Scorpio or Taurus, for example, there is much greater likelihood of sexual experimentation than if Venus is in Libra, Gemini, or Leo; for Venus in some signs needs *physical* expression more intensely than Venus in other signs in order to gain a feeling of closeness and emotional release. There *is* usually a desire to experiment with many kinds of relationships and to insist upon an extraordinary degree of freedom in one's intimate contacts; and, in some instances, this need *will* be expressed as homosexual, bisexual, orgiastic, or other types of culturally unconventional behavior (for Uranus, after all, does urge us to break through cultural norms in a radical fashion!). However, most people who have such aspects, especially the flowing angles, will express what Tobey calls a "gentle unconventionality;" they will have a strong interest in the opposite sex in most cases and almost always an active social life which includes a wide variety of not always conventional people.

The flowing aspects of Venus and Uranus often reveal the ability to get along harmoniously with all sorts of people in an open-minded way. The main problems indicated even in these relatively harmonious aspects are the changeability and impersonality which can make the person tire easily of any relationship that ceases to be especially exciting. The combination of impersonal, aloof Uranus with personally oriented, sensitive Venus is not the most compatible of interchanges; but the flowing aspects do not as a rule manifest with nearly the problematical quality exemplified in the challenging aspects.

The emotional restlessness of this combination reaches its most intense stage in the dynamic aspects, where we often find people whose self-centeredness, coldness, insensitivity, and insistence on their right to experiment without regard for others creates havoc in their most important relationships. The conjunction, square, quincunx, and opposition can all manifest in somewhat similar ways; but the opposition between Venus and Uranus is especially indicative of severe relationship problems since not only Venus itself but also the nature of the opposition aspect symbolizes *relationship*. The self-centeredness that characterizes these dynamic aspects has often been pointed out, but it has rarely been explained in terms of the inner dynamics at work. These people are often afraid to love on an intimate, personal level; for they often feel that such a commitment will restrict their emotional freedom. There is an erratic, tense quality in the emotional energy field, manifesting as a high-strung "touchiness" and insecurity, although it may not be immediately obvious. There is a tendency not to let oneself be loved (except erratically) because of the habit of spasmodically jumping back from any emotional commitment. Feeling afraid of being hurt insures that one *will* be hurt, and a fear of rejection is extremely common in those who were born during any of these dynamic aspects. Hence, these people unconsciously try to cope with their feelings by giving their partners, lovers, or friends the subtle message: "I don't really need you." And they therefore tend to grant the other person a great deal of space in the name of freedom. However, it is sometimes too much space, and a gap begins to grow between the two people. The partner may get the message: "I'm bored with you. I don't have any need of your presence." And hence, people with these aspects are in effect *eliciting* rejection or forcing the partner to go elsewhere for deep, personal affection. In some cases, a person whose chart has one of these aspects manifests extremely self-centered, insensitive behavior while simultaneously complaining that "Nobody loves me." In this instance, one might assume that this way of approaching relationships is a karmic carryover from past lives, but the important fact is that it is a living energy pattern in this very lifetime. And the individual is creating his or her misery in the present by acting out the old patterns. It often seems that one of the transformative purposes of being born with such an aspect is that one should learn how to give (Venus) freely (Uranus), but to do so with some degree of balance and sensitivity—without detaching oneself from human feelings.

Mars-Uranus Aspects

Any interchange between Mars and Uranus is indicative of an extremely dynamic flow of energy, usually manifesting as decisiveness, drive, and exceptional energy resources. Any such aspect tends to indicate a strong restlessness and a quick excitability, especially in the area of sexual drive, physical movement, and ambition. There is usually considerable courage, inventiveness, daring, leadership, and personal independence. As Carter writes, the person tends to "know his own mind excellently well;" however, one cannot necessarily deduce that the person always *understands* what is really motivating him, since these are aspects of compulsive activity, adventure, and excitement. This person is stimulated by new frontiers of knowledge or activity (note the sign position of Mars), and there is often engineering or mechanical skill. (For example, the only two women engineers I know have Mars-Uranus oppositions). It is an interchange of great—often excessive—tension; and, especially with the dynamic aspects, the tension erupts now and then in displays of anger, violence (physical, verbal, or emotional), purposeless destruction, or sexual activity bordering on violence. However, while these aspects' reputation for violence is not without foundation, the powerful energies symbolized do not have to take that form. For example, interchanges between Mars and Uranus are common in charts of healers, inventors, and "super salesmen" who simply overpower the potential buyer of their products. The healer called "Mr. A" in Ruth Montgomery's excellent book *Born To Heal* was born with Mars in square to Uranus, and his biography reveals the incredible cures he was able to effect through the use of these formidable energies. A great deal depends on how Mars and Uranus are related to the other planets in the chart and on the sign position of Mars. If either or both of them is in a flowing aspect with one of the other personal planets or with Saturn, the likelihood of the individual's expressing violence is lessened. The questions which must be considered when evaluating these aspects in any chart are: How well controlled and directed is that energy, and is the person involved in activities which can absorb such intense energy? One of the best characteristics of this kind of energy release is that the person is usually capable of handling all sorts of challenges and emergencies. In fact, he or she often seeks them out, sometimes unconsciously. As Carter states, "Often the character shows best in moments of danger. . . ."

The dynamic aspects in particular tend toward a total lack of patience, and the person's inability to slow down and temper his or her extremism is perhaps the worst trait of this combination. The willfulness is nothing short of fanatical in some cases, and the need for rather crude excitement is often overwhelming. As Carter writes, such a person *"wants his own way* at all costs." If the individual is able to experience the excitement he or she wants in a more refined and concentrated form, these aspects can be unusually creative. But, in most people, the desire for freedom and total disregard for any kind of restriction is so strong that it sets up a distinctly irritating and troublesome vibration in the person's energy field. In such cases, Carter's evaluation is appropriate: "the native . . . is frequently not well fitted for ordinary existence; it is distinctly unfavourable for married life or for any restricted or ordered way of living. . . ." I have often wondered if these aspects are not in many cases a carryover from pastlives' experiences of warfare or from the person having been trained in extreme forms of physical or psychological harshness.

In summary, we can say that Uranus aspects with all of the personal planets (and particularly the challenging aspects) indicate phases of growth wherein our attitudes, energy attunements and basic life structures are radically transformed, thus enabling us to break free of old patterns of being which may be inhibiting our development. Uranians are thus challenged to learn how to balance their need for freedom with the responsibilities to which they are committed. By being electrified and intensely stirred up, a specific dimension of experience (symbolized by the planet aspecting Uranus) undergoes transformation, thus hastening our growth by enabling us to gain an extraordinary breadth of experience in a comparatively short time. Through the influence of Uranus, we are propelled into the future and launched out into new, high-potential experience rapidly and with the possibility of great openness and objectivity.

Aspects with Neptune

Like Uranus aspects, Neptune aspects also indicate specific dimensions of our lives (depending on the other planet involved) wherein we have an urge to experience a new level of freedom. However, there is a subtle but highly important difference in the kinds of freedom that Uranus and Neptune represent. Whereas Uranus symbolizes an individualistic, ego-centered, willful urge for freedom of expression, Neptune ideally represents an urge toward ultimate, transcendent freedom wherein we lose the limitations of the ego-personality and become free from the boundaries of both intellect and ego. Neptune indicates a yearning to experience a state of oneness with all of life, a merger with the whole of existence, and the dissolution of all boundaries, feelings of separateness, and ego-centricity. Perhaps the most practical way of expressing Neptune's essential nature is to say that its aspects represent ways in which we try to escape from all limitation: tradition, ego, the material world, and the harshness of everyday life. Although many books have accurately stated that Neptune aspects are related to imagination and that the challenging aspects often reveal deception, confusion, and dissipation, they usually fail to emphasize the most important fact about Neptune aspects: namely, that any close aspect of Neptune with a personal planet or with the Ascendant indicates the possibility of coming to an immediate realization of the spiritual dimension of experience and the oneness of all creation; and that the challenging aspects more often than the flowing ones manifest as an individual's taking definite steps to incorporate spiritual ideals into his or her everyday life. It is true that such aspects can be expressed in negative ways such as self-deception, pseudo-spiritual egotism, self-destructive escapism, and the habit of evading all responsibilities to self or others. However, even such negative manifestations of these aspects are often an indication that the person is at least beginning to feel the stirrings of the soul's deepest yearnings but that he or she has not yet learned the essential meaning of these feelings or how to discriminate between the various ways of dealing with them. There is often confusion due to the fact that the person still looks to the outer world for the fulfillment of higher states of awareness or for a full experience of a spiritual ideal. This naturally leads to disillusionment since in essence Neptune represents an attunement to the boundless resources of the *inner* world and to the reality of intangible levels of experience. In fact, we can define Neptune's challenging aspects as phases of life wherein we learn about spiritual values and realities in a subtle way by experiencing disillusionment to the full! The dimension of experience wherein we confront this disillusionment is symbolized by the planet in close aspect with Neptune.

As we mentioned in Chapter 3, the challenging aspects of Neptune are often more creative and productive than the flowing angles. We could in fact call the dynamic Neptune aspects with personal planets "spiritual seeker aspects." This of course does not mean that *all* those who have such aspects in their charts will be consciously pursuing a spiritual orientation in their lives; but it does indicate that when an astrological counselor sees a close challenging aspect between Neptune and a personal planet in an individual chart, he or she should be sure to explore the person's deeper spiritual inclinations in an emphatic way, rather than simply concentrating on the everyday life problems with which such aspects often correlate. By so emphasizing the deeper meaning of such aspects and the significance of the individual's most profound yearnings, the astrologer will often find that the client is helped to gain a totally new perspective on various difficulties by being encouraged to view such areas of confusion as spiritually meaningful and—in fact—as spiritually desirable! For, when one takes a spiritual point of view, our entire perspective changes radically: what was once viewed as a major problem becomes a blessing, and what was once seen as an affliction to be painfully endured becomes a path toward greater openness to a more transcendent and inspiring reality.

Since the general meaning of Neptune and its aspects was explored in Chapter 3, we can now proceed to establish certain basic principles to guide us in understanding these aspects. The reader may therefore want to review the latter section of Chapter 3 before reading the following principles.

a)   Neptune aspects indicate areas of one's life where one is being *opened* to the infinite and boundless. As one begins to experience this opening, thus encountering a realm of life that is infinitely promising but totally unformed and unintegrated into established mental structures, there is often some confusion and, as Carter writes, a "tendency to 'sit on the fence' and to avoid definiteness in judgment and action." This state of uncertainty tends to remain problematical until one realizes that it is necessary to act in a definite way and to make commitments from our necessarily limited viewpoint as long as we are in the physical body. In other words, as long as we are in the relative plane, we have to act in the relative plane, although our spiritual attitude may tell us that such limited perception is unreal and illusory. We can never know all the subtler implications of any action or the totality of our future karma; so we have to live in the present, just doing our best and leaving the rest to the Lord. As one spiritual teacher says, in this plane we should be "*sincere* actors," thus playing our allotted roles to the hilt: being in the world but not of it. Acute and extremely refined spiritual discrimination is necessary in order to handle any strong Neptune influence if we are not to fall victim to the intriguing but self-deceptive allure of its magic.

b)   Anyone who has strong Neptune attunement (whether through aspects to personal planets, planets in Pisces, Neptune situated in the first house, or Pisces rising) desperately needs to find a *definite* and *disciplined* way of expressing his or her urge to transcend and to escape. Unless such a person finds and becomes committed to a particular ideal, program for self-development, or spiritual path, it is very unlikely that he or she will be able to achieve any sense of peace or order in this life; for the divine discontent will persist until definite steps are taken to deal with it.

c)   Close Neptune aspects of any type can (but don't always) indicate that the person is capable of tuning in on extremely subtle levels of perception. Such insight seems to come not only from the person's attunement with spiritual dimensions of consciousness in general, but also in some cases from actual help and instruction from various spiritual guides, astral forms, or spiritual teachers. This is what Dr. Davidson has called the "angelic benediction," i.e., actual protection and guidance from other planes of being. For example, it is very common to meet Americans (especially young people) who know that they have spiritual guides who have in past incarnations been American Indians and who are particularly well versed in communication between the different planes of life since their training while on earth prepared them for such work. However, when one begins to speak of spiritual guides and similar phenomena, we should take note of the fact that this is one area of Neptunian experience where absolute honesty and sharp discrimination should be used; for many Neptunian people obviously become lost in self-delusions of this type and become ego-involved with how spiritual and "clairvoyant" they are. This is so since, unless we are thoroughly grounded and honest with ourselves, Neptune induces us to believe what we want to believe and to see what we want to see. There is a very fine line between "imagination" (based only on mental *images*) and actual direct experience of spiritual realities.

d) As pointed out in section c above, certain aspects involving Neptune can indicate a misunderstanding or misapplication of spiritual forces. A challenging aspect of Neptune with a personal planet often reveals a karmic pattern of having misunderstood, misused, or misapplied spiritual energies and truths in past lives, although by no means am I inferring that these aspects always indicate such a karmic pattern. But in those cases where this interpretation does make sense, it therefore follows that the person in this lifetime needs to confront those tendencies and to deal with spiritual energies and ideals very directly and actively; in other words, he or she needs to build a new structure through which the attunement to Neptune may be practically expressed in a more uplifting and refined manner. By doing so, the confusion, self-destructive escapism, and ego-involvement prevalent in the past may be slowly reduced as the person becomes more grounded and more aware of the subtler implications of his or her ideals.

e) Any planet in close aspect to Neptune is highly sensitized and the dimension of experience that it symbolizes is open to being refined, inspired, and—in some cases—even "spiritualized." However, by giving us this heightened sensitivity and by opening us to unknown and transcendent levels of experience, the Neptune attunement also makes us prone to *oversensitivity* which depletes our energy and to *gullibility* if our increased openness leaves us too defenseless and trusting.

The refinement and sensitivity which Neptune represents are, of course, positive qualities in their essence, but such qualities and the attitudes toward life which result are not particularly at home in the material world. Such subtlety and receptivity must be guarded and protected if we are not to be manipulated by others and thus have our energies dissipated. The way to live in the material world if one has this degree of sensitivity is to be "wise as a serpent, but as gentle as a dove." The Neptune vibration leaves one so vulnerable to being used, being taken advantage of, being deceived, and feeling responsible for things that are not really our concern (due to an abundance of compassion) that we must learn how to protect ourselves without closing off to the positive aspects of such sensitivity. A wise man once told a serpent not to bite anyone ever again since that was an evil thing to do. The serpent followed the advice but soon found that it was constantly being harassed by the local people and hit with sticks by children who had discovered that the serpent would no longer bite. So the serpent went to the wise man and complained of his dilemma: how can I remain so inoffensive and without intent to injure if my gentleness will then be taken advantage of? The wise man replied: "I told you not to bite; but I didn't tell you not to hiss!" Perhaps Neptunians should cultivate the ability to hiss!!

We can now examine the various interchanges between Neptune and each personal planet, emphasizing the meaning of the dynamic aspects as we did with Uranus in the earlier section.

Sun-Neptune Aspects

These aspects are exceptionally common in those whose lives are guided by a larger, more-encompassing vision than normal. This broad vision can be humanitarian, political, artistic, or spiritual in nature. According to Carter, the Sun-Neptune conjunction is the most common aspect in astrologers' charts, and the other interchanges between these planets also appear unusually often in the charts of those who are particularly open to and interested in the intangible forces of life. These aspects are common in the charts of artists and those who, although perhaps not productive artists themselves, are keenly sensitive to aesthetic stimuli of all types. This is a person for whom *vibrations* are an immediate reality, whether perceived through music, colors, auras, unusual types of healing, or other means. A combination of these two planets does not always mean that the person is impractical (contrary to many textbook interpretations), and in fact the person often displays unusual gifts in his or her worldly abilities. (Granted, however, that *some* people who have these aspects are totally "spaced out;" but the entire chart must be examined in order to understand the other contributing factors.)

People with these aspects in their charts usually have a visionary quality which exerts a fascinating pull on them; and it is quite surprising to see how many of these individuals actually fulfill that vision! The lack of clarity which traditional books usually ascribe to these interchanges seems to be focused not so much on the person's way of dealing with the *outer* world as on his or her perception of the self. There is often a strong current of self-delusion; and, especially in the case of the challenging aspects, there is almost always a lack of clear self-awareness and of realistic perspective on oneself. Accurate and practical self-knowledge is rarely evident, for the person has difficulty seeing him or herself objectively. This person needs feedback from others in order to begin to develop a clearer sense of self. Since the person has so little insight into his own self and his motives, he is often particularly easy to fool. As Carter states: "The native is as a rule easily played upon, either through his vanity or his sympathies, or both." The person is, however, usually compassionate and sensitive (at least in a general, impersonal way) and is often characterized by high spiritual, aesthetic, or humanitarian ideals. The main problem is that the person so often refuses to face the truth about self, even if this truth is positive and encouraging; and therefore, he or she may neglect to actualize creative potentials since one's abilities are commonly underestimated.

Moon-Neptune Aspects

Many of the characteristics mentioned in the general sections and in the Sun-Neptune section above naturally apply in these cases also. A few specific things stand out, however. Since the Moon and Neptune are both particularly sensitive, intuitive, and receptive, such combinations tend very strongly toward mystical, intuitive, or idealistic leanings. There is often a great devotion to an ideal. (Note that the Moon and Cancer, along with Neptune and Pisces, are particularly associated with *devotion*.) And, since both of these planets are associated with unstructured, constantly changing energy flow, it is natural that these combinations often manifest as a profoundly deep inner restlessness and a state of "divine discontent" that sometimes approaches total dissatisfaction with self and everything else. These people have great difficulty *settling down* to anything; for they seem to intuit that the tides of change will simply wash away their efforts.

There is often a great idealization of one or both parents (not always the mother!); and, in men's charts, a challenging aspect (including the conjunction) often indicates great difficulty in finding a mate who measures up to their unreachable expectations and to their unrealistic idealization of women (usually including the mother). There is thus a hunger for emotional nourishment, caring, and comfort that is extremely difficult to satisfy; for no imperfect human being can ever fulfill the totally giving and selfless image that Moon-Neptune people project on others. And yet, this is often the kind of person for whom such a person is unconsciously looking. Since the Moon symbolizes the *subconscious* pattern of conditioning, the capacity for self-delusion is even stronger here than in the aspects between Neptune and the Sun (*conscious* self). Hence, any close dynamic aspect of these two planets calls for an unrelenting determination to be honest with oneself and to avoid the path of evading situations which reveal the harsh truth about one's real desires and needs. If the individual with such an aspect successfully actualizes his or her devotion to an ideal by *living* it rather than just looking for it, such a person can become a channel for unlimited spiritual insights and indeed divine compassion.

Mercury-Neptune Aspects

Interchanges between these two planets always reveal a particularly sensitive, intuitive, and even visionary quality of mind; but the expression of such an attunement ranges from inspired thought and marked artistic ability to a subtle talent for manipulation or the habit of rationalizing any deception. There can be an attunement to higher dimensions of life and thus an acute sensitivity to beauty, colors, music, and mystical truths; and the imagination is unusually active. The person may be capable of acquiring information and insights that cannot be explained rationally and which are difficult to express in words. This is because Neptune opens the mind to the realm of the infinite and to the immediate perception of subtleties which can be expressed more easily in images, symbols, or art than by means of logical phraseology. In fact, these people often find words to be frustrating, with the exception of those who develop a poetic ability. There *is* often talent for writing, but it is usually poetry, fiction, fantasy, or occult-mystical genres rather than systematic treatises or essays. Due to the fact that the perceptions are sensitized to the level where the person finds it hard to organize his or her thoughts, such people often seem less perceptive and intelligent than they really are; and, from casual observation of such an individual's attempts at communication, you may deduce that the person is hopelessly lost in chaotic thoughts. But, at the same time, this person may be tuning in on you at subtle levels and picking up your own subconscious desires and motives. This very intuitive power is what enables the person to evade other people's intentions, or even in some cases to manipulate people, while not revealing his or her own true thoughts; for the person can read others like a book while simultaneously keeping his own perceptions and desires totally secret. (Similar qualities are also found in *some* people who have Pluto/Mercury aspects.) Naturally, true *communication* is impossible with such behavior; and easy relationship on a clear and authentic level is inhibited by nebulous fears and subconscious desires to believe what one wants to believe regardless of the facts or opinions which others may express.

The challenging aspects often manifest as the individual being unable to control his wandering mind as it endlessly and aimlessly gathers in all sorts of unrelated and tangential perceptions without any trace of discipline. A noted lack of concentration is often evident, and trying to communicate clearly with these people is especially infuriating to those who demand that all thoughts be expressed with some degree of logic and precision. In fact, real communication is sometimes impossible with such people, unless one can tune in on the subtle impressions that the Neptunian mind is trying to express. The habit of evading simple and clear facts inclines these people to all sorts of problems. For one thing, there is often much pointless worry, some of which could be alleviated if the person would face up to the immediate realities of the present moment. Deception (often unconscious) is especially common with these aspects, especially the challenging ones, since Mercury is the planet of communication *and* rationalization. Hence, there is often the ability to rationalize anything while not facing up to the truth about one's own motivations. At best, however, even when the aspect is a dynamic one, the person can have an extraordinarily creative mind, attuned to high ideals and clear visions of the future, and inspired by spiritual or religious feelings. Such a person often manifests a great aura of mystery and charisma when he or she speaks, which highly-charged energy comes from the attunement to higher planes of awareness.

Venus-Neptune Aspects

We quoted Carter's description of the Venus-Neptune challenging aspects in Chapter 3; hence, there is no need to repeat those ideas here.

We should only emphasize that the Venus-Neptune challenging aspects are, *par excellence,* primary indicators of true spiritual seeking and mystical yearnings. This is due to the fact that the planet of "love" (Venus) is highly sensitized and idealized to the point where a person with such an aspect finds it impossible to satisfy in any worldly relationship his or her yearnings for a high state of union with a beloved. And hence, usually after repeated disillusionments about what love really is and what its limitations are in the material world, such a person is often drawn toward spiritual pursuits. In other words, the person yearns for the experience of a state of ideal love, and this very longing for an experience which is not of this world often compels such a person *unconsciously* to try to avoid commitment to *any* intimate human relationship. It is as if the person's attention is preoccupied with the ideal dream love, the non-existent but remotely possible perfect union; and this emotional preoccupation leads to evasive behavior toward any person with whom there *is* an immediate relationship. One could say that nebulous dreams (and sometimes nebulous fears!) inhibit the person from establishing real relatedness; and then the person wonders why his or her relationships so often fail! Naturally, it is impossible to have a one-way relationship, and anyone trying to relate honestly and completely to a person with the Venus-Neptune orientation cannot help becoming frustrated at the other person's evasiveness and noncommittal behavior. The problem is not that a person with such an attunement is unloving; in fact such an individual is usually extremely kind-hearted and compassionate. Rather, the problem is that the love the person feels is *unfocused* and diffuse (Neptune!!). The feelings are too general and all-encompassing to be channeled easily to just one person. The same general attunement is found in those who have Venus in Pisces. As a friend of mine once described this type of person, "Yes, they are loving; but how can you know that *you* mean anything special to them since they are that way with everybody?" Thus, it seems that the Venus-Neptune combinations are most at home when the affections can be dispensed to many persons rather than limited just to one individual.

Because of the open-heartedness and the intense compassion that such people feel, they often have their feelings played upon by others. It is relatively easy to gain their sympathy and even to have them act lovingly simply out of pity. Especially in the case of the challenging aspects, one finds an emotional and sometimes sexual orientation that lacks discrimination. They are easily fooled by others since they want to believe the best about everyone. (Note that Neptune can, as it were, idealize one's view of other people [Venus] and their motives.) They therefore often involve themselves with others whose characters are, to say the least, less than high-minded, thus leaving themselves open to emotional—if not physical—harm. The unfocused quality of the emotions is also a cause of the sexual difficulties which often arise; for how can one be an involved and active lover if the mind and emotions are wandering through all sorts of fantasies related to everyone but the real person who is present? A number of women I have seen, although very attractive to the opposite sex, have great difficulty getting "turned on" with anyone with whom the relationship has become at all routine. In order to allow themselves to become emotionally (and sexually) involved in an intense way, either the partner must fit the romantic image of the ideal lover or some form of artificial stimulation (such as music, candles, incense, alcohol, or drugs) is often used. In other words, something is needed to inject intrigue into relationships that have become too mundane. Perhaps the above helps to explain why some of the people who, at first meeting, seem so kindly and so loving are the ones who have the most difficulties in keeping a relationship satisfying and vital.

Lastly, the artistic abilities shown by these aspects should be mentioned; for, as Carter writes, "It is pre-eminently the artist combination and is more nearly related to beauty than to either the moral or the scientific spheres." The artistic abilities can be expressed in music, drama, drawing, painting, poetry, or other fields; and it is common to find people with these interchanges who excel in expressing themselves through a wide variety of media. Not all people will use this attunement productively, for Venus-Neptune aspects can often show a tendency toward being markedly passive and sometimes lazy (depending on the sign placements and other aspects). But there is almost always a great aesthetic sensitivity and often highly refined tastes. Those with the square between these two planets are often the most productive since they tend to be more inclined to work at developing the expressive abilities.

Mars-Neptune Aspects

With these combinations, there is perhaps a wider gap between the constructive and the self-destructive, the positive and the negative manifestations of the energies than in any other kind of aspect involving Neptune. This is probably due to the power of Mars and its correlation with *definite action*, rather than simply with perceptions or feelings as in the above interchanges. Hence, how these energies are expressed is dependent upon a number of factors: 1) the ideals and level of consciousness of the individual; 2) the signs involved; and 3) other natal chart factors, such as the other natal aspects which tie in with one or both of these planets. The positive and negative forms of expression are, however, often found simultaneously in one person, especially as he or she works at refining (Neptune) the expression of the coarse Mars energy. These interchanges stimulate the imagination tremendously, leading in some cases to great ambitions and aspirations (sometimes practical, sometimes not) and in other cases to evasive, self-deceptive, or fearful behavior. But no matter which type of pattern dominates, the person is usually slow to see or to admit his faults or failures since he is so intensely caught up in the uplifting currents of his far-off visions. Carter succinctly captures one essential quality of this type of person when he writes: "Ordinary life is too humdrum and colourless for the Mars-Neptune native; hence he seeks pursuits that are capable of appealing to the romantic and grandeur-loving elements of the soul."

Hence, it is not surprising to find these combinations more often than usual in charts of artists, movie and TV stars, and publicity-prone athletes. Those with these combinations often have a particular charisma which seems to be at home in public displays of their talents, although by no means do all those with these aspects prefer a publicly involved lifestyle. Especially the men with these combinations evoke public attention to a marked degree, and it is often because of the image (Neptune) which they are able to project (Mars) of their masculine powers. [Examples are Paul Newman (trine); Mark Spitz (conjunction); and O.J. Simpson (trine). Both of the latter not only excelled in athletics (Mars) but also became TV commentators and actors; and Paul Newman, in addition to acting, has achieved some success in one of the most Martian of all sports: auto racing.]

But the above comments by no means capture the broad range of qualities symbolized by these aspects. This combination of energies can manifest on so many levels that focusing on just one characteristic expression of these forces is sure to lead to a great many misunderstandings. Hence, it is most useful to emphasize the psychological dynamics involved rather than the observable behavior alone. In its most positive expression, this combination can indicate that the person has the ability to act on his or her conscious ideals, to intuit a far-off possibility, to actualize a distant vision, whether in worldly achievements or in spiritual aspirations. At its worst, this combination is expressed as action motivated by fears or irrational subconscious desires, as complete self-delusion about what one really wants (Mars!), or as the tendency to evade any confrontation which will bring the person down to harsh reality from the elevated planes of his or her personal visions. Almost invariably, the person must learn to deal with unfinished business on psychological/emotional levels and to face uncertainties in a practical way. The ideals which guide their actions and desires need to be clarified if they are to have any peace of mind.

An entire chapter could be written about the sexual dimension of these combinations, but there are a few points to note since they are so common. We mentioned above that Mars-Neptune combinations are often found in men who become particularly attractive to the public and who symbolize an idealized form of the masculine image. However, the sexual attractiveness is also found in many women with these aspects; and both sexes share the tendency to indulge in a great deal of sexual fantasy. Also, in people of both sexes, one often encounters a sense of confusion about their sexuality, about what kind of sexual life they want, and about what kinds of sexual activities they find proper. Since Neptune tends to open things up to infinite possibilities, at least on the subconscious levels, these people are often perplexed about the feelings and fantasies that they find themselves entertaining. The sexual identity and—in men—the male ego (Mars) is often an area of great inner conflict, especially when the aspects are challenging. Hence, one often finds that these people are easily led into sexual involvements that, upon reflection, they didn't really want; sometimes, they do it out of pity for the other person, sometimes out of fear, and at times in order to prove their sexual powers. But in almost all cases, there is an urge to use one's powers (Mars) in an idealized or exaggerated way (Neptune). These combinations are pre-eminently aspects of seduction; in some cases, the person is actively involved in seducing others, and in other cases, the person is clearly open to being seduced, usually rather indiscriminately. In any case, sexuality is idealized and is experienced as overwhelming and greatly intriguing. It is common to find men with these aspects who have an absolute abhorence for homosexuals and who thus take every opportunity to criticize or demean those with that lifestyle. (These aspects are occasionally found in charts of people who actively pursue homosexual relationships; but, in my experience, they are not common.) In some cases, men with these aspects seem to be compensating for their own fears about their sexual identity by developing a *machismo* complex and cultivating behavior that is culturally regarded as super-masculine (e.g., hunting, other gun fetishes, risky and dangerous recreational activities, etc.). From the spiritual point of view, however, all of the fears, doubts, and psychological confusion correlated with these aspects become clearly purposeful; for, as Isabel Hickey writes, "Neptune dissolves the animal nature." In other words, there is a strong urge toward developing a higher application of the Mars energy. Some people who have these attunements therefore live or try to live a life of celibacy (another manifestation of wanting one's sexual expression to meet a high ideal!). How can one have intense desire (Mars) for a *particular* person if the expression of that energy and desire has become universalized (Neptune)? One could say that these combinations reveal the need for the narrow expression of Mars energy to be broadened to the universal level. Hence, as this learning process proceeds, one eventually begins to realize that one cannot *have* everyone who strikes his or her fancy, although some people take a long time to learn this. And thus, the person often begins to see sexuality as an all-or-nothing realm of experience; and a few give up all such desires entirely. (Neptune always symbolizes the potentiality for surrender.)

This section would become unduly long if I were to mention here all of the other qualities associated with these combinations, but I do want to encourage the reader to study Grant Lewi's interpretations of Mars-Neptune aspects in his book *Heaven Knows What*. Lewi is one of the few authors who seems to have understood these aspects' association with 1) powerful personal magnetism, i.e., the ability to *make things happen* almost magically, and 2) spiritual thought and spiritual leadership. At the highest level, an interchange between these planets can indicate the potential for tremendous self-refinement, spiritual dedication, and for becoming a channel for action based on a transcendent power.

Aspects with Pluto

Since Pluto's nature and aspects were considered in some detail in Chapter 4, there is no need to elaborate upon the general principles involved in any Pluto aspect. We can therefore immediately proceed to mention some of the distinctive qualities shown by specific interchanges between Pluto and the personal planets. The reader might, however, want to review the section on Pluto aspects in Chapter 4 before going on with the following explanations.

Sun-Pluto Aspects

Individuals with these interchanges in their charts exemplify qualities that are usually associated with the Sun in Scorpio: the urge to remold oneself, a strong willfulness, a great intensity, often an infatuation with power, a pronounced secrecy about their motives and desires, and at times a notable ruthlessness, both with others and with themselves. There is often an urge to do something or to express self in a powerful and extreme way, especially if the aspect is a challenging one. These people often feel the need to transform themselves in a radical way and to eliminate old patterns of life which no longer measure up to their ideals, although effecting this transformation seems to come a bit easier to those with the flowing aspects, *once they become aware of the transformative process.* Those with the flowing aspects seem better able to let go of the old smoothly and to understand the laws of life which necessitate that old forms die away before the new can be born. Whether the aspects are challenging or flowing, a compulsive streak is almost always present, in which the person is driven by unconscious factors toward some goal which he or she cannot clearly fathom. In fact, the word "unfathomable" is often an appropriate description of the types of experiences which befall these people, for they often experience "coincidences" and mysterious connections and meetings which defy rational explanation but which are clearly related to some purposeful life pattern. The dynamic aspects almost always manifest as intense power struggles occurring periodically in the life; and the person's entire identity is often subject to periodic crises and radical alterations, not just in how the person sees self but also in how the self is *expressed* in every-day life.

These aspects often seem to be more difficult when found in women's charts than in men's, although most of the characteristics mentioned above will be true for both. In women's charts, however, I have repeatedly found these aspects (especially the challenging ones) to correlate with the person's having experienced great difficulties with the father and usually with other men as well. There is often a lack of attention and true communication from the father, which leads to resentment and a feeling of being deprived of love. This seems to be one reason why such women often seek a powerful husband (even a ruthless, criminal type), one who promises (in their fantasies) to be the authoritative source of both strength and love in their lives. However, these people are themselves incredibly demanding and sometimes impersonally ruthless to the point where they drive away the very love that they want so badly. Self-glorification is a tendency in both sexes with such aspects, and humility is rarely in evidence. So naturally, close relationships for people who have these planets in dynamic aspects are rarely harmonious unless they work at them with great effort; and those with the opposition seem especially prone to making unreasonable (and unconscious) demands on those with whom they are intimately involved. They seem to want the other person to be different from what he or she really is, and they usually give out the message (though they rarely realize what they are doing) that they will not fully accept the other person until he or she has become someone entirely different, an obvious impossibility! Thus, severe disappointments in close relationships are extremely common with such oppositions; and the Pluto oppositions involving Venus or the Moon share this tendency.

It is primarily the challenging aspects that manifest as the kinds of problems that most people consciously recognize. Since Pluto is related to forces within us that are at least partly unconscious, the power and tension of the dynamic angles seem to be required in order to force a person to realize that there *is* some inner conflict or need for transformation. By contrast, although the flowing aspects do indicate that the individual will more easily accommodate self to life's transformations if he or she is *aware* of such an ongoing process, the benefits as well as the creative potentialities shown by the trine and sextile are never fully realized or dealt with by many people. Hence, the comments in this section apply most specifically to those who have the dynamic aspects in their charts.

One more comment on the correlation between these aspects and the relationship with the father seems worthwhile. I have repeatedly found that not only the Sun's aspects with Pluto but also the Sun's natal position in the eighth house (the Pluto house) very often manifest as a separation from the father that leaves deep psychological scars. This separation may be either physical (where he is simply not present due to his having left, died, or—in an amazing number of cases—simply disappeared with no trace) or it may be a psychological separation wherein the father was physically present but very distant and aloof from the child. In a few cases, this father complex manifests as the person idolizing and doting on the father and having unrealistically positive feelings toward him. In either case, the person is compulsively "hung up" on the father, with subsequent difficulties in establishing a clear individual identity. Another point worth looking into is the fact that Charles Jayne's research relates the Sun-Pluto aspects in *men's* charts to an extra close tie with a woman (often the mother). In any case, one should understand that the kind of closeness shown by Pluto *and* by Scorpio is the closeness of *absorption*, wherein one person is absorbed into the other one, thus leaving the one absorbed (or, in some cases, even *consumed*!) with no individual identity or faith in one's self. (Note that a person with such a Pluto aspect can be either the "absorber" or the "absorbee.") This closeness leaves no room for individual uniqueness and true growth; and it is therefore a pattern which can be severely inhibiting as the person grows older and tries to attain individual maturity and independence. It is a type of closeness which is based on tremendously intense karmic attachment rather than on real love and caring; for real love is always supportive and encouraging rather than possessive and manipulative. And yet we see this kind of manipulation and impersonal domination of another person day in and day out, usually posing under the garb of love. Hence, anyone with natal challenging aspects involving Pluto and the Sun, Moon, Venus, or Ascendant would benefit by gaining an objective perspective on all his major relationships and especially on what his parents were really doing and what their real motivations were in their behavior toward him.

Moon-Pluto Aspects

Many of the qualities described under Sun-Pluto aspects apply to these interchanges as well, but the primary difference is the greater emotional extremism of the Moon-Pluto aspects. These people manifest qualities that are strikingly similar to those with the natal Moon in Scorpio: intense, even explosive sensitivity; a deep dissatisfaction with themselves and the urge to remold themselves in a new way; a strong psychic attunement and the need to probe both the mysteries of life and other peoples' motivations; and an urge to break through the taboos that were established by their particular kind of upbringing and parental influence. There is usually a profound capacity for intense effort, unrelenting commitment to an objective, and self-discipline; and the person is usually attuned to survival needs so acutely that he or she can be incredibly resourceful in times of crisis. (Note that Cancer & Moon principles, as well as Scorpio & Pluto principles are combined here; and both of these principles are attuned to self-preservation.)

Since the Moon symbolizes the self-image and how the person *feels* about self, and since Pluto (especially in challenging aspects) reveals a tendency to destroy and eliminate the old, their interaction often manifests as ruthlessness and harshness towards oneself; for there is an urge to destroy one's old self-image and identity since the person is not at all comfortable with the old pattern of emotional conditioning. In extreme cases, this can even manifest as suicidal feelings, the ultimate symbol of self-destruction. In any case, periods of self-hatred and intense emotional turmoil are not uncommon. This person needs, more than anything else, a concentrated program of self-transformation based on re-programming his or her instinctive response patterns in order to be able to adjust to any life experience with more flexibility and objectivity.

A "mother-complex" is also often evident in people with these combinations. Sometimes, this is experienced simply by having a domineering or subtly demanding and absorbing mother who projects all of her fears onto the child. (One occasionally finds these aspects to also correlate with a demanding or rejecting father.) In other cases, a woman may feel the need to become "super-mother," either by having many children herself (in order to impress others with her maternal *power*) or by playing the role of head mother over a group of people in an organization or group living situation. Such a case might be a woman who becomes or wants to become the "Mother Superior" in a convent, or the head of an orphanage or school. This same tendency is found even in those women who have the *Sun* closely aspecting Pluto; for, as Charles Jayne has observed in his rectification and progression studies, *the mother is often symbolized by Pluto.* So naturally, when the Moon— the traditional symbol of motherhood—is combined with Pluto, one might expect to find this emphasis even more strongly. This is not to say that all such desires will be realized but simply that people with these aspects often feel these kinds of urges to be particularly dominant. One could in this regard characterize Pluto as identical with the archetype of the "terrible mother" found in various myths, such as the goddess Kali in Hinduism. Such a mother image is all-powerful, nurturing her children with one hand while devouring them with the other. The *power* to give *and to take* life is worshiped in such deities, and the impersonality of such a power should be readily apparent.

These combinations (especially the opposition) also indicate a tendency to identify with others subconsciously and then to demand too much of them since one sees them merely as extensions of one's self. One then tries to have one's sense of identity confirmed by subtly demanding that others pay total attention to oneself. There is thus a strong need either to absorb another into oneself, or to be absorbed into the other person. In either case, one destroys (Pluto) one's own separate identity or at least tries to do so through such a merging.

Mercury-Pluto Aspects

These combinations are expressive of a similar mental attunement to that found in the Scorpio position of Mercury. Profound powers of concentration are common, as are deep interests in the occult, sexuality, and other "taboo" areas of life. Psychic sensitivity and intellectual intensity are usual here, although at times the mind gets out of control and manifests in an unusually secretive and fearful way. In those cases, there is a tendency to fear the worst and to think that one is being "psychic" when one is actually at the mercy of negative emotions. There is often an awareness of the ability to use mind power in a directed and purposeful way, even to the point of being able to overpower the minds of others through either sheer force of will or subtle manipulation. Hence, those with such a combination should surround their "occult" studies and practices with a strict code of ethics and spiritual ideals.

Those with the challenging aspects are especially prone to compulsive talking, opinionated ideas, and using power to foist their ideas insistently onto others, even though the ideas themselves may not be particularly meaningful when viewed in calm retrospect. In other words, the power behind the words is really what makes the impression; for people tend to think that any idea so forcefully expressed must have something significant about it. It is as if the emotions boil over into the communication channels, flooding them with a torrential release of verbiage which—though perhaps quite impressive in quantity and power—may be incompletely thought out or even entirely disconnected and irrelevant. In some cases, the compulsive quality of the person's ideas is so dominant that the person doesn't bother to examine the ideas with a critical eye, thus allowing himself to express concepts or beliefs that are totally devoid of clear logic. In certain people, so much inner tension is felt that they find it difficult to express what they feel to be the truth with any degree of consistency or clarity. Occasionally, one finds that these people therefore develop a noticeable inhibition of verbal expression, although Mercury is also usually in a challenging aspect with the Moon, Saturn, Uranus, or Neptune in such cases. However, the primary thing that we can tell from Mercury-Pluto aspects is *how the mind works*; but we cannot prejudge the quality of the person's perceptions from one aspect alone since *what the mind produces* ultimately emanates from the wholeness of the individual's total consciousness.

Venus-Pluto Aspects

These aspects share many of the qualities and characteristics evident in the Scorpio placement of Venus: magnetism, charisma, and attractiveness; an urge to break through all taboos in love, sex, or forms of relationship; and a compulsive, intense, and somewhat impersonal approach to emotional involvements. There is usually a secretive, judgmental, and jealous quality in such aspects, although the signs involved must be evaluated since a Venus placement in Libra or Aquarius, for example, will often refuse to indulge such feelings. Like Venus in Scorpio, however, almost all those who have these aspects—and especially those with the dynamic angles—feel the urge to delve into emotional and sexual mysteries, to probe the rock bottom depths of emotional and relationship experience regardless of pain, and to exert their emotional and sexual powers to the full. Emotional satisfaction and deep feelings of closeness are felt to be an absolutely necessary part of life, an area of experience and expression that *cannot* be neglected or avoided. Although some such people will try to evade their deeper needs and feelings, they never feel happy in such escapism or repression since such an intensely vital part of them is not being lived. But, on the other hand, such a person will rarely feel emotionally satisfied even if he or she *does* break through every restriction and taboo. The key to these interchanges is that one is insatiably greedy for emotional nourishment; it is as if the person is trying to fill up an inner reservoir of love that is so empty that it never becomes full. Part of the difficulty with trying to gain a feeling of satisfaction is that the person does not know how to approach love; the tendency is to try to fill up one's need by taking more and more, by consuming more and more, rather than by learning how to let go and give of oneself. This leads us to the essential meaning of Pluto-Venus interchanges: the potential to transform one's entire approach to love and relationship. In this transformative process, old values are destroyed and relationships inhibiting transformation are either terminated or themselves become transformed into a new level of authenticity. The understanding of "pleasure" and "happiness" becomes refined as—through the fires of emotional torment—the inner alchemical transmutation becomes a personal reality.

This kind of transformation is of course the ideal, but what are the kinds of things that the person experiences on the way to this ideal? We have already mentioned some of the common experiences and tendencies. Also worth noting is the proneness to use one's attractiveness or friendliness to gain power, money, or simply to inflate one's ego. Often, the person does not recognize what he or she is really doing, although many other people will see such behavior as premeditated and devious. Those with the challenging aspects between Venus and Pluto frequently relate to others with impersonal, compulsive forms of affection. They may seem very loving, kind, or friendly at first, until one begins to see that their real motives are not particularly selfless or even conscious. In a few cases, I have seen people with the Venus-Pluto conjunction put on the most phony smile and veneer of sensitivity that you can imagine, seemingly trying to distract me from the demands that they were making of me at that very moment. It is as if they are saying: "Well, of course I will do whatever you want since I'm so caring and considerate and nice, but you better do what *I* want or else!" Putting out these kinds of vibrations naturally attracts similarly attuned people into one's life, and those with these aspects (especially the opposition) tend to attract into intimate relationships others who exemplify Plutonian characteristics, therefore aggravating their already compulsive situation. Hence, the person often comes to feel lonely, unloved, used, neglected, dominated, or utterly emotionally exhausted and consumed. But it is just at these times of despair that such a person can begin to tune in on the depths of his or her inner resources in order to really understand the need for a deep, fulfilling love.

There are often sexual problems or maladjustments in people whose charts have these aspects. Homosexual or bisexual inclinations are not uncommon; and, even in those who don't act out all of their urges, there is very often an intense emotional resentment toward either the person's own sex or toward those of the opposite sex. And it should be emphasized that this form of resentment is also found in those whose sexual *behavior* is exclusively heterosexual. Since Pluto commonly manifests as a simultaneous attraction-repulsion, we often find these people engaging in self-destructive behavior or engulfed in feelings of disgust for having been attracted to the very types of experiences which at other times repel them. One last note, which should not be considered applicable to all those with Venus-Pluto aspects but which I have often seen when Venus is either conjunct or opposite Pluto, exemplifies how completely some of us have to let go of old emotional attachments. In a number of cases, the person with such an aspect has repeatedly had lovers or fiancés die or disappear. One particular man was actually engaged to be married four different times; and each time, shortly before the wedding, the partner-to-be died. This is what I would call the "unfathomable" nature of Pluto; for there is obviously a purpose behind such a sequence of events, although one would be at a loss to explain it logically.

Mars-Pluto Aspects

Similar to the nature of Mars in Scorpio, this combination of energies represents perhaps the most intense expression of raw power to be found in any chart factor. Since Mars is the energy available to accomplish specific tasks in the outer world and represents desire and will, and since Pluto symbolizes the energy available to accomplish work in the "underworld" and is correlated with *unconscious* desires and willfulness, this interchange invariably indicates a boundless potential for either constructive or destructive action. Like Mars in Scorpio, such an energy combination tends to be expressed in extreme ways, as the raw power is released from the depths of one's being. This extremism results primarily from two facts: first, the person has an almost inexhaustible reservoir of energy at his or her disposal, functioning at least partially in an unconscious way; and secondly, a person with such an attunement almost always seeks to keep a firm control over such compulsive energy flow, thus encouraging an explosion when the lid is removed. There is a particularly secretive— sometimes even devious—method of getting things done (which can be especially effective in some activities) and the person's method of operation is unusually thorough. Such behavior, though, tends to elicit charges of "ruthlessness" from others since this individual hates to do anything half way and has a propensity to cut to the core of any problem without flinching from the potential repercussions. Hence, while impatience, ruthlessness, and an uncompromising willfulness are common traits of those with this attunement, there is also limitless courage and an unusual capacity for resourceful and decisive action in any emergency. Those with such attunement are particularly capable in situations where rapid, deep-acting commitments and decisions are called for.

Anyone born with the challenging aspects between these two planets must confront the nature of power head on; and the personal values which guide the expression of this power are of the utmost importance. Coupled with a humane and compassionate sensitivity, such energies can make the person a channel for the expression of the decisive actions and reforms for which many people long but which few have the capacity to actualize. If the expression of the energies is well disciplined—and those with these combinations have an incredible capacity for self-discipline—mind and will power can be dedicated toward the thorough transformation of either worldly structures or one's own self or of both. However, if the power is not guided properly and if the individual is infatuated with his or her personal strength for its own sake, there can be a compulsive desire to *win* at all costs and a "might makes right" attitude which can lead to cruelty, anti-social and even criminal behavior, and an utter disregard for all moral, ethical, and social values. The desire to accomplish things through power alone can lead to a type of willfulness which can be expressed as: "I'm going to do whatever I want regardless of anything!" The strange part of this attitude is that the person rarely knows what he or she really wants. The individual is merely driven by compulsive forces—one might say *possessed* by an overwhelming power which demands expression. This state of being "possessed" applies to those who use this power constructively as well as to those who use it for destruction; a similar sort of obsession and discontent is found in both. However, the person who is dedicated to an ideal (whether or not it is a positive ideal) will feel this "possession" as a sense of mission which drives him on relentlessly toward the goal. Furthermore, such a fanatical dedication and commitment to a life mission can be a great asset in any path of self-transformation which demands that we reform ourselves thoroughly and deeply and that we transmute our desires into higher aspirations.

When an individual who is attuned to these energies commits self to a path of transformation, however, there are certain problems that he or she must face. First of all, when impatience and ruthlessness color one's approach to the slow process of personal evolution, the person tends to become excessively harsh with his or her own limitations and failures. Instead of focusing one's demands on others or on society as before, the person now demands too much of self. It is therefore important that such a person see this compulsive power within the self as an objective force which wants expression and which (like a wild beast) must be controlled and directed. If the person identifies too much with success or failure in a spiritually-oriented path of development, he or she will incessantly create an even greater inner tension and a higher level of frustration. The first step is thus simply to acknowledge one's need for reforming; the second step is beginning to *understand* the intricacies and subtleties of such a process; and the next step is beginning to act upon this understanding *gently* while cultivating a sense of contentment in the present moment. Another problem often confronted is the anger and resentment that surfaces after the person has begun to work on gaining self-knowledge. The explosive and even violent quality of these emotions comes from the person's having been unaware of his or her deepest desires and frustrations for such a long time. These combinations do show a tendency toward self-repression, and the individual is thus often completely unaware of the forcefulness of his own nature and the power of the karmic tendencies which have motivated so much of his behavior for lifetimes. One antidote for anger and resentment is to work on cultivating forgiveness; and this forgiveness should be directed not only toward others but also toward oneself.

Lunar Aspects

Although this chapter's purpose is to discuss primarily those aspects involving the outer planets, we cannot leave the subject of aspects which are related to transformation without at least a brief mention of the aspects involving the Moon. It is particularly necessary to touch on this subject here since the Moon is so intimately connected with past conditioning—and hence, with karma.

The basic principle we must understand if we are to interpret lunar aspects accurately is that the Moon's interaction with the other planets shows how one is able to make use of and to express the results of past experience and conditioning. In other words, these aspects reveal whether our feelings and instinctive reactions hold us back and interfere with the expression of our urges and the fulfillment of our needs *or* whether they give us support and encourage our self-expression with a foundation of inner security and tranquility. A flowing aspect involving the Moon usually means that one's karmic pattern in that area is characterized by an easy flexibility and an accurate sense of our capabilities, thus allowing us to tap inner resources and to make use of spontaneous reactions in a creative and expressive way. The challenging aspects with the Moon often reveal areas of life where the karmic pattern is problematical and sometimes quite rigid. Where we are rigid and thus unable to adjust easily, the life force cannot flow. We then experience constant tension in that area of life, and this inner tightness manifests in everyday life as our reacting to experience with too much sensitivity. In fact, one might easily devise key-phrases for the various dynamic lunar aspects by focusing on the word "oversensitivity": Moon-Mars means that one is oversensitive about asserting self; Moon-Mercury indicates oversensitivity about one's ideas and opinions; Moon-Jupiter shows oversensitivity about one's ego, since one wants to give the impression of generosity and great capabilities, etc. If a planet (especially one of the other personal planets) is in a challenging aspect with the Moon, there is a generalized tension and fear of losing one's roots, of leaving one's emotionally secure foundations, or of becoming vulnerable if one steps outside the old patterns of self-expression and behavior (the Moon) to express an energy which is attuned to a radically different vibration (shown by the other planet). The flowing aspects involving the Moon are, on the other hand, indicative of an easy and spontaneous *flow* of our emotional and supportive energies into the channels of expression indicated by the other planets involved. With these aspects, our expression of these energies is unencumbered by fear and enlivened by positive emotional involvement, for there is a feeling of being naturally comfortable with those dimensions of everyday experience.

Another important point about lunar aspects is that any close aspect involving the Moon colors how we feel about ourselves—what is commonly called the *self-image*. When the aspect is flowing, we usually have a fairly objective sense of our real nature and our abilities in that area of life. When the aspect is more dynamic (especially in the square and opposition), we usually have a rather inaccurate sense of ourselves and tend to lack objectivity in the area indicated. Naturally, when we express ourselves in a way that is obviously natural, comfortable, and flowing, other people react to us with ease and enthusiasm. When we express discomfort, tension, or fear, others also pick up those vibrations. The lunar aspects are therefore the key to understanding how other people and the public in general will react to us and how comfortable they feel with us.

One last interpretive guideline for dealing with lunar aspects is explained in Robert Jansky's book *Interpreting the Aspects*. When I came across this brief—but extremely useful—classification, it clarified my feelings that lunar aspects operate in markedly different ways, depending on the other planet involved. To put this concisely:

A. The Moon in challenging aspect to Sun, Venus, Mercury, and sometimes Mars shows a feeling of being unable to *express* something that one feels.

B. The Moon in challenging aspect to the other planets reveals a feeling of being inadequate to cope with life's demands.

If the reader applies this principle to the various interchanges with the Moon, its usefulness and accuracy should be readily apparent.

Understanding Themes in the Birth-Chart

Once one has gained an in-depth understanding of the meaning of specific aspects, one can then begin to apply this familiarity with the various interchanges between the twelve fundamental principles on an even broader scope. As mentioned in the introduction, the key to a holistic approach to charts is the ability to detect various themes that dominate a person's life by synthesizing the chart factors into relationships between the twelve basic principles. With a particular chart, one has to use not only the aspects themselves but also the sign and house positions of the planets involved. This is a great deal more difficult than simply isolating a particular aspect and reading a set interpretation from a textbook; and it is an ability which cannot readily be taught or written about in the abstract since the combinations of aspects, signs, and houses are so numerous. Each specific aspect is modified in its expression according to the signs involved, and each planet's energy is expressed in a way that is colored by not only its close aspects but also by its sign placement.

For example, if one's chart not only has Mars in Scorpio (an interchange between astrological letters 1 and 8, thus coloring or *toning* the expression of the Mars energy with a Pluto quality) but also includes a close Mars-Pluto aspect (another interchange of letters 1 and 8), there is a double emphasis on the same combination of energies; and hence, the expression of Mars energy will be powerfully characterized by Plutonian qualities. If Mars is also in the 8th house or if Pluto is in the 1st house, this theme will be even more dominant.

Another example might help to explain this mode of synthetic analysis, especially for beginning and intermediate students of astrology. Suppose a person has Mercury in Capricorn; this person's attunement of the conscious mind will inevitably share some *fundamental* qualities with *all others* who have this Mercury placement. But suppose this particular person also has Saturn in close aspect to Mercury. This gives us two different emphases on the same theme: an interchange of astrological letters (or principles) 3 and 10 (or between 6 and 10 if the

Virgoan dimension of Mercury seems strong for this person). With such a double emphasis on the same fundamental dynamic, we know that this individual will have a strong propensity toward handling exacting detail, toward a serious and practical mode of thinking, toward nervous tension, and toward working hard to develop certainty about their ideas. If this person has other factors in the birth-chart which also represent interchanges between these same principles (such as Mercury in the 10th house or Saturn in the 3rd or 6th house), there would be even greater dominance of this theme in the person's life; and the astrologer could therefore know with certainty that this would have to be one of the major things discussed during the consultation.

Another area of aspect interpretation which students of astrology find difficult is the entire question of *configurations* between many planets, involving a number of different aspects. Ultimately, only years of experience and practice will enable the student to overcome this seemingly insurmountable obstacle; for one must develop the ability to see configurations in a chart as a whole and to *blend* the meaning of all the planets involved in such complex combinations. However, many textbooks are so filled with abstract theory about various configurations (grand trine, T-square, grand cross, kite, etc.) that they make the whole process seem much more difficult than it really is. What is usually ignored is the fact that all those various factors and details simply symbolize facets of *one whole, living person.* And, in such configurations, there are primarily three basic things to keep in mind which are much more important than the exact type of configuration involved:

A. Rather than focusing upon the type of configuration being considered (for example, a grand trine, yod, kite, etc.), one must primarily understand the meaning of the *planets* involved and their specific interchanges with other planets in that configuration. One is then able to blend these meanings in a way which accurately reflects how an individual actually *experiences* these energies. *Any* of the traditional configurations can be productive and creative, regardless of beliefs to the contrary, since they *all* represent *particularly intensified interactions* of the energies and principles symbolized by the planets involved.

B. One should concentrate on particular planets in a given configuration according to the importance of those planets in the person's overall chart. For example, if the planet is the ruler of the Sun, Moon, or rising sign or the dispositor of many other planets, it will always be especially important. In other words, if a planet participates in the major themes of the chart and therefore symbolizes an attunement which the individual expresses in a dominant way, its role in a given configuration is worth special attention.

C. Most of all, one should focus one's attention on any personal planet (or the Ascendant) involved in a configuration, for that factor symbolizes the most immediate mode of expression for the energies of the *entire* configuration; and it reveals a dimension of the individual's being which is usually at least partially conscious and therefore has a particularly direct impact on his or her everyday experience. An individual will be able to *identify* with the meaning of a personal planet, and thus will be more able to understand and perhaps to modify the expression of that energy. In other words, since the individual's approach to those dimensions of experience can be consciously adjusted, the expression of the entire energy pattern of a given configuration can be modified.

If all else fails to elucidate the meaning of a given aspect, there is one technique which is often especially revealing, not just for the astrologer but also for the client—the technique of "inner dialogue." We can play the role of each planet, working toward expressing in words, actions, or emotions how each energy manifests within us. As a person acts out the primary urges and needs shown by each planet in a given aspect, it is as if the two parts of the self are getting to know each other, to learn to accept each other for what they really are. This technique is especially valuable in working with the kinds of blockages or conflicts shown by challenging aspects, for it is in those areas that the individual needs some kind of integration. The inner dialogue technique has been used with great success in both Psychodrama and Gestalt Therapy for many years, and it is a procedure with which the counseling astrologer should be familiar. Such a procedure often provides an *immediate experience* of a particular problem which an aspect symbolizes, and such immediacy has much more power and generates much greater awareness than a mere intellectual discussion of abstract principles.

Libra

7

Karma & Relationships

Human relations are for self-revelation, not self-gratification. People, especially true friends, are mirrors in which we begin to discover ourselves.
— *H. F. Weekley*

It could easily require an entire book to explain all the various astrological factors pertinent to relationships and their karmic implications. Hence, in this chapter, I will concentrate on those major factors encountered in comparing individual charts which are *commonly* problematical and could therefore be dealt with more effectively by a consideration of the karmic patterns involved. By focusing primarily on the aspects of Saturn, Uranus, Neptune, and Pluto and on their corresponding houses, I do not mean to infer that no other factors in a comparison or in individual charts have karmic implications with regard to our relationships. In fact, as mentioned earlier in this book, one could indeed view the birth-chart as indicating nothing but karma! If the Law of Karma does guide everything in an individual life— at least in its general pattern, structure, and circumstances—then this would seem to be especially true in our relationships with other human beings, in which there is an endless give and take through a spontaneous interchange of energy. One might say that there is a constant crediting and debiting of our karmic account within any particular relationship, a continual paying off of debts and refining of attachments. In some cases, we primarily have to give to another person; and in other cases, we primarily have to receive. And then there are relationships wherein there seems to be a fairly even exchange of energy, as if the scales of karma were being ever so subtly balanced through the people's periodic interaction.

As an astrologer and marriage and family counselor, I have seen many hundreds of relationships, and this experience has clearly revealed one inescapable fact: when doing chart comparisons, although the astrological factors which symbolize various types of attraction and compatibility are almost innumerable, the inter-chart factors which symbolize definite problems in making a relationship work in a healthy way can in many cases be reduced to a few key elements. Namely, these problematical factors are the challenging inter-chart aspects involving one person's Saturn, Uranus, Neptune, or Pluto and the other person's personal planets or Ascendant.* These aspects reveal areas of life wherein the two people may experience striking conflict, discord, disillusionment, oppression, mistrust, or manipulation. They each reveal a specific interchange of energy which is experienced as a major difficulty in the relationship and as a major obstacle in trying to achieve harmony and cooperation. This is not to say that such aspects cannot have positive effects or that they cannot be adjusted to; for these very areas of tension within the relationship can indicate the greatest learning experiences for both parties. In most cases, the presence of such aspects in a chart comparison will indicate the need for both people to gain a heightened perspective on their interaction and to begin to develop new ways of relating if the relationship is going to be a lasting and satisfying experience. In some cases, the tensions are too great for the people to adjust to; their individual natures are so different that no amount of effort will enable them to develop a mutually harmonious attunement. But in cases where there is an essential harmony of the primary energies, objectives, and ideals (especially shown by at least a few flowing aspects between both people's personal planets and Ascendants), such challenging aspects can provide the stimulation the people need both to grow in self-awareness and to gain an appreciation of each other's individual identity and uniqueness.

As in work with individual charts, one should focus in chart comparisons on those aspects which are closest to exact; and, as always, the conjunction is considered the most potent of all possible aspects. Even more clearly than in individual charts, the challenging aspects involving the personal planets or Ascendant in comparisons reveal conflict and discord, with the exception of certain oppositions which—in chart comparisons alone—can indicate strong attraction, stimulation, and a feeling of completeness. (Such oppositions are Moon opposite Moon, Sun opposite Moon, Venus opposite Moon, and Venus opposite the Sun or Venus in *some* cases.) More regularly and reliably than in individual charts, the challenging aspects in chart comparisons tend to manifest as *overt* and *immediate* problem areas which the two people are almost always aware of to some extent. These aspects constitute such a reliable factor for understanding relationships because, when such an aspect is present within a single birthchart, the individual encompasses the entire energy interaction within him/herself and can, even at an early age, begin to integrate the conflicting tendencies and learn how to manage the energies. However, in a relationship with another person, we cannot modify our partner's energies; we simply have to relate to that person in whatever way we can. If his or her expression of the Sun, Moon, or Venus energies, for example, does not harmonize with our own, there is not that much we can do about it

---

*I am assuming here that the reader is already familiar with the basic procedures of comparing charts, namely 1) finding the close aspects between the two people's planets; and 2) seeing which houses in one chart are activated by the planets in the other's charts. Another highly important procedure is that of looking at the general harmony of the two people's personal planets and Ascendants according to the elements, for discord between two personal planets (e.g., Mars in an earth sign compared with Mars in a fire sign) can also indicate definite conflicts.

except to learn to accept that person without judgment, criticism, or demands. We can learn to adjust *ourselves* to his or her way of being, but we cannot change it. In fact, if we demand that the other person try to fulfill our needs by adopting behavior which is not authentic and spontaneous, we often feel even more frustration later since our dependency on that person has become painfully obvious and since his or her mechanical behavior is invariably unsatisfying to both of us.

It may help to give an example of the difference between a particular aspect in an individual chart and the same aspect in a chart comparison. If a person is born with Mercury square Saturn, he or she may cope with this tension by working extraordinarily hard to learn facts and skills, to develop a mode of self-expression which is characterized by an orderly and efficient mind, or to adjust his or her priorities (Saturn) about intelligence and verbal abilities. Such personal efforts may indeed take time to bring about obvious results and personality changes, but there is no doubt that some kind of personal adjustment may be consciously made. In a relationship, on the other hand, where one person's Saturn is square the other person's Mercury, the Mercury person feels the pressure of the Saturn person's criticism, demands, or reservations, regardless of what he may do to avoid or to change it. The Mercury person may find that changing his attitude toward the Saturn person is a successful way of dealing with the problem, and in fact he may eventually realize that he has greatly benefited from the imposed need to discipline his thoughts and mode of communication. However, the interaction of energies indicated by this aspect will still be present, and the Mercury person may find that living with or having extensive interaction with the Saturn person is placing heavy burdens on his nervous system and may be reducing his confidence in his own intelligence. How heavily the Saturn person expresses criticism will of course affect what the Mercury person experiences, but unspoken negativity is negativity nevertheless and may be felt by the other person as a threatening impact on his or her energy field. Likewise, the Saturn person will be unable to change the way the Mercury person thinks, no matter what measures he may take. And so, if he feels threatened by the Mercury person's ideas, he can only withdraw from the relationship *or* open himself to the ideas to see what they can contribute to his understanding. The Mercury person's ideas may in fact benefit his work or ambitions by giving him a different viewpoint and helping him to loosen up the rigidity of some of his opinions and prejudices, for Mercury is flexible where Saturn is constricted. There is no denying that such an aspect can indicate many extremely positive qualities, but I am primarily using this example to show that a particular aspect is expressed in a more predictable and overt way in a relationship than when it is found only in the chart of a single individual.

When there is *more than one* conjunction, square, or opposition involving *one of the outer four planets* in a comparison, we should be careful to evaluate whether this hints at a dominant theme in the relationship. For example, if Mary's Saturn conjuncts my Moon *and* squares my Venus, it is obvious that my emotional reactions to her might be criticized, frustrated, or ignored and that my way of relating to her emotionally may activate her Saturnian fears and defensiveness. If my Uranus is, for another example, opposite Nancy's Sun *and* square her Mars, my aloofness and unpredictably self-centered behavior might easily leave her feeling that she can't rely on me or that she can't ever plan anything which requires my cooperation since I am likely to divorce myself from her activities and aspirations at any moment. She may even become very resentful toward me because of the frustration I cause her. Such themes in any relationship are almost always indicated by at least two—and sometimes more—dynamic aspects involving a particular outer planet on one hand and the personal planets or Ascendant on the other. These themes can also be shown by the repetition of the identical (or at least a very similar) interchange involving one of the outer four planets in *each* person's chart. For example, if my Uranus is square Jerry's Mars and *his* Uranus is opposite *my* Mars, the explosiveness of this interchange is doubly emphasized. I remember one comparison I've used in synastry lectures which includes three of these double emphases (what I often call in lectures "double whammies"); and, having known this couple for a number of years, I have observed that the themes shown by these double interchanges have indeed been the dominant themes in this relationship. To list them briefly:

His Venus is conjunct her Neptune; and her Venus is conjunct his Neptune.

His Saturn is opposite her Venus; and her Saturn is square his Venus.

His Uranus is opposite her Sun; and her Uranus is square his Sun.

The meanings of these various interchanges should become apparent in the following sections; and, in fact, anyone familiar with Lois H. Sargent's book *How to Handle Your Human Relations* will immediately sense how these interchanges have manifested. But, suffice it to say that the compassion and sympathy shown by the Venus-Neptune combinations was not enough to enable these people to tolerate the emotional frustration of the Venus-Saturn combinations and the sporadic, unstable energies of the Sun-Uranus combinations. They divorced only about two years after they were married, although they lived together off and on (Uranus!) for a number of years before the marriage.

Another important factor to focus on in considering the aspects in a comparison is: how do one person's planets connect with the major configurations in the other person's chart? For example, if someone's Ascendant activates the closest square in my chart, conjuncting one planet and squaring the other, that person's role in my life—at least in part—will be to challenge me to deal with an area of life which may be extremely problematical for me. I may not like the frustration of such a confrontation nor the pain of gaining the necessary self-knowledge, but that does not mean that the relationship is "bad" or that we are ultimately "incompatible." For if I am consciously working at resolving the tension and conflict indicated by that square aspect, I may in my more reflective and spiritual moments appreciate the challenge which the other person has presented me. If, for another example, someone's Mercury activates that same square in my chart, I may become more aware of my problems through *dialogue* with that person; and, in fact, communicating with such a person may be especially effective as a therapeutic experience since he or she so readily tunes in on my inner conflicts. Another type of interchange in which one person's planets tie in with the other person's major configurations might be exemplified as follows: If someone's Venus trines one of the planets involved in a close square in my natal chart, that person may have the ability to help me harmonize the expression of energies that usually give me trouble. That individual may therefore have a particularly soothing and encouraging effect upon me as I seek to express myself in ways that are usually rather difficult. All of the above points should be kept in mind when analyzing aspects between two charts; for if one does not do so, the explanation of those interchanges will often be somewhat shallow, rather than exploring the relationship's meaning at the deepest level of experience. Moreover, the aspects will not be understood sufficiently to enable the people involved to gain a real working perspective on their relationship.

In the following sections, I will use the term "interaspect" rather than the more cumbersome term "inter-chart aspect" to signify a close major aspect between the planets of two different charts. I first heard this term used when I attended excellent lectures on synastry given by Mr. and Mrs. Kenneth Negus at the 1976 AFA Convention. It is a useful and concise term and contributes toward the development of a specialized language relevant to all forms of chart comparisons.

Saturn's Challenging Interaspects

When I began doing chart comparisons and was still under the sway of traditional notions about Saturn's dynamic aspects in comparisons being "bad" and dooming a relationship to failure (and probable divorce in the case of a marriage), I could not understand why almost every marriage comparison—including those which lasted for decades!—included at least one and often more of these aspects. The most common are Saturn interaspects with the other person's Sun, Moon, Venus, or Ascendant. However, after seeing such interchanges repeatedly in hundreds of comparisons and after gaining a better understanding of Saturn's essential meaning and its relationship to karma, I began to realize what this was all about. For one thing, Saturn often symbolizes things that last, or—in other cases—it reveals an *urge* to establish a secure life structure that will endure for a long period of time, even if experience proves that it won't. Saturn's correlation with specific karmic attachments (often rigid attachments in which one or both people's security is bound up) is also a relevant meaning of Saturn interaspects in comparisons, especially when one begins to see all important relationships in one's life as ultimately karmic in nature. Hence, if one views serious relationships (especially marriages) as structured arrangements and deep commitments wherein the two people must learn to work out their attachments, expectations, and debts to each other, the meaning of these aspects takes on an entirely new dimension. Some of the key words, therefore, for these interaspects are: security, respect, authority, and responsibility. Let us examine each of these terms in regard to relationships and their karmic implications.

Saturn interaspects with personal planets or the Ascendant often manifest at first encounter as a feeling of caution about the other person. Usually, it is the person whose personal planet or Ascendant is involved in the aspect who is cautious and even fearful of entering into a relationship with the Saturn person, as if he or she senses subconsciously that there is some intense karma to work out with that person. Avoidance of the relationship, or even an attempt to run away from it entirely, is thus quite common at the initial stages of the encounter. However, once this initial hesitation is overcome and the person enters into the relationship actively, there is often a feeling of extremely deep security on the part of both people. Even if they don't believe in reincarnation, they often feel that they have known each other before since they feel so comfortable and secure in each other's presence. There is often a feeling of familiarity, even, in some cases, as if one has been reunited with a long-lost part of oneself. The bonds of attachment indicated by these aspects are incredibly strong, and it often seems that one is kept in the dark about the negative dimensions of the relationship until some commitment has been made, thus ensuring that the people will be tied to each other for a period of time in order that they will *have* to deal with the karma involved. But, as is so often true with anything Saturnian, "time will tell"; and the passage of time slowly reveals levels of the relationship which were not immediately apparent since they lay *beneath* the evident sense of security. As these factors in the relationship become apparent, the sense of security for both people becomes jeopardized. The Saturn person especially begins to feel his security being threatened as the other person's growth proceeds. Often the Saturn person then begins to demand (usually unconsciously) that the other person remain the same as he or she was in the past, or at least behave as if no change or growth has taken place. But the fact of the situation is that the other person has been growing and changing for a long while and doesn't want to be restricted to the old pattern of life which the Saturn person wants to impose. These demands take the form of criticism about new ways of doing things, restrictive and seemingly arbitrary uses of authority (for the Saturn person usually has the authority in the relationship), or simply defensive, fearful behavior. Hence, what was once a source of security becomes a burdensome habit; for the feelings of security were based on past associations, subliminal memories, and an old pattern of interaction—all of which are no longer appropriate for the present realities of each person's state of development. The primary way these types of problems can be adjusted to is for the Saturn person to learn how to refrain from his fear-induced demands, to turn *within* to become more self-sufficient and inwardly secure, and to use his disciplinarian tendencies in working with himself rather than imposing them on the other person. Likewise, the other person can learn how to avoid expressing certain things that he or she has found through experience to be unsettling or anxiety producing for the Saturn person; and, in fact, he or she may find that some of the authoritative advice or criticisms heard from the Saturn person are valuable and ultimately beneficial.

If someone's Saturn conjuncts, squares, or opposes your personal planets or Ascendant, you may feel that this individual has something *over* you. In extreme cases, you'll feel "under the thumb" of that person; and, in other cases, you'll feel an awe or great respect for his or her authority. You will tend to look up to and admire him or her (at least for a while). This may also be experienced if someone's natal planets activate your own 10th house, for that is a Saturnine house and has similar connotations. In such a relationship, one might deduce that the other person still holds power over you, coming perhaps from a pastlife situation in which he wielded the authority. In such a situation, you may feel responsible to the Saturn person and seek to please him in order to gain his favor. The Saturn person likewise may feel responsible for you; and there can be either a mutual or a one-sided feeling of indebtedness, a deep sense of owing something to the other person. This feeling of indebtedness persists until the debt is paid off, a process which usually takes a considerable period of time but which is often accomplished in a particularly concentrated manner during important Saturn transits. However, it should be pointed out that the feeling of indebtedness is a *psychic* pattern, that it is in itself an attachment which endlessly generates karma. Hence, only when you are ready to totally let go of the attachment to the other person can that feeling be resolved; and the time often becomes ripe for such a realization when Saturn returns to its natal place, or when Saturn conjuncts your Sun, Ascendant, Moon, Venus, or Ruling Planet. It should also be emphasized that, although the feeling of indebtedness is often felt by both parties, the person with the personal planet or Ascendant involved in the interaspect is *usually* the one who feels most obligated to give to the other person for a long period of time, even if nothing is received in return.

These interchanges are most problematical in relationships wherein important duties and responsibilities are being shared, such as business contracts and partnerships or marriage. In other words, when you are trying to accomplish definite aims and to manage your life, your money, your energies, and your priorities in unison with someone else, there is always a need for leadership and delegation of authority. It is in such goal-oriented relationships that the conflicts about authority and power most readily and quickly surface. Some such relationships can be extremely productive and in fact quite happy *if* the rest of the comparison reveals mutual harmony, caring, and sensitivity, and if the two people are mature enough to face the negative patterns of the past with objectivity and flexibility. Almost any kind of relationship wherein one finds such interaspects is characterized by a great loyalty and sense of duty to each other, although it must be admitted that these positive Saturn qualities sometimes degenerate—into hate, resentment, and devitalization, especially in marriage—since that life structure is probably the greatest test of cooperation and compatibility that exists. (Note that Saturn is *exalted* in Libra, the traditional sign of marriage!) One finds many enduring friendships between people who have these interaspects, where the loyalty and sense of duty predominate without becoming too heavy and exhausting; for, in a friendship, both people are able to go their separate ways now and then, to cultivate their independent space and lifestyle, and to fulfill their various needs with many different people. In a marriage, the people often look to each other too exclusively to satisfy their needs and desires; what starts as a healthy enjoyment of the ways their natures fit together often becomes an unhealthy, isolated state of dependency. At best in such relationships, the Saturn person can use his experience, wisdom, and authority to help the other person structure the expression of his or her energies and to become more organized and efficient; but this positive experience results only if the Saturn person is loving, patient, and not heavy handed!

Although it is impossible to deduce the specific nature of past life relationships solely from astrological data (since the chart reveals primarily the archetypal karmic patterns carried over from the past rather than precise correlations with various interpersonal roles), it seems that the patterns so indicated can be classified in one of two groups. First, the Saturn interaspects may show simply a repetition of an old pattern of interaction to which both people are still attached. Or secondly, they may reveal that there was a *lack* of definite commitment or a shirking of responsibility in the past and therefore that the people must now compensate for that lack of commitment by assuming specific duties in relation to each other. In either case, the fact that these interaspects are so common in marriage comparisons leads us to deduce that they symbolize extremely deep involvement with each other and that the nature of this involvement in the past has not been entirely positive or growth-promoting. Therefore, it is now time to face the results of our past actions, and without making demands, to work toward building a relationship based on both love and responsibility.

Uranus' Challenging Interaspects

These interchanges can also be considered to indicate two rather different karmic patterns: either a repetition of an old pattern of sporadic and unpredictable interaction—or—a compensation for lack of freedom in the past. I feel, however, that these interaspects are *usually* indicative of a repetition of the same spasmodic, unpredictable rhythm of relating to each other that characterized the people's past association. As far as I can tell from various psychic readings which clients have had and from my own intuitions, people who in this life are experiencing a repetition of a past pattern fall into one of two categories. The first is the type of relationship in which there was in the past too much freedom and too much impersonality; in some cases the people seem to have been friends with each other but not particularly reliable in their behavior toward each other. The second type of past relationship shown by such aspects is one in which circumstances prevented the people from maintaining a consistent and stable relationship, for example, cases where the people lived in times of constant warfare during which they were repeatedly separated. In these cases, the individuals saw each other only in passing or at sporadic moments; and so they became used to expecting little consistency but a *great deal of excitement* whenever they saw each other. Hence, in this lifetime, the people again experience this excitement when they first meet, and the relationship tends to develop with great intensity and speed, sometimes manifesting as a marriage or other type of commitment within only a few weeks or months of their initial encounter. However, both people expect that the same level of excitement will be maintained throughout the course of the relationship; and so, both are usually disappointed within a short time when the relationship seems to be settling into routines which can hardly be described as "exciting." One or both people then try to maintain the old feeling of excitement by re-enacting their previous separations and/or by emphasizing their individual freedom.

There is always a pronounced tone of freedom in any such relationship, and—since some amount of individual freedom is necessary for any relationship to be authentic and growth-promoting—this can manifest as the people being best friends to each other, with a large measure of respect for each other's individual needs. However, Uranus is the planet of extremism, and this tendency toward personal freedom is often taken to extremes, in which case the people find themselves so free within the relationship that they often wonder if there is indeed any relationship at all. With some of the Uranus interaspects, the one with the personal planet or Ascendant involved will resent the Uranus person's insistence upon freedom, impersonality, and aloofness; and the Uranus person may rebel against any constraints which the other person tries to impose to limit that freedom. When there are a number of challenging Uranus interaspects in a comparison, involving *both people's natal Uranus,* the tone of impersonality and independence is likely to be so dominant that each person ignores the other's needs and desires much of the time, leading in some cases to their living together physically but having hardly any meeting of the minds and emotions. In any case, there tends to be a characteristic expression of the Uranian sporadic, spasmodic rhythm: a consistent alternation between distance and closeness wherein the people get as free from each other as they can, then become frustrated with the lack of closeness that ensues from such self-centered living, then rebel or explode with frustration and loneliness, and then finally achieve a rapid and exciting togetherness once again. This togetherness is, however, highly unstable, and the reunion no sooner occurs than the same patterns begin to reappear and to bring about a widening gap between the two people once again. A good example of this unstable, sporadic rhythm is seen in those common relationships which are forever on the brink of separation but which never actually terminate. The on-again-off-again types of marriages and love affairs with which we are all familiar exemplify this vibration. Such relationships are characterized by a tone of uncertainty and unpredictability; and, especially in the early stages of such a relationship, this feeling may be very disconcerting to both people. However, once they become accustomed to that particular rhythm in their relationship and once they accept the need for their periodic separations (which requires a certain amount of flexibility and self-sufficiency!), the relationship may endure and may be quite excellent. It will always be an unconventional union, and the people simply have to accept it for what it is, rather than always trying to make it fit the mold of whatever traditional relationship patterns seem "proper" to them. Naturally, if the Uranus tone of the relationship is too strong, shown by too many challenging Uranus interaspects, the people will become more and more independent of each other and more and more resistant to any form of cooperation, to the point where the relationship will in fact cease to exist.

One or both people in this type of relationship often feels like he has to get away from the other person now and then, that he is going to be absolutely suffocated if he doesn't do something new and exciting by himself. If the other person resists this temporary separation, the tension already being felt simply increases. In other words, if someone's personal planets or Ascendant activate my natal Uranus strongly by conjunction, square or opposition, that person's very nature stimulates my need for excitement and change. If the other person resists my expressing the Uranus needs and urges, that activates my Uranus all the more! Hence, it should be clear that such relationships can thrive only if a great deal of space and freedom is given to the Uranus person (can be one or both people). Uranus (like its sign Aquarius) detests all forms of jealousy and manipulation. So, if you are in a relationship with someone whose natal Uranus is in a challenging aspect to any of your personal planets, and if you feel that he or she is getting rather bored with you, you should remember that attempts to dissuade him or her from experimentation and independent activity will nearly always create even more problems. If the person can act out his or her needs for freedom and change, then— by contrast—the old routines may eventually seem like an exciting change also, thus generating new enthusiasm for involvement in the relationship that was once felt to be so boring.

Neptune's Challenging Interaspects

Under the category of "challenging interaspects" in this section, we will be referring primarily to the square and opposition since those are the angles that manifest as the most problematical areas in chart comparisons. The conjunctions involving Neptune in comparisons can in most cases be classified as flowing aspects since most of them (in a manner similar to the flowing aspects of Venus in comparisons) smooth things out and round off the rough edges in any relationship. This harmony is due to the fact that the flowing aspects (including the sextile and trine) are sympathetic and compassionate vibrations which allow one to tune in to the needs and feelings of the other person telepathically. Of all the conjunctions involving Neptune and a personal planet, the only one that is *commonly* problematical is the Mars-

Neptune conjunction; and even this can manifest in positive ways in some relationships. The other conjunctions *can* be problematical, but this is primarily due to an excess of compassion or, in some cases, pity. Usually, the conjunctions of Neptune with personal planets in comparisons symbolize a strong mutual identity with the other person and often a feeling of obligation toward him. (One also often feels this obligation if one's twelfth house is activated by someone else's natal planets.) There is an *idealization* of the other person in some cases, which prompts us to give to him without desire or expectation of repayment. From the viewpoint of karma, one might say that we do indeed owe the other person something from a past life, and there is a powerful subconscious commitment to pay him back through any means available. Hence, since we feel this obligation so strongly, we tend to be forgiving, generous, yielding, and incredibly tolerant with such a person; and we often feel like he owes us nothing in return. Hence, we learn not to expect *anything* from him. This feeling of obligation is not the same as the feeling of obligation we experience with Saturn interaspects, where we often feel that we *have to* pay back the other person. In the case of Neptune aspects, there is something deep within us that tells us that we *want to* pay this person back for something he or she gave us or helped us with in the past. We need only to be careful that such a feeling does not lead to resentment when we never get anything in return or to an obsession with owing something indefinable which never *can* be paid back, in which case the other person could begin to use us at will since we could always be counted on to yield to any demand. The karma involved in such relationships is extremely subtle; and hence there is no easy way of explaining in detail what such aspects might mean in a particular case. We should simply take these interaspects as clues that we do have some kind of karmic tie that focuses on a particular area of the relationship, but we should also keep our eyes open in order to discriminate clearly between a real feeling of indebtedness and vague feelings of confusion which will lead to later resentment.

With the squares and oppositions, the above feelings will be evident in some cases; but more often, an entirely different pattern emerges. The Neptune square and opposition interaspects are experienced most often as the Neptune person's feeling the need to escape from the other person's influence in the way indicated (shown specifically by the personal planet involved with Neptune). There is usually a powerful wave of confusion and disorientation encountered by the Neptune person whenever he or she is confronted with the other person's challenging mode of expression. The only way that the Neptune person feels able to function clearly and with focused concentration is if he or she is able to escape from that energy. For example, I was once working with an editor whose Mercury closely squares my natal Neptune. She is an excellent editor, and we had always been quite compatible in our common work efforts. However, at one time, we experimented with going over particular chapters together, after she had already read the material and made some notes. The idea was that she would show me the various sections that she thought needed changing, I would then read them over, and we would together decide on corrections, new phrasing, and so forth. However, by working so closely with her, I found that her Mercury intensely activated my Neptune; and, as she showed me various sections of the material, I would lose all concentration and just space out into a state of utter confusion. Trying to do the editing in this manner eventually became so frustrating and time-wasting that we stopped it. While still trying it, however, I found that I had to get at least ten feet away from her, to get out of the influence of her energy field, before I could sufficiently concentrate on the material at hand. Once out of the range of her aura, I could again concentrate and think about it clearly. So, over time, we found that the work could be done most efficiently, and in about one-fifth the time, if she simply submitted a list of suggested corrections to me and I went over them alone. Hence, with Mercury square Neptune, my Neptune was activated in the way stated above; but also, her Mercury expression was frustrated since I couldn't understand what she was saying, and she started to become extremely nervous and on-edge whenever we started the editing.

In Neptune interaspects, the sort of confusion mentioned above almost always manifests to some degree. Occasionally, it is only a mild irritation, as in the above example; but at times it manifests as misinterpretation, major misunderstandings, and even as deception. The deception that can occur comes from the tendency of the Neptune person to evade facing something with complete honesty. Things are left unsaid, or things are said ambiguously in order to induce the other person to assume something that is not the whole truth. The Neptune person wants to maintain his self-deceptions and is made uncomfortable and uncertain if he has to deal with the problem in concrete terms. By being vague or by evading the question at hand, he is able to fend off the other person's influence while not committing himself to anything. If these Neptune interaspects involve the other person's Sun, the interchange can be tremendously dominant in the relationship, often manifesting as habitual evasion and escapism on the part of the Neptune person and as considerable frustration on the part of the Sun person since he or she gets no direct response or recognition when expressing authenticity and creative energy. The *conjunction* of Neptune and the Sun can share some of these qualities, but it usually also shows a strong mutual identification that at times borders on the mystical, wherein each person feels like he or she is one with the other person. Sometimes, extremely close relationships have such an aspect, and there is often a powerful—but highly refined—flow of love between the two people. The opposition will sometimes share this mystical quality, although the problematical elements mentioned above are almost always somewhat evident. But the square is by far the most frustrating aspect and most prone to produce major conflicts; for, while there may occasionally be a strong mutual identification, the relationship is often based on an unrealistic idealization of the other person and the identification is therefore often based on illusion or subconscious prejudices.

Pluto's Challenging Interaspects

The general nature of these interchanges may easily be inferred from the characteristics of Pluto already described in previous chapters. In those chapters, I gave examples of Pluto's association with manipulation and absorption and also its symbolism of potential transformation in a total and highly positive way. All of these meanings are likewise applicable to Pluto's interaspects in chart comparisons. In fact, we can easily outline the alternative ways such aspects can manifest because— since Pluto, like Scorpio which it rules, is a planet of emotional extremism—the energies tend to be expressed in rather extreme ways, either positively or negatively. However, it should be remembered that Pluto, like any astrological factor, manifests in terms of *polarities;* what may at one time be extremely negative may in a short time become transformed into an extremely positive mode of expression. And, specifically in relation to Pluto, it is impossible for us to know the ultimate outcome of various types of behavior or experience which may seem at first glance to be quite negative. For Pluto always wants to penetrate into the depths of experience, to delve into the core of meaning underlying surface appearances, and to confront all manner of experience ruthlessly and intensely. Therefore, to outline the essence of these interaspects, Pluto's interchanges with personal planets may focus upon either manipulation or transformation. In other words, the Pluto person can either pull the other person down spiritually and even in some cases help to degrade the other person (or to encourage self-degradation); or, the Pluto person can encourage the other person toward self-transformation in a concentrated, determined way. The latter manifestation is totally dependent, however, on the Pluto person having attained some degree of spiritual awareness in his or her own life. We can hardly expect that one who is still spiritually unawakened and still entirely at the mercy of unconscious compulsions can be of much help in encouraging the spiritual growth of another individual.

Trying to understand the meaning of Pluto interaspects in any chart comparison is always difficult and always involves either considerable guessing and intuition or at least some extremely penetrating knowledge of the two people's interaction; for Pluto rarely operates entirely on the surface of life, and—unless we know the people intimately *and* have been able to witness their way of interacting for some time—it may be impossible for us to describe how such an aspect is manifesting except in general terms. Understanding these aspects is also made difficult by the fact that Pluto's meaning is so complex; if we tend to judge things by their surface appearances, we are almost certain to evaluate a Pluto interchange incompletely. One reason this is true can be illustrated as follows. Suppose John's Pluto is square my Mercury; other people may see John as pulling me down by influencing me to think about "forbidden" things, to study taboo subjects, or to express ideas which are socially unpopular and threatening. A judgmental observer therefore might say: "Look how John is influencing that fellow's mind; he's just overpowering his common sense and reason! What a nasty person that

John is!" However, what I am experiencing through the association with John may be of great value to me. He may be pulling me down into the depths, but perhaps I need a journey into the depths of life and of my own mind and emotions in order to purge myself of useless psychic waste, old fears, outmoded attitudes, or compulsions. From my journey into the depths, I may come back to the surface with a great wealth of inner understanding and with more courage than ever before. Even if John's motivations are entirely negative in such a relationship, who is to say that I will not grow from this confrontation? Once I have gained all I can from the experience, I may feel quite comfortable telling John to get lost!

Another reason that one should be cautious about the interpretation of these aspects is that, since Pluto moves so slowly, we share the same interaspect with literally millions of human beings. For example, if I am born with Pluto exactly opposite my Sun, my natal Sun will also be in opposition to the natal Pluto of every other person born within a number of years of me. Does this mean that I will share the same basic pattern of relationship with all those millions of people? I would have to say no. The problem represented by that opposition in my natal chart is merely activated most intensely by people of my own generation; but the main problem is mine, not theirs! Hence, when I see that a natal aspect involving Pluto (or, to some extent, Uranus or Neptune) is repeated in a particular comparison, I usually place very little emphasis upon it and prefer to look at other, more individually unique, dimensions of the relationship. It is only when a particular Plutonian *theme* emerges in such a comparison, shown by a number of challenging Pluto aspects (and sometimes including one person's planets falling in the other person's natal eighth house), that I focus special attention on the potentials symbolized by Pluto. And, in order to be considered especially important, such combinations should include at least one aspect that is not found in either natal chart. In comparisons between two people of the same approximate age, this usually means an aspect involving one person's Pluto and one of the cardinal angles of the other chart. In comparisons involving people of widely different ages, the chances of finding such an aspect are much greater; and, in those cases, *any* conjunction (and, to a lesser extent, any square or opposition) of one person's Pluto and the other person's personal planet should be viewed as tremendously significant in characterizing the quality and meaning of the relationship. However, it should be re-emphasized here that—even if there are no important Pluto *aspects*—a strong emphasis on one or both persons' eighth house *in the comparison* will often reveal a Plutonian quality in the relationship. The person whose eighth house is activated by the other person's natal planets is usually the one who feels the urge to manipulate, to absorb, to reform, or to transform the other person.

In terms of karma, the only pattern that seems to appear regularly in relationships characterized by a strong Pluto theme is the need for one or both people to learn how to live independently and to allow the other person simply to be and to grow in whatever way is spontaneous and natural. But this lesson is difficult to learn in such cases because this Pluto emphasis seems to indicate that the people shared past lives of absorption into one another, situations where the identities were largely merged or where mutual dependency, closeness, or manipulation were overemphasized. One naturally thinks of the mother-child relationship in some of these cases, but the present karma could also be accounted for by certain other types of pastlife relationships. Examples might be pastlife experiences as "lovers" almost *owning* one another or relationships as husband-wife or slavemaster-slave where one did indeed own the other person (according to the laws of the society at that time). Another dimension of this type of relationship is *power*. In most cases, one person (usually the one whose Pluto is involved) has a tremendously powerful hold over the other person, especially if the Sun, Moon, or Ascendant is involved with Pluto. Although this control is rarely overt, it is there nevertheless, and it is maintained by the magnetism which the other person feels from the Pluto person. In many cases, unless the Pluto person voluntarily relinquishes the power that he or she has over the other individual, the other person may eventually find it necessary to remove self entirely from the presence of this disturbing energy in order to be able to live and breathe freely.

Composite Charts

Since in this chapter we are dealing with factors that reveal the karma involved in specific relationships, we should also mention the complementary side of this approach, namely the *dharma* or essential purpose of a particular interaction. I was not especially interested in composite charts* until rather recently, although I had experimented with them somewhat. My lack of interest was due to the fact that none of the explanations I had read of what composite charts were supposed to indicate seemed to apply to the composite charts with which I had experimented. The absence of a meaningful philosophy and theoretical framework to illuminate such charts therefore led me to think that the entire technique was purely speculative and, in fact, probably quite worthless. These feelings were strengthened when I tested the interpretations in some books that deal with composite charts; for they simply did not fit my experience of certain relationships.

However, then I met an astrologer named Judy Weinstein, who had done considerable work with composites. She explained to me that I should view the composite chart as indicative of the *purpose* of a given relationship. With this new approach in mind, composite charts began to

---

*For those not familiar with these charts, a composite chart is comprised of the midpoints between the two people's Suns, Moons, etc., thus creating a chart which shows focal points of energy expression which may not have been dominant in either of the individual charts. A composite chart can best be interpreted by emphasizing the Ascendant and the occupied houses as symbolic of the specific types of activities engaged in, and by de-emphasizing aspects and signs. This approach to composites naturally requires that both charts being used are based on accurate birth-times.

take on clear meaning. Those factors which had made no sense at all before, since they did not describe my *experience* of the relationship as traditional chart comparisons do, now appeared to be meaningful. They clearly symbolized specific activities that the two people engage in together, as well as the way the unit formed by the two people expresses itself spontaneously. Soon thereafter, while on a trip to Seattle for some lectures, another astrologer, June Marsden, told me that she had also found this approach to composite charts to be especially useful and accurate, regardless of what the various books on the subject led one to believe. My experience since then tends to confirm this view that a composite reveals a relationship's essential purpose. So, if we meet another person who seems to have some important role to play in our lives, and especially if the traditional method of comparing charts does not sufficiently illuminate what the interaction is based on, we might then do a composite chart with him or her. By doing so, we can perhaps get a better perspective on the purpose of the interaction and the ultimate way in which the two people's combined energies will be expressed.

Scorpio

8

Cycles of Transformation: Part I
Progressions

The unexamined life is not worth living.
—Socrates

Live life as life lives itself.
—Lao Tsu

This chapter and the following chapter on transits examine some of the most important features of these two methods of understanding the cyclic nature of human growth and development. Whereas transits have been dealt with quite thoroughly in a number of contemporary books, the subject of progressions—although it is talked about glibly in even the mass-market astrology magazines—has not been treated with the same depth or the same quality.* Hence, at this time in the evolution of a modern approach to astrology, we still need to develop a language that is appropriate for understanding progressions from an *experiential* viewpoint, rather than from the traditional approach of seeing progressions solely as indicators of outer events. It is primarily this new language that I want to focus upon in this chapter. But first, we need to define what kind of progressions we are going to discuss, and we also need to differentiate between the meanings of transits and progressions.

There are at least a dozen different methods of progressions currently used by astrologers, and this very fact should impress upon us the subtlety of experience which some progressions indicate; for, if progressions invariably corresponded with definite, observable experiences or events in our lives, one would think that only a few methods would be used since they would have proven their validity through years of testing. To some extent, a preference for only a few particular methods does exist among the majority of astrologers; but whether this preference arises from the greater reliability of those methods or whether it merely comes from the fact that only a few methods are taught by most schools of astrology is not entirely clear. But it is evident that the progression methods used most widely by Western astrologers are: the system of Secondary Progressions (or "day-for-a-year method") and, especially in recent years, the Solar Arc method. Since these two methods are the primary ones with which I have considerable experience, I will limit my explanation to those two

---

* *Noel Tyl's The Expanded Present* is an exception to this statement, for it is a valuable and instructive book that not only outlines different methods of progressions and their application but also takes a large step toward expressing the meaning of specific progressions in a dynamic, experiential language.

methods alone. As far as I have been able to determine, the secondary progressions are best for understanding psychological developments and periods of personal unfoldment and intensive growth, although they often correspond with specific events and major experiences as well. The reliability of such progressions (i.e., whether we can know for sure that a particular secondary progression will manifest in a noticeable way) is fairly good when using the progressed Sun and progressed Moon aspects, but it becomes more questionable when we begin to use these progressions of the other planets. This may indicate simply that people are more *in touch with* those growth and development cycles shown by the progressed Sun and Moon, rather than that the other progressed planets have no meaning or practical value. An exact aspect of, for example, progressed Mars, Mercury, or Venus will often correspond with noticeable trends in the individual life, but by no means will all people be able to identify with or relate to its supposed meaning. Hence, it becomes a question of how aware the individual is of his or her inner changes and dynamics, for some people claim that they can notice a definite "influence" from almost all the secondary progressions' exact aspects, whereas others only tune in on those of the progressed Sun and Moon (and perhaps an occasional progressed aspect of another planet).

The solar arc progressions, on the other hand, seem to be slightly more reliable than the secondary progressions, primarily due to the fact that the solar arc progression of *all* the planets, not just the Sun and Moon, seem to have equal power since each is progressed through the chart at the same rate. The solar arc progressions seem consistently more indicative of definite events than most of the secondary progressions (the main exception is the conjunction of the Moon by secondary progression to a natal planet), and they have therefore been increasingly used by event-oriented astrologers. However, since the primary application of solar arc progressions is in understanding or predicting events and definite changes in outer circumstances, it is my feeling that those whose main interest is the inner life of the individual should emphasize secondary progressions over (but not to the exclusion of) solar arc methods. Since solar arc measurements are based on the planets being moved at the same rate as the secondary progressed Sun (*approximately* 1° per year of life is a rough estimate), they bear strong resemblance to the progression method which simply moves each planet and important point in the chart by exactly 1° per year of life. And therefore, the following quotation from C.E.O. Carter's writings would seem to apply to solar arc progressions:

> If I abandoned all others [i.e., all other progression and "direction" methods], I would at least retain the 1°=1 year measure . . . in my own case, I have never found them to fail to work . . ." (from *Some Principles of Horoscopic Delineation*, p. 75)

One must, however, keep in mind that the reliability of solar arc progressions is easier to test than that of the secondary progressions, for the latter often symbolize life-developments which—although extremely important—are of such subtlety that their meaning is not always immediately evident. Since my focus in this book is upon the "inner dimensions" of the birthchart and the individual's personal experience, my comments about the meaning of specific progressions are primarily applicable to secondary progressions. And, since the progressed Sun and Moon are—of all the progressed planets in the secondary system—the most reliable and the most indicative of important inner developments, I will concentrate on the meaning of the secondary progressions of the two luminaries.

One more preliminary matter needs discussion before we proceed with the details of interpreting specific progressions: namely, the difference between transits and progressions both in meaning and in scope of application. The first thing which should be emphasized is that the oft-repeated statement that progressions show only inner developments and that transits show primarily environmental and circumstantial changes is an attempt to oversimplify the situation by ignoring many important facts. Attempting to discriminate between these two techniques in this way is based on an artificial dichotomy between inner and outer, personal and environmental. The outer world is a reflection of our karma and our inner situation, and we have all experienced how a change in mood or attitude can give us an entirely different view of outer circumstances. A particular progression sometimes corresponds with events in the outer world, at other times with changes in our consciousness, and often with both; and the same can be said for transits. As I pointed out in the Introduction, how much of one's karma and destiny is manifested in the outer world as circumstances which seem to happen *to* us depends a great deal on our level of self-awareness. In the excellent introduction to his book *Planets in Transit*, Robert Hand elaborates on the artificial distinction between "inner" and "outer" experiences:

> The point is that what we call an objective description is nothing more than a collective subjective experience. There may be an absolute reality outside of anyone's experience, but it is quite irrelevant to our daily life. We act upon our universe, and we receive reactions from it in a continuous field of consciousness. (p. 5)

Hand goes on to compare progressions to transits in some detail, and I urge the reader to study his observations. The following quotation is an excellent summary of his remarks:

> A given set of astrological symbols can manifest themselves in many ways. Transits indicate how the symbolism of your life unfolds in time, exactly as do progressions, although transits give greater detail over the short range. The progressions indicate a more general structure over a longer time. (p. 6)

We also find that transits refer to *a more specific attunement of energy* which can actually be felt with great immediacy, whereas most progressions are indicative of moods, new interests, and new life-orientations that usually are not accompanied by an awareness of a different mode of energy flow within the total energy field. It is as if the planets at birth set up our initial attunement or "cosmic conditioning" energy pattern, and we then continue to vibrate at that rhythm and frequency throughout our lives. However, changes in the cosmic environment (transits) indicate periods when we vibrate (or *resonate*) either in harmony or in discord with our basic natal attunement. A transit can in fact *temporarily* alter our natal energy pattern by adding another vibration to our usual way of being. At times, this new energy flow will simply end after the transit is over, revealing that little change occurred during the period when it was in effect. In other cases, however, the individual will seem to have assimilated some of that new energy (manifesting as an altered approach to some dimension of life), and— although the natal energy pattern will be generally maintained—major personality change has obviously occurred. Progressions, on the other hand, reveal the set periodicity or cyclic pattern which we all go through during our life; in other words, the energy field we are attuned to from birth naturally and regularly undergoes periodic rhythmic changes from within, and these changes are indicated by the progressions.

It seems to me that progressions are over-emphasized in many schools of astrological thought, sometimes even to the total exclusion of transits. I personally cannot understand how anyone who uses transits consistently for a few years could possibly dismiss the uncanny and incredibly useful insights that a knowledge of transits can provide. Some astrologers also place what I feel is too much emphasis on a so-called "progressed chart" by setting up a chart based on current progressions and then interpreting it in the abstract, unrelated to the individual's natal chart. Along with many other astrologers, I feel that all progressions and transits must be related to the natal chart since such techniques reveal development and unfolding of the potentials symbolized most clearly by the birthchart itself. I would also agree with Carter that transits show important life changes more often than do progressions, and in that sense, transits are more practically useful in everyday astrological counseling than are progressions. As Carter writes:

> So far as personal experience goes, I believe that three-quarters, at least, of the events of my not uneventful life could be adequately accounted for by transits, properly understood. (*Some Principles of Horoscopic Delineation*, p. 73)

The last two words of Carter's quotation, "properly understood," hold the key to this entire controversy; for once a person has begun to get a feel for the proper application of transits, a perspective that develops only after much study and practice, he or she will find that approximately 90% of the important experiences and time periods can be clearly and *specifically* understood through the use of transits. In the following chapter, I have included many pointers for using transits properly which I have found to be significant and which are only rarely mentioned in most astrological textbooks. But there are indeed times when no method of understanding life cycles seems to adequately account for a particular experience. Such times are rare, but we must admit that they do occasionally come to our attention if we are intellectually honest and therefore refuse to stretch the meaning of cycles that *are* present simply in order to try to account for every life experience. Carter addressed this question in his pamphlet *The Seven Great Problems of Astrology* as early as 1927, and his comments could be applied to transits as well as to progressions:

> When we see a thousand diverse causes leading up to the precise time a direction falls due and closely corresponding to the nature of that direction, we are apt to think that it is always so, and that we have a wonderful example of the all-coordinating unity of nature.
>
> But we must remember, to begin with, that directions (i.e., progressions) do not always work out in this marvellous way; sometimes we have to admit that events occur without appropriate directions, or, on the other hand, directions fail to act, or act at the wrong time or in the wrong manner or with more or less power than astrological rules would lead one to anticipate. Very many systems have been advocated and fresh ones still appear from time to time, but it is doubtful if any approaches perfection. The reason lies in the infinite complexity of life, not only with respect to the individual, but in his endless relationship with others. . . . To expect perfection of any directional system is manifestly over-sanguine. Especially is this the case when many persons are affected by one event: if an employer dies and numerous employees are affected, are all to have appropriate directions to their M.C. at the same time? If this were so, then the perfection of Astrology would mean the enmeshment of man in a rigid, mathematically exact machine. (p. 10)

The truth of Carter's statement should lead us to a clearer realization that the practice of astrology is an art, a highly refined art in which the astrologer is not only the artist but also the primary medium of expression; the transits, progressions, and other techniques are merely the tools utilized in the practice of the art. Another important point, which beginning students of astrology usually take a long time to learn and which even many experienced practitioners of astrology don't seem to understand, is that all of the processes symbolized by transits and progressions are merely parts of the one grand process: the individual living person. Those cycles and change periods indicated are not isolated events that come out of the blue. As I wrote in the introduction, they are all aspects (or dimensions) of a *unified and developing consciousness* (the individual person) *which is operating simultaneously at many different levels of being.* In other words, there is really no such thing as a person *having,* for example, a progressed Sun square to natal Mars. It is not something that you can go out and buy at a department store or that someone can give you. It is a direct outgrowth of *YOU,* your nature, your current life situation, and your future potentials. What is really happening could be better expressed by saying: "*YOUR* Sun has progressed to the point where it is activating *YOUR* Mars." This simply means that *your* identity, consciousness, and use of your creative energy (Sun) has progressed (or developed) to the point where you are ready to tune in on your capacity for initiative and self-assertion (Mars). Hence, you can further integrate the Mars energy into your conscious life and grow by assimilating and becoming more in control of this energy from now on.

Our interpretation of progressions, in other words, has to become personalized, i.e., related to the individual's fundamental nature (and hence to the natal birthchart). It is only in this way that the use of progressions (and transits) can be a constructive and insightful technique for better self-understanding. To put this another way, the effect of any progression or transit depends on the nature of our natal attunement to the energies involved in the particular configuration being considered. For example, a progressed Sun or Moon aspect to natal Saturn can indicate a time of deep satisfaction and rapid growth for someone who is harmoniously attuned to (and thus not resistant to) the Saturn principle. Some effort may still be required, but such a person takes the necessary effort for granted and in fact gains great satisfaction from it. If Jupiter is involved, although the progressed aspect may be a "harmonious" angle, the outcome of that time period may merely be missed opportunities or wasted effort if the individual is not attuned to Jupiter in a healthy, flowing way. More than anything else, the secondary progressions (especially those of the Sun and Moon) give us an opportunity to integrate different aspects of our nature and to become more conscious and more in command of our energies. Hence, an understanding of these progressions can give us keys with which we can unlock the secrets of self-transformation and which help us to flow with the maturation process through which time is leading us.

I mentioned above that a proper understanding of transits would in most cases enable an astrologer to "account for" approximately 90% of the important time periods in a person's life. One might therefore ask why it is necessary for a practitioner of astrology to bother with progressions at all, especially since there are well-known and highly respected astrologers who never use them. My approach to all astrological methods is that one should familiarize oneself with a variety of methods, experiment with them for a while, and then concentrate on those methods which give the best results for one's own particular purposes. I personally advise students to learn both the Secondary Progressions system and the Solar Arc method and then to focus especially upon the progressed Sun (the same in both systems) and the progressed Moon in the secondary system. For, although progressed Sun and Moon aspects symbolize only a small percentage of the important experiences and time periods in one's life, those that *are* symbolized are usually of extraordinary importance. There are, however, also a few other types of secondary progressions that are worth paying attention to, and these will be mentioned at the end of this chapter.

The Progressed Sun

Although the aspects of the progressed Sun to natal planets may be interpreted in many ways and with many different sorts of language, the following information represents those ways of expressing and understanding such aspects which I have come to find meaningful myself and which clients with no knowledge of astrology seem to be able to relate to with little difficulty. My main emphasis in using the progressed Sun is upon the aspects which it makes to natal planets or angles. Unlike some astrologers, I pay little attention to the sign and house position of the progressed Sun since I feel the importance of these factors is often overestimated. Although there may be some significance to the progressed Sun's current sign and house position, it is far too general to be particularly important to the person in a counseling situation since it will remain in each sign and house approximately thirty years or so. However, I do pay attention to those times when the progressed Sun is *changing* signs or houses, for these transition periods are often important and are felt by the individual to be phases of reorientation and changing values. But, whatever the progressed Sun's position by sign or house may mean, the person inevitably adjusts to the change in one way or another within a year or two and therefore is no longer aware of such a factor as a *dynamic* focus of current concern. And so, in using the progressed Sun, the *aspects* yield the most valuable information about the present orientation and focus of the individual. Although emphasis should be placed upon the conjunction, square, and opposition, *all* exact aspects of the progressed Sun to natal points may be used with good results, even to the extent of using "minor" aspects such as the semi-sextile and semi-square. The speed of the progressed Sun is so slow that an aspect will remain within 15' (or ¼ of a degree) of exact for around six months. During such a time, when there is a dynamic interaction of two powerful energies for an extended period, it is almost inevitable that an individual will begin to be aware of some degree of inner intensity and promptings toward change, even if the symbolic indicators of this development are the so-called "minor" aspects.

The above comments bring to mind the question of what orbs to use when interpreting progressed Sun aspects. In other words, how should one express and how can one understand the probable length of time that a given progressed Sun aspect will be particularly active? As the widely different preferences of various astrologers should indicate, this is largely an individual matter, for some people are more sensitive than others to inner changes and to new trends and vibrations in their lives. More material on this question of orbs will be found in the following chapter, but I personally use much smaller orbs for the progressed Sun than the 1° orb often recommended. If one uses a 1° orb applying to and separating from the exact angle, then a progressed Sun aspect would be felt for two years. Although this sometimes applies, in my experience it is not usually the case since most people are much too busy to pay attention to any important change until it forces itself upon their consciousness with a degree of intensity which cannot be ignored. I prefer to give a *maximum* orb of 30' (or ½ a degree) applying and 15' (or ¼ of a degree) separating. This merely indicates that *most* people won't begin to feel the effects of a close progressed Sun aspect *strongly* until six months or less before the exact aspect is formed. And then, once the exact aspect begins to separate, the immediacy of the experience indicated will usually begin to fade out rather quickly (often within three months), although it may take much longer for the person to assimilate its significance completely. As far as I have seen, most people seem to go through the experience indicated by a progressed Sun aspect within a time span of six months or less. It is during that time that the most intense phase of the experience will be *predominant* in their lives.

The meaning of progressed Sun aspects can best be understood by defining the astrological principle represented by both the Sun and Leo as "the urge to be, to *become*, and to express one's self." If we can see the progressed Sun in this light, we can then describe all progressed Sun aspects as indicative of periods when one is assimilating new qualities of being and developing new modes of self-expression. As the progressed Sun aspects other planets, we have the opportunity to become more *consciously* attuned to the potentials shown by those planets and thus to learn what those symbols mean in our lives in a highly personal and specific way. Just to clarify what I mean by "assimilating new qualities of being," let's look briefly at the sign Leo and examine how that energy operates. A Leo person says, in effect, "I will *be* something," and then Leo proceeds to become whatever was envisioned. They play to the hilt whatever role represents what they want to become. The fact that they are not *now* what they want to *become* does not hinder them in any way; they simply start becoming it by acting it out. And so they demonstrate one of the secrets of self-transformation. There are other ways of changing oneself, but Leo demonstrates the Sun principle's mode of operation. To relate this concept to the progressed Sun: as the progressed Sun aspects a natal planet, you *become* more like that planet's nature. Such an aspect shows a period of *becoming* more than you were before. And this process of becoming happens whether or not the person is conscious of it. One might indeed say that both the Sun and Leo represent the urge to be more than you are, the will to become greater and more complete than you now are. Hence, if we see the Sun as essentially a symbol of *becoming,* then each of the progressed Sun's exact aspects indicates a time period in which we will be actively involved in rapid development and growth; our entire personality can change during such a period, and the scope of self-expression with which we feel comfortable can be expanded considerably at such a time.

A few examples from my files should help to explain this approach to progressed Sun aspects:

Progressed Sun conjunct Mars (male, 25 years old): he began to get in touch with his masculinity, personal strength, and power. The fears and inhibitions (shown by a natal square of Saturn to Mars) which previously had prevented him from going after what he wanted began to have less and less power over him; and, in fact, this was a period of great growth in confidence and courage. He never returned to the old fearful, doubting way of acting and speaking, for he seemed to have fully assimilated a strong dose of Mars energy. He *became* more like the nature of Mars: more forceful, assertive, fearless, and inclined to initiate new projects and activities, even some involving considerable risk. It was a period of radical self-transformation.

Progressed Sun conjunct Venus (woman, 48 years old): never married and with almost no experience in love or sexual relationships, she began to awaken to this neglected part of her nature during this time. She became involved sexually with two different men and, although the relationships did not last very long and although she was troubled by numerous conflicts about her actions and desires, it was a period of tremendous growth since she *became* more in touch with her Venus needs, capacities, and desires, thus giving her more confidence in her femininity and attractiveness and opening her up to the entire dimension of experience symbolized by Venus. During this time, she *became* more Venusian—with enhanced sensitivity and greater emotional depth.

Progressed Sun square Jupiter (male, aged 19): this was a period of great expansion, self-improvement, and adventure. He began at this time to experiment with new lifestyles, ideas, ideals, and ways of relating which opened up many doors for greater self-knowledge. It was a period of "finding himself" and *becoming* more confident, happy, and independent. He also found new religious interests at this time since he was then first exposed to Eastern teachings about reincarnation and Taoist philosophy. Financial protection was also present since he was given a car and a monthly stipend for college.

Progressed Sun conjunct Neptune (woman, aged 26): marked a period of *becoming* more idealistic and of actually trying to live up to those ideals. There was a spiritual awakening and an increased awareness of many subtle, intangible factors in her life that previously had been ignored. The beginning of this period was marked by her quitting her job and retreating from the world for about three months, during which time she began to develop a plan for her future which would be more fulfilling and inspiring than her previous lifestyle. During this progression, she began to take an interest in a career in the medical field, which she has pursued for many years since then and finds extremely satisfying. She also *became* more Neptunian during this time in the sense that she became more open to such spiritual factors as karma, destiny, etc.

Progressed Sun conjunct Uranus (male, 27 years old): marked a period of great changes both in his outer life and in his inner sense of purpose and individuality. He moved to a different state at the beginning of this period in order to pursue a radically new ambition: a graduate program in music (although his bachelor's degree was in psychology). Then, after only a few months in his new location, his restlessness prompted him to quit the program and to return to his former residence in order to pursue astrology and counseling, another radically new approach for him since he had previously done no counseling and had only periodically dabbled in astrology. He *became* more Uranian, as evidenced not only by the numerous changes in his outer life, but also by the tremendously increased interest in astrology.

Progressed Sun square Pluto (male, aged 30): a period of leaving behind the old, realizing that he was no longer a "young" person whose values and orientations grew out of his experiences in college. It was a period of assimilating the fact that the past was irretrievably gone and also that the compulsive, mechanical approach he had toward many life situations was no longer fulfilling or even interesting. This period coincided with a three-week illness that heralded a major rebirth since, once recovered, he completely ended all the work activities with which he had made his living for a number of years, thus clearing the way to begin an entirely new career. For, during the illness, he had realized that he absolutely couldn't continue to perform the meaningless, uninspiring activities of the past. He *became* Plutonian at this time by being much more ruthless (in a positive way!) in his method of conducting his life and much more concentrated about his goals.

Progressed Sun square Saturn (male, aged 25): a period in which he became much more conservative in his views and values. During this period, he assimilated many Saturnian qualities, some of which were confronted through his dealings with an older professor with whom he had conflicts. He felt the need to withdraw from his work and from graduate school programs for about five weeks in order to assess whether he should continue to pursue what had once been his main ambitions. Once this period had passed, he was resigned to many practical realities for the first time in his life, and he had *become* much more Saturnian, with increased patience and greater acceptance of older members of the "establishment."

The above examples should give the reader sufficient acquaintance with this approach to progressed Sun aspects to enable her to test this method in actual practice. One can then see if its emphasis on psychological growth is appropriate for the kind of astrological work she is doing. Although the progressed Sun's "minor" aspects and its trines and sextiles don't always indicate major psychological developments, paying attention to them is nevertheless worthwhile. But one can *always* know in advance that a conjunction, square, or opposition of the progressed Sun will mark a major phase of self-transformation and potentially a time when the person is able to *consciously* integrate a prominent part of his or her nature. If the person is attuned to the subtler dimensions of everyday experiences, he or she may be aware that a major karmic pattern is being activated and brought into the light of consciousness. For those who are not so sensitized to the progress of their inner life, these periods will often begin with some major event or experience which, as it were, forces them to deal with a particular part of themselves. And it initiates a phase of personality development and increased maturity which they would not consciously have thought was necessary.

The Progressed Moon

The progressed Moon by secondary progressions is an especially valuable tool since its relatively rapid speed makes it possible to use not only the aspects that it makes to natal points but also the house position that it occupies as interpretive guidelines. In addition, the time period of the progressed Moon's complete cycle through an individual's chart

(approximately 27-28 years) serves as a perfect complement to the cycle of transiting Saturn (28½-30 years). The house position of the progressed Moon indicates, among other things, that you are becoming aware of that area of your life and that field of experience; you feel *pulled* toward it and your mind tends to dwell upon those matters almost constantly.*
By contrast, the house position of transiting Saturn, as described in Chapter 5, specifically represents an area of life and expression that you are either consciously working on or which circumstances are compelling you to make effort toward. The progressed Moon's house position can also indicate any of the following:

a) that past patterns of response and subconscious attitudes (karma from past lives) toward that area of life tend to become apparent.

b) that much attention will be focused upon that area of experience for the entire time the Moon is in that house.

c) that changing interests will become evident as the progressed Moon changes houses (and especially when it aspects various natal planets).

d) that new contacts, meetings, or relationships will also tend to occur either when the Moon is changing houses or when it makes close aspects to natal planets.

e) that one's overall mood will be symbolized by the progressed Moon's house position, and therefore that definite psychological developments tend to occur as one assimilates this new experience. (Note that the Moon is closely related to nourishment, feeding, mothering, and thus *assimilating* sustenance; hence one might say that we *feed* on that area of experience during the time the Moon is in a certain house.)

f) that the progressed Moon's position in some cases shows, as many authors state, the everyday circumstances and environment; but in almost all cases it reveals what is preoccupying your mind.

g) that the progressed Moon's house position shows where your vital energies are going, toward what field of experience and types of interests you are being *drawn,* and to what area of your life you're particularly responsive and sensitive.

When the progressed Moon (or transiting Saturn as well) is in an angular house, it tends to correspond with a period of marked activity, when in a succeedent house with a time of consolidation and building or searching for security, and when in a cadent house with a great deal of new experience and learning, sometimes coming through travel or educational involvements. The movement of the progressed Moon (and to some extent this is also applicable to the transits of both Saturn and Jupiter) can be further explained by classifying the houses according to the elements of the signs they correlate with:

Passing through the air houses (III, VII, & XI): stimulates planning, new ideas, new relationships, interchange of ideas, and gaining a detached perspective on things.

---

* Note that the Moon is symbolic of the "mind" in Hindu astrology, i.e., the constant flow of thoughts, feelings, impressions, moods, images, needs, and memories that characterize our *general* "state of mind." Differentiated from this type of "mind" is the conscious, rational mind symbolized by Mercury, which is actually just a particular faculty of the *conscious* mind alone. It is therefore incorrect to ascribe the keyword of "mind" to Mercury although there is no denying that Mercury's function is indeed totally mental.

Passing through the fire houses (I, V, & IX): stimulates a strong urge toward action and commitments to things you'll do or create or aspire toward. Strong involvements with the outer world.

Passing through the water houses (IV, VIII, & XII): stimulates reflection, a need to retreat from the outer world, and in-depth learning. Can be a period of marked spiritual growth and increased psychic sensitivity.

Passing through the earth houses (II, VI, & X): stimulates an awareness of immediate necessities and matters concerned with work, practical duties, and—in general—how you fit into the outer world. Will also at times show periods of having to bear burdens or pay off specific karma through heavy effort.

It should be noted that the progressed Moon's position in a fire or air house is usually indicative of a lighter overall mood in day to day living than is the Moon in an earth or water house. In fact, it is often striking how noticeable the mood change is when someone's progressed Moon changes houses. The vital energies seem to flow more freely and spontaneously when the progressed Moon is in a fire or air house, whereas they seem to be held down or inhibited when in a water or earth house. For example, suppose a person who has had the progressed Moon in the 8th house for two and a half years is now experiencing the Moon's entrance into the 9th house. That person's entire demeanor is likely to change, from a heavy, intense, introspective mood to one of optimism, adventure, and even playfulness.

As mentioned in Chapter 5, another factor relevant to the use of the progressed Moon's house position is the common phenomenon of a decisive event or experience taking place just before the Moon is about to leave a certain house and enter the next one. I would not suggest that such a transition of the Moon from one house to another will always correlate with an important and definite experience, but—using the Koch system of houses—I have so often seen such an occurrence just as the Moon gets to within six or eight degrees of the next cusp that I always keep alert to the possibility. The journey of the progressed Moon through any given house may be described as follows, and this pattern applies also to Saturn's transit through any house: When the planet is at the beginning of a house, we often have to "make decisions" or at least come to a more conscious realization of a new direction for our energy and growth; when at the end of a house, the results of our plans and efforts (as well as the pattern of our karma in that area of life) are manifested, often quite definitely and concretely. It is as if the potentials that at first were just abstract—alive only on the level of ideas and imaginings—become catalyzed in a specific form. And, once this has happened, one often finds that the entire area of life shown by that house has become more settled and that it now feels more comfortable and familiar to the person.

There is also another parallel between transiting Saturn and the progressed Moon: namely, the return of each to its natal place between the ages of 27 and 30. Whereas the Saturn return deals with accepting your destiny, especially in relation to the outer world, the progressed Moon's return is a more private, subjective matter. Somewhat like the Saturn return period, it is a time of learning to accept your self as you really are and to accept your inner needs and feelings as real and vital. But perhaps the most important implication of the progressed Moon's return is that it gives you the opportunity to become *comfortable* with yourself at last! Parental, social, religious, and educational pressures have all combined to make us uncertain of who we are and indeed uncertain whether it is even all right to be what we are. Therefore, most of us develop a mistrust of parts of ourselves, and we often feel vaguely uncomfortable with those parts of our nature which have not received the stamp of approval from some authoritative source. But, as the progressed Moon returns, we can begin to leave behind our childhood insecurities and to settle into being what we have come to know that we are, without guilt, tension, or self-conscious awkwardness. The sign and aspects of the natal Moon are important to note in this regard; for the Moon's natal sign shows certain qualities that we can now begin to express more freely and its aspects reveal the degree of tension that can now be released and transformed into constructive, creative energy.

The Progressed Moon through the Houses

Rather than repeating the traditional meanings of the various houses or attempting to describe all the possible manifestations of the progressed Moon in a certain house, in this brief section I simply want to outline a few of the general trends that seem to be experienced most often by all sorts of individuals.

House I: the beginning of a new cycle, when people often feel they are "coming into their own" after having been held back by all sorts of factors beyond their control (especially when the Moon was in the 12th house). More independence and confidence is apparent, and one relates to the outer world and experiences life in general with greater immediacy and spontaneity. Can be a feeling of liberation!

House II: settling into a rhythm of work, making a living, and planning your life with more consistency. Laying the groundwork for many kinds of security (especially material security), based on deeper and more practical values.

House III: one is responsive to other people spontaneously, for one is aware that he or she can learn from anyone. There is often a new openness and a strong desire to have a wide variety of experiences, as well as the awareness that one needs to learn to become more versatile.

House IV: one becomes aware of the end of a cycle and the stirrings of a new one. A time of retreat, preparation, perhaps staying at home more than before. Almost always a reflective time when one needs privacy and some kind of social, domestic, or familial "womb" in which new parts of one's self may incubate and develop in a protective atmosphere.

House V: more confidence and exuberance. Sensing your abilities more accurately and more clearly realizing your potential for success and creativity, you begin to take risks in expressing yourself and in satisfying your needs for recognition, love, and pleasure. A time of "taking your measure" to see how much you really can accomplish if you are given *and give yourself* the chance.

House VI: purification of self. Can give new meaning to your life through self-analysis, dealing with your state of health, or setting yourself on a disciplined path of personal development or discipleship. Sometimes sets you back physically in order to prompt you to re-evaluate self and improve self. Sometimes a bit depressing, when you notice all that's wrong with you. Happiness during this time comes mainly from devoted work or service which can absorb your mental energy.

House VII: feeling a strong pull toward sharing and companionship. More energy goes into either one-to-one relationships or into dealings with the public (or both). New relationships start and old ones end, especially as the Moon gets toward the end of the house. More proclivity toward social involvements of all kinds.

House VIII: a deep orientation toward all life issues. For many people, one of the heaviest and most profound times in their lives. Occult, metaphysical, and spiritual interests are common, as is preoccupation with the negative polarity and its manifestations: lust, egotism, stinginess, and power-trips, all of which often cause strong inner conflicts and suffering. At best, a time of refining one's self and searching for deeper values after having broken through enough taboos that one's old socially-conditioned values have been seen to be shallow and empty. Often feels like being in purgatory.

House IX: an orientation toward expanding one's horizons, learning what is ultimately *true*, developing and improving self, and seeking some definite, idealistic way of life or set of beliefs. For those who are *seeking*, this is a period of incessant searching and questioning. For those who think they've found something, this is often a time for sharing that with others through speaking, lecturing, publishing, etc. Wide-ranging travel, inwardly or outwardly, is a strong urge.

House X: an ambitious orientation, constant thinking about attaining something or working toward something. An impersonal approach to life, wherein other people either fit into your practical aims or don't fit into your life at all. A strong urge to achieve something or to make your place in the world. This more often indicates a peak in *striving toward* achievement than actually attaining it (as many books indicate), especially so for people under 35 years old.

House XI: developing an increasing sense of social involvement, social responsibility, and duty, wherein one realizes one's *purpose* in relation to many other human beings (i.e., how you fit into their lives and which of their needs you meet). Often a sensitivity to one's popularity or lack of it and to being accepted by others. Can be a time of service to many people, sometimes by pouring out one's knowledge to them.

House XII: an important time when you are thrown back on yourself and feel cast adrift from all old moorings that once gave order and meaning to your life. Can be a time of loneliness (either because of circumstances or because of your inner need to retreat from the world). A time when all that can pass passes, leaving you with just the essence and the spiritual meaning of past experiences.

The sign position of the progressed Moon should also be given some consideration in every chart, although in my experience it rarely symbolizes anything extraordinarily important if considered separately from the Moon's house position. However, since a birthchart is an integrated whole, the ideal way to analyze the progressed Moon's meaning is to combine the sign's qualities with the characteristic significance of its particular house location. Some astrologers have told me that they seem to attract and often to become involved with people who are generally described by the progressed Moon's current sign position. I have not noticed that to be an invariable occurrence, but I have seen enough instances of this kind of trend to make such an idea worthy of future study.

The Progressed Moon's Aspects

The most important aspects formed by the Moon as it progresses through any chart are, as mentioned before, the conjunction, square, and opposition. In most cases, when the Moon makes these aspects to natal planets, there will be a perceptible development or experience, although there are occasional exceptions. However, in my own experience, the conjunctions of the progressed Moon have never failed to correlate with significant and noticeable events, experiences, or realizations; and so, I consider the conjunction to be by far the most powerful and reliable aspect, followed in order by the opposition and then the square. In addition, it is useful to note any other exact aspect made by the progressed Moon (including even the sextile and quincunx), for—while such aspects do not regularly correspond to important developments—they also will be seen to "act" decisively in some instances. For example, I was married when the progressed Moon sextiled my Venus *exact to the minute*, although at the time I had no knowledge of progressions; and it was in fact the only indicator of a possible marriage which was even close to exact at that time. But all in all, I feel that just focusing on the conjunctions, squares, and oppositions of the progressed Moon can give the practitioner most of the *useful* data which may be derived from this progression technique. The progressed Moon is so significant, not only because it often correlates with inner changes but also because its aspects so often mark important outer events: meetings with new people who will be important in your life for some time to come; new interests and activities which will develop in the future; and important transitions, journeys, and decisions. In fact, the progressed Moon aspects will manifest as definite *outer events* even a greater percentage of the time than do the progressed Sun aspects. It is as if the progressed Moon symbolizes the hand of a clock which ticks off karmic events and situations which we need to meet in the outer world. By no means will all such important events be symbolized by the progressed Moon's aspects; but the most powerful progressed Moon aspects do often symbolize important events or experiences not shown by other methods.

Using a rigid orb of 1° or 2° for these aspects is not nearly so useful as utilizing an orb of *time*. As a general guideline, I recommend using a *maximum* of a one-month orb (before and after the exact aspect) during which time the potential situation indicated may manifest. This seems to be an accurate approach, according to my experience; and the rationale for it is simply that many progressions (and transits also) don't seem to "act" until the transiting Moon trips them off. Hence, by using a one-month orb, there will be two different times when the transiting Moon conjuncts each point involved in the progressed aspect. My overall view of timing the progressed Moon's duration of power confirms C.E.O. Carter's observation. He says that the progressed lunar aspects *usually* act for a month or so, unless it is a conjunction or opposition, which he calls "the most potent contacts" and which, he says, can occasionally act for a somewhat longer period.

Other Important Progressions

The only other progressions that I want to mention in this chapter are those which involve one of the four angles of the chart. These are of two types, and both of them often correlate with major life developments. They may be described as follows:

1) Aspects formed by the progressed Ascendant or Midheaven to natal planets, which therefore simultaneously involve the progressed Descendant or Imum Coeli as well.

2) Aspects formed by a progressed planet as it conjuncts the angles of the natal chart.

The first classification of progressed aspects can be confusing to students of astrology since there are so many ways of progressing the Midheaven or Ascendant. I always advise beginning students simply to use the Solar Arc method of progressing these points, i.e., just adding to the natal Ascendant and Midheaven the total degrees and minutes of longitude that the progressed Sun has traveled. The other most common method of progressing the Ascendant is to look up the Midheaven (as progressed by the Solar Arc method) in a table of houses and find the Ascendant that corresponds to your given latitude. In his book *Some Principles of Horoscopic Delineation*, C.E.O. Carter places great emphasis on these types of progressions:

> The aspects formed by the progressed ascendant and mid-heaven . . .
> are known to be amongst the most potent of all stellar indices,
> producing, almost if not quite invariably, events of an epochal
> character. The aspects of the progressed Sun can alone vie with this class
> in respect of importance and somewhat lower in the scale perhaps,
> come aspects by progressed bodies to the radical angles. (p. 74)

When one's progressed Ascendant or Midheaven contact natal planets
(especially by conjunction), one begins to absorb the qualities, energies,
and activities symbolized by those planets into one's life with
immediacy; and these aspects often mark periods of decision-making,
new realizations, or important events.

The aspects formed by various progressed planets to the natal
Ascendant and Midheaven (again, especially the conjunctions) usually
indicate that the dimension of experience represented by the
progressed planet is coming to one's attention in a particularly direct
way. The aspects to the Midheaven usually represent factors that have a
bearing on your long-range plans, ambitions, or life-structure; whereas
the aspects to the Ascendant tend to indicate a new development in your
personal life, a shift in awareness, an important new interest, or an
alteration in your mode of self-expression. For example, if progressed
Venus conjuncts the Midheaven, there may be some development in
your long-range plans, in your vocational outlook, or in your place in
society which seem promising and pleasant. On the other hand, if
progressed Venus conjuncts the natal Ascendant, it is more likely that the
dimension of experience symbolized by Venus will come to your
attention in some immediate personal way, e.g., a love affair, financial
developments, artistic activities, or pleasant social contacts, any of which
may awaken you to the significance of Venus in your particular
birthchart. The progressed planets' conjunctions to the other angles (the
Descendant and Imum Coeli) can also be important and should also
be given consideration. Such conjunctions often signify noticeable
developments in one's relationships (Descendant) or one's homelife
and living situation (Imum Coeli), as might be expected from the
traditional meaning of these points. However, since the
Ascendant/Descendant and the MC/IC form axes of power and energy
flow within the birthchart, a conjunction to any of the four angles will
often manifest in a way that is obviously reminiscent of the opposite
point. In understanding such progressions, therefore, it is advisable to
take into consideration the polarity action between opposite points and
opposite houses. For example, a conjunction to the Midheaven may well
manifest as buying a new home (Imum Coeli). This is simply one more
indication of the fact that the birthchart is not an assemblage of unrelated factors but rather a unified, resonating *whole*.

Sagittarius

9

Cycles of Transformation: Part II
Transits

There is no coming to consciousness without pain.
—C. G. Jung

In this chapter, I primarily want to present a rather brief synthesis of a vast topic, emphasizing the transformative and growth-promoting potentials of transits. Hence, I will attempt to explain certain essential meanings of various types of transits, elucidating their practical use both as symbols of specific types of experience and as timing indicators of rather predictable phases of intensive personal change. Since there are a number of excellent books which deal with transits in a systematic way, and since a few of them are quite comprehensive, I feel there is no need to illustrate the various principles by listing set interpretations of each possible transit. Such a treatment of transits can only be presented in a fairly sizeable book devoted to nothing but that topic. Among the best books on transits are: Lewi's *Astrology for the Millions,* which after more than thirty-five years is still worth detailed study; Robert Hand's *Planets in Transit;* and a new and extremely interesting treatment of transits from a humanistic and holistic perspective by Swiss astrologer Alexander Ruperti, *Cycles of Becoming.** Therefore, rather than boring the reader by repeating many factors which have been discussed in other books, I am interested here in providing a concise overview of the value of transits for understanding transformative periods in life, as well as some guidelines for using transits which I have found to be meaningful and reliable.

I would like to emphasize here something that is rarely pointed out in published writings on transits and which has taken me many years to realize: namely, the essential simplicity of transits. All of astrology is really very simple; it deals primarily with four fundamental energies (the four elements), and each planetary principle shows a focal point of energy flow. Hence, all transits merely stimulate (or activate) these energies to flow in a certain way and with a certain rhythm. For example, all transits to natal Venus are similar in that they *all* activate the Venus principle in your chart; in other words, they all energize the dimension of experience shown by Venus and affect the flow of the elemental

---
Cycles of Becoming: The Planetary Pattern of Growth is due to be published by CRCS Publications in the summer of 1978.

energy shown by Venus' sign position. But each planet's transits activate or affect this energy flow and experience in a different way. The most important transits are those of the outer five planets (with the exception of close aspects made by the New Moon to natal points) since they stir up the unconscious and bring you into touch with the essence of the natal factor. All transits of the outer five planets, as it were, put pressure on the unconscious, in order to prompt you to change, to transform, to let go and—more than anything else—to be aware! Indeed, one might say that all transits are *ultimately* the same. Although this generalization will no doubt elicit a response of bewilderment or outrage from many astrologers, it may seem less radical if one considers the following points:

1) Each individual person is a living *unit,* and all transits to a particular chart reflect changes taking place within that particular person. If a transit affects one part of the whole, it affects the whole; hence, while a specific transit focuses upon one or two particular dimensions of experience in that person's life, in reality it affects the whole person.

2) All transits confront you with experiences that you are ready to deal with; whether or not you consciously *know* that the time is ripe for such experiences, transits tend to bring to awareness those parts of yourself and those dimensions of your life that are ready to be realized and assimilated. If you align yourself with your true pattern of being and rhythm of growth by realizing that life is a *learning* experience and that whatever you may experience is *good for you* from the viewpoint of your higher self's development, very few transits (if any) will totally surprise you because you'll have sensed the *need* for such an experience. In fact, you may have consciously wanted it beforehand, even if you knew that it would entail considerable stress, work, or even suffering. But in many cases, the person's conscious orientation is rigidly opposed to what is really needed. In those cases, the individual's response to unforeseen or challenging experiences seems to be: "I don't want it! Take it away from me!" and his or her behavior is similar to a child's throwing a tantrum.

The simplicity of transits is also shown by the fact that there are only twelve fundamental principles in astrology. Hence, all transits *of a particular planet* to your natal planets or important points are similar since that specific vibration is especially active in your life during the time the transit is in effect. For example, all Pluto transits connote somewhat similar periods in your life, since during that time the Pluto vibration and function will be especially powerful. That basic Pluto force will be felt to some extent whether the transit is to the Ascendant, Sun, Moon, Venus, or another planet. (Although the transits to the personal planets and Ascendant are *usually* the most important, there are many exceptions.) Therefore, when we see a particular transit approaching, we should indeed try to understand it as thoroughly as possible in all its possible ramifications; but we should not lose sight of the fact that, if for example transiting Pluto is aspecting *any* natal planet, this will be a *Plutonian time* in the person's life! Being aware of the overall quality of a given time period is just as important as being able to list many details of the possible experiences that may accompany a particular transit. And, especially in the common cases when many major transits are active during the same time period, an astrological counselor who attempts to explain to a client (who has no astrological knowledge) all the details of each current transit can easily fail in his or her duty to outline some pattern of order in that individual's life. The counselor may in that case merely be temporarily substituting a mass of confusing details for a mass of confusing emotions. But on the other hand, if the astrological counselor slowly and clearly explains the *general* vibrations that are active at that time *in the person's entire life* (rather than just in various unrelated conceptual categories of experience), the counselor will have taken a great step toward revealing some semblance of order which the person can grasp and draw strength from.

I would estimate that more than 70% of my clients in the past five years first called me for consultations when they were experiencing at least two (and often three or four) major transits. Although one important transit can indeed symbolize a radical change and a crucial transition period, it seems that most people who reach a level of tension, conflict, or confusion which prompts them to seek out professional help are going through more than one such transit simultaneously. If, for example, George is having Jupiter transiting in conjunction with his Ascendant, transiting Pluto square his Venus-Mercury conjunction, and transiting Uranus squaring his Moon all at the same time, he will inevitably undergo major changes, powerful stress periods, and radical re-orientations for more than a year. It may be appropriate to explain each *specific* transit in enough detail that he can relate to it; but such an elaboration of details should be followed by a *summary* of the entire time period's *general* quality and tone. George can then recall as much of the detail as he finds useful during the next year or so, but he will be especially likely to remember the counselor's summary of that entire period, thus giving him an overall perspective on that time of his life.

I mentioned above that some people's reactions to "unpleasant" experiences during various transits are like a child's temper tantrum, an emotional resistance to dealing with pain. An excellent explanation of the entire subject of one's attitude toward pain appeared in a series of articles by Donna Cunningham in *Horoscope* magazine a few years ago. The series was called "A Spiritual-Psychological Perspective on Transits," and it is one of the best things I have ever read on this topic.* In Part I of that series, Cunningham writes that "some of our emotional pain is actually a kind of temper tantrum at not being given what we want when we want it" and that "much of the pain of transits seems to come from resistance to change." She also explains a positive way of viewing pain in terms of growth potential:

> ....pain is the proverbial cry for help; if we heed it, if we do something constructive about it, we can prevent further complications and enter a healthier time of our lives.
>
> Pain often comes during the process of readjusting to a greater demand, but the organism grows to accommodate the demand; soon the higher

---

*These articles have been expanded and included in Donna Cunningham's new book, *An Astrological Guide to Self-Awareness* (published by CRCS Publications). This book also includes valuable treatment of many other astrological subjects from a psychological, growth-oriented perspective; and it is written in positive, down-to-earth language that is indeed refreshing.

level of functioning is no longer painful, but actually feels normal to us. On the spiritual level, too, we may experience some pain as we try to stretch ourselves; but we soon function better than ever. It is often a hard transit that gives us the impetus to stretch ourselves or that provides the conditions under which we are forced to stretch ourselves if we are not doing so voluntarily.

....a great deal of the pain of transits is, I believe, no more than a side effect of the process of strengthening, healing, and growing that goes along with any major transit. We err in focusing our attention on the pain rather than on the growth process.....

Cunningham also explains that "transits are not isolated events over which you have no control but instead are part of an integral psychological process that you are participating in." In fact, as she points out, a good way of using transits in counseling is always to ask the person what has been going on for the past year or so, while looking up the major transits that were in effect during that earlier time period. By doing so, we can not only get a feeling for the momentum of personal changes that the individual is still feeling even now, but we can also get important clues about how the person usually deals with such cosmic promptings toward growth by judging how he or she faced such challenges in the past. Once we understand the individual's habitual way of approaching critical phases of life, we can more easily adjust our way of expressing what he or she is going through in the present. And also, such questioning can begin to show us how the abstract symbols in the person's natal chart are actually manifesting in everyday experience. Without some feeling for the way the dynamics of the birthchart are expressed in actual experience, it is very difficult to fully understand specific transits, let alone predict what such celestial facts will represent in the future. But of course, I personally am much more interested in *understanding* than in predicting, for by focusing on predictions we take the person's attention off the real ongoing process at hand. Cunningham, who is a licensed social worker and who has a great deal of experience in what constitutes effective counseling, says much the same thing in her writings:

Too much attention is paid to events in astrology and not enough to the process that brings them about. Actually, events are more like signposts—more visible than the process, naturally. But you didn't jump from one town to the next; you covered the distance gradually. Events may be the culmination of a process or may be a catalyst that starts a process, but they are most useful to study as outer indicators of an inner trend. Transit readings that focus only on events miss out on a potent tool for self-knowledge and change.

During important transits, one can feel an inner urge toward change (if one is in touch with oneself) or one can encounter the promptings toward change through outer circumstances, *or both*. Transits may be viewed as barometers which *reflect* the changes in one's inner "environment," and often outer circumstances will also reflect the inner state, especially if one needs encouragement to look inward. The transits cannot be separated from the person or from his or her growth processes. Especially during the important transits of the outer five planets, which are the ones we will concentrate on in this chapter, you can allow yourself to be transformed and thus to go *through* the experience thoroughly and deeply, or you can dwell on outer circumstances and try to escape from them and from the inner pressure toward change which corresponds with them. A person who takes the latter approach will probably try to go on acting out old patterns of thought and behavior once the transit passes, but in a new situation. Such an attempt is likely to have bewildering results since the old behavior patterns will now seem awkward, empty, and unnatural, creating considerable frustration and disorientation. And what's more, the person will be compelled to face these same issues again the next time a similar transformative cycle is set in motion.

Transits & Karma

Transits show *how* one's energies (and karma) are released, not necessarily *what* is released. In other words, they reveal a characteristic *quality* of experience, although we can't usually know in advance precisely what experience is indicated. The transits tick off the karmic clock, each one activating a current of energy (or wave of karma) in a certain way. They vary in the speed, quality, intensity, depth, and force with which they bring things to awareness. (See the following section for specifics on how each transiting planet differs.) During any transit, we may be either sowing seeds of new karma or harvesting karma that was activated previously. In most cases, it is impossible to know whether we are simply encountering karma from the past or whether we are creating new karma with which we will have to deal at a later time, or a mixture of both. Therefore, we should approach all experiences assuming that we are creating new karma and thus use some degree of caution when the situation seems to call for it. But, if our *best* efforts fail to keep us out of a certain entanglement or activity which we feel to be a negative influence upon our spiritual growth, we might assume that this is past karma coming ripe for payment.

As Donna Cunningham's above quotation indicated, events may be either a culmination of a process or a catalyst which starts a process. Similarly, although there is no certain way of knowing whether one is harvesting karma or sowing new seeds, there is a general distinction among some transits that should be pointed out. Transits of Saturn and Pluto are very often harvesting times, periods when we are confronted with the results of past actions and thoughts. In fact, this is how Saturn came to be known as the "planet of karma" throughout the ages, for its transits often correlate with obviously destined events. And Pluto's transits often reveal a somewhat similar pattern of experience which not only seems destined but indeed often seems completely unfathomable.

The transits of Jupiter and Uranus, on the other hand, very often correlate with seeding times, when potential future developments are revealed to us. During certain Jupiter transits, especially when Jupiter conjuncts the Ascendant, we are often given prophetic glimpses of the future, either through dreams, intuitive flashes, or simply through a new future-oriented train of thought that comes into mind strongly at such periods. I have also witnessed this trend toward having prophetic dreams, hunches, or visions while transiting Jupiter was aspecting the natal Sun, either by conjunction or trine; and future developments in both instances have born out the truth of these prophetic glimpses. The connection of Jupiter transits to prophetic experiences correlates with the fact that the Jupiter sign Sagittarius has always been known as a sign of prophecy and future-oriented aspirations. (Note for example the visionary, prophetic poems and drawings of William Blake, who was born with Jupiter conjunct the Sun in Sagittarius.) One should naturally be careful about accepting such an experience as a divine revelation of absolute truth, especially if one is inclined to be overly Jupiterian or Neptunian. But such glimpses *can* be extremely valuable not only as guidelines for future plans and activities but also as a source of the strength and confidence which only some kind of inner knowledge can provide. It should also be stated that not all people will readily tune in on such future intimations, for some people are not sufficiently open to perceive them, some are not aware enough to recognize them, and some people simply think too much to allow the comprehensive nature of Jupiterian visions into their analytical minds.

Likewise, during Uranus transits (especially to the Ascendant, Sun, or Ascendant's ruling planet) one may also receive flashes of insight which constitute a seed for future developments. What is experienced then may take ten years or more to be actualized in the material world, but the excitement and quickness with which such an experience is received is often felt to be a reliable indication of the fact that whatever seeds are being planted then will inevitably bear fruit in some time to come. Experiences such as these during Jupiter and Uranus transits are further examples of the phenomenon that I mentioned in Chapter 5: namely, that we often get messages and instructions during periods when important transits are active. Whether one says that such messages come from the planets themselves, from spiritual agencies, from the unconscious mind, or from some other source really makes very little difference. The fact is that what we *experience* at such times can often be described as a particular planet's having a dialogue with us and providing us with specific information which is immediately useful.

We can also derive some information about transits' relation to karma by looking at the houses occupied by transiting planets. The most important houses in such a consideration are almost always the ones where we find transiting Jupiter and Saturn. The personal planets travel through any given house much too quickly to regularly indicate important trends, although occasionally the house where one finds transiting Mars will indicate a significant focus of activity. And, on the other hand, the house positions of transiting Uranus, Neptune, and Pluto are not usually very useful factors for the astrological counselor's purposes (with the exception of times when these planets change houses, especially when they cross one of the four angles of the chart). This is so because each of them stays so long in one house; an individual therefore gets used to that vibration in a particular area of his or her life within a relatively short time. However, Jupiter remains in one house for about one year, and Saturn for about two and a half years, periods of time which the client can see as marking significant phases of life. The house positions of Jupiter and Saturn are therefore of chief importance since they reveal so much about the structure, quality, and rhythm of one's cyclic participation in the world at large.

How one experiences the Jupiter and Saturn transits of the houses either above or below the horizon depends almost entirely on one's fundamental orientation to life. If you are a rather introverted, reflective sort of person who prefers to live a private, inward lifestyle, then you may well feel that the transits *above* the horizon correlate with activities that you *have to* do rather than things you personally *want to* do. When Jupiter and/or Saturn transit above the horizon, you may find that you have to deal with all sorts of outer necessities, obligations, and circumstances. (One whose natural inclination is more extraverted may find such a time extremely satisfying, since outer objectives and duties play a larger role in his or her life.) If you are an inwardly-oriented person, then when Jupiter and/or Saturn transit the houses *below* the horizon, you tend to become involved in and work at those areas of life at least in part because you are more personally motivated to do so by your own need for security and happiness. A more extraverted person may feel at such times that he or she is being *forced* to turn within, away from the distractions and energy-consuming activities of the outer world.

In general, when Jupiter is transiting above the horizon, you have to expand your activities toward greater involvement in the outer world, in order to feel confident and in tune with life's rhythms. You are more sensitive to *other* people's needs, desires, and expectations, and you feel the need to get along with them. *Much of your support comes from outside yourself.* But when Jupiter begins to transit the first house, and while it is under the horizon, you feel more confident about doing what *you* want to, simply because it's *you* and without so much regard for others' advice and approval. You gain inner assurance and confidence while Jupiter is under the horizon. You feel the expansive and protective vibration of Jupiter *within* you at that time, and hence you don't have to care so much about what others do or say. Likewise with Saturn, whereas Saturn's passage through the last six houses may involve you in many outer duties, obligations, and karmic burdens, its journey through the first six houses marks a time when your serious work and concerns are found mainly at a personal and rather private level. Saturn's transit under the horizon is thus a time when you work out karma related to personal anxieties, insecurities, and basic capacities and abilities.

Keynotes of Transits' "Influence"

Experiences corresponding with the transits of the various planets are often described in terms of the "influence" an individual feels in his or her life at that time. The following is a concise series of key concepts related to each *transiting planet:*

PLUTO: brings to the surface and transforms, often ending an old form of life or expression completely.

NEPTUNE: undermines, dissolves, sensitizes, refines, and spiritualizes.

URANUS: speeds up the rhythm of nature, hastening change; disrupts, revolutionizes, & brings to awareness whatever was just below the threshhold of consciousness.

SATURN: delays and slows the rhythm of nature, thus concentrating your experience; constricts; confronts one with a realistic approach to life.

JUPITER: opens doors for new plans, aspirations, and improvements; tunes you into future possibilities; urges you to expand into new areas of experience.

MARS: upsets the usual rhythm of nature, energizing it and giving an urge toward action; often makes one impatient and temper-mental.

VENUS: harmonizes, smooths out the flow of experience and the expression of one's energies. Sometimes corresponds to pleasant news or a sense of relaxation from tension.

MERCURY: rarely important, but corresponds at times to communications & meetings that are significant.

SUN & MOON: must be taken together as a unit; hence, the New Moon's position is most important since it energizes anything it aspects. The Full Moon can also activate natal planets.

A few more words of explanation are in order concerning the use of the Sun and Moon as transits. Although many books list the "influence" of the transiting Sun or Moon alone, the transits of the Moon are rarely significant *in themselves,* although they do seem to activate other transits (and progressions) which are in effect at that time. The transits of the Sun are likewise rarely significant in themselves, although they do occasionally correspond to noticeable qualities of experience for a day or so. However, the Sun and Moon constitute a complete polarity and unit of energy flow together, and so they must be used in relation to each other in transits. Any study of transits should therefore include the use of the New and Full Moons. The New Moon especially is extremely powerful in that it often strongly activates a natal planet if it aspects it by conjunction, opposition, or—to a lesser extent—by square. The New and Full Moons seem to have no characteristic quality or "influence" in themselves; they simply energize whatever is shown as potential in the natal chart. Very often, the New Moon aspecting a natal planet will be the only indicator of an important experience.

Some of the New or Full Moons will also be Solar or Lunar Eclipses, which celestial phenomena are traditionally supposed to be far more powerful than other Lunations and Full Moons. However, my experience leads me to believe that eclipses *for work with individuals' charts* are greatly over-rated. One should remember that the astrological traditions concerning the power of eclipses were developed during a time when the primary use of astrology was the forecasting of mundane events; and, in fact, those traditional rules may still apply to mundane astrology. I simply do not have enough experience in mundane astrology to judge; but some researchers have found significant meanings associated with not only eclipses themselves but also with eclipse paths as they cut across various nations. My feeling is that, in relation to individuals' charts, eclipses are not any more powerful than ordinary New or Full Moons, with the possible exception of those eclipses which are *visible* in one's current locality. Geocentric astrology is based completely on our vantage point from the earth's surface, and we should therefore be somewhat consistent in the application of this fundamental assumption. This means that we should see an eclipse as a specifically powerful message for us personally only in cases where it not only aspects an important natal chart point but also is visible where we are living. Otherwise, my feeling is that we should simply view eclipses as similar to any other New or Full Moons.

A New Moon is sufficiently powerful that it can energize some field of experience (symbolized by a natal house) even if it makes no close aspect to a natal planet. Such experiences are not usually as important as those shown by close aspects, but there is often a pronounced mood, type of activity, or tone during that period. For example, if the New Moon falls in the 3rd or 9th house, it is not uncommon to travel more during the following month. If the Lunation falls in the fifth house, we may have stronger urges toward pleasures, gambling, free spending, and other 5th house matters. The New Moon falling in the 12th house each year marks for some people an annual period of reflecting on the past or of confronting the results of the thoughts and desires of the previous year. The New Moons, in other words, constitute the key for understanding those yearly cycles that many people (even many who don't "believe" in astrology) notice as regular patterns in their lives. For example, we have all heard friends say something like: "All the important things in my life have happened to me in the fall" or "Every year at about this time I have trouble with my health." The use of the Lunation cycles will enable us not only to understand these annual trends, but also to time such periods more precisely.

Keynotes of Planets Activated by Transits

In this section I want to outline some characteristic meanings of the various planets *being activated by transits.* In other words, what is the general significance of a transit *to* a particular natal planet or point? When a specific planet is being aspected by any transiting planet, the dimension of experience shown by that natal planet is energized in some way. As mentioned earlier in this chapter, I feel that this kind of approach is useful as a way of sensing the simplicity of transits. For example, any number of transits to natal Mercury can manifest in somewhat similar ways: transits of Saturn, Uranus, or Pluto in challenging aspect to Mercury can all be felt—at least in part—as the urge to leave old friends and acquaintances behind. The motivation or the rationale behind such an urge will in each case be different: with Saturn, one doesn't want to waste time and mental energy on people who don't serve one's practical needs; with Uranus, one is impatient with the slowness and lack of excitement in such relationships; with Pluto, one is dissatisfied with the shallowness of the relationship since one needs more depth and intensity at that time. But in all cases, the *overt* behavior that grows from those inner urges may be almost identical.

PLUTO: Transits to natal Pluto affect one's use of one's inner powers and resources. Sometimes psychic experiences are evident, and in other cases various compulsive thought and behavior patterns are activated. Transits to Pluto are often not evident to those who have little awareness of their inner life. These transits sometimes mark the end of an entire chapter of life, especially if the transiting planet is Saturn, Uranus, or Neptune, leaving as a residue only an empty shell and distant memories.

NEPTUNE: Transits to Neptune are especially important for spiritually-oriented people. Since Neptune by itself represents a state of extreme passivity, it has to be activated by other planets (especially Saturn, Uranus, Pluto, or the New Moon) in order to manifest strongly and constructively. The specific transits just mentioned often indicate a time of transforming or defining one's ideals, facing one's escapism, or heightening one's psychic sensitivity. I have seen many people who experienced a particularly high level of consciousness when Uranus conjuncted natal Neptune. There is often a mild crisis when Saturn or Pluto activates Neptune, for both give an urge to *integrate* one's ideals or to purge oneself of escapist activities and self-deceptions. Often during these times, some circumstance compels us to face something that we have wanted to ignore. And often, but by no means always, it is a sexual problem (especially with transiting Pluto) since Western culture seems to specialize in self-deceptions, unrealistic ideals, hypocrisy, and major hang-ups in this area of experience; for Western cultures possess no vital myth or other way of accurately understanding the connection between the sex energy and spiritual realities (Neptune).

URANUS: Transits to natal Uranus affect how free one feels, how one expresses one's uniqueness and originality, and how one deals with restlessness and desires for change and excitement. These transits also have an impact on any exciting new ventures in which one is participating. One's concept of precisely what constitutes real independence often undergoes an important change when Uranus is activated by Jupiter, Saturn, Neptune, or Pluto.

SATURN: Transits to natal Saturn can have an impact on one's entire life structure and on all of one's long-term ambitions, but the emphasis is usually felt in the area of life which is most related to one's feelings of material security. Hence, whatever constitutes one's job, vocation, or daily work is most often the focus of these changes; and this includes the role of housewife and mother just as much as any role in the professional world. While a transit of Jupiter to Saturn often correlates with an improvement or expansion of one's vocational situation, a transit of Uranus, Neptune, or Pluto is often felt to be a period of marked insecurity and uncertainty about one's work and social status.

JUPITER: Transits to Jupiter primarily affect one's future plans and aspirations, whether that specifically involves business or financial ventures, educational or travel plans, or the general direction of one's efforts at self-improvement through religious, philosophical, or metaphysical activities. Therefore, the transits of the outer four planets to Jupiter often have the effect of significantly altering one's future plans and one's awareness of their true potential.

MARS: Transits to Mars are felt as changes in the way you assert yourself and in the methods you are using to attain your goals. An increased clarity about *what you want* is usually evident (except in the case of a Neptune transit), as is a marked change in your physical and sexual energy flow. For men, there is often a striking change in their feelings of strength and in their confidence in their masculinity, and in both sexes there is often an increased sense of competence and the capacity to assert their own desires.

VENUS: Transits to Venus are experienced as changes in one or more of a number of areas: relationship and emotional activities, financial affairs, aesthetic tastes, and personal values. These transits are also correlated directly with how happy and contented one is feeling in everyday life. For both sexes, there is often a marked change in their feelings of attractiveness and social ease; and women often experience important transitions in the development of their sexuality and confidence in their femininity.

MERCURY: The importance of transits to Mercury is often underestimated since they do not usually correlate with *immediate* radical changes in circumstance or with particularly painful crises. However, since transits to Mercury affect the very way one thinks and expresses his or her perceptions, and since "as ye think that shall ye become," these should receive just as much attention as any other important transit. Especially when the outer five planets aspect Mercury, there is a powerful effect on the way the conscious mind functions, in many cases eventually leading to an entirely different attitude toward life (even though the change may be subtle and not immediately evident to others) and/or an involvement with a new skill or area of study.

MOON: Transits to the natal Moon affect how one feels about oneself, how comfortable one is both with oneself and in one's current living situation, and how one views his or her involvements with children, parents, family life, or other areas connected with one's "roots." Security factors are uppermost in one's mind at this time, and one is often preoccupied with thoughts about where one *belongs* (i.e., where one feels truly comfortable). Women often develop a new awareness of their womanliness and what its implications are for their future plans. Both men and women, however, have the opportunity at this time to intensify their awareness of their own lunar nature: the gentle, yin, nurturing qualities of being.

SUN: Any transit to the natal Sun can be important, even those of Venus, Mercury, and Mars since anything that aspects the Sun comes to your conscious awareness immediately. These transits most often affect the way you seek to express yourself in a confident and integrated way, as well as having an impact on your creative potentials and sense of well-being. They are important in your overall attitude toward life and in your way of expressing your entire self; they also have a direct impact on your physical vitality.

A transit to any planet may be important for a particular individual, depending upon how that person is attuned to that planetary vibration. If a planet is the ruler of the Ascendant, Sun sign, or Moon sign, the impact will almost always be greater than if that planet is relatively unassociated with the major themes in the chart. The area of life symbolized by the house that a specific planet "rules" will also very often come to one's attention when that planet is being transited by other planets. For example, if Mercury rules your 6th house, a transit of one of the outer planets in challenging aspect to Mercury will not only manifest as the sorts of changes found in almost all Mercury transits, but it will also often correlate with important developments in your work, employment, or health. Any conjunction of either the Ascendant or Descendant by one of the outer five planets is usually significant, often in a dramatic and immediate way that has long-term ramifications. Such transits affect not only your approach to life in general and your confidence in who you are, but also your state of health and your level of vitality. Transits to the Ascendant's ruling planet are of similar importance and also have a powerful effect on one's health and overall tone of self-expression. As an ancient astrological law states: When a planet transits over the Ascendant, it brings the concerns of the house(s) it rules to your personal attention. I have found that rule to be quite accurate, and therefore it is worth paying attention to all transits over the Ascendant; for even a Venus or Mercury transit over the Ascendant may be extraordinarily significant if that planet is especially powerful in your chart. It should also be added that any planet in the natal chart closely aspecting the Sun and/or Moon or in the first house is highly sensitive since you are especially attuned to its energy. Transits to such planets are therefore unusually important and are strongly felt.

Transits of the Outer Five Planets

In the following sections, I want to recapitulate some of the essential principles of these transiting planets and present these principles in a concise way in order that they can be used quite readily even by new students of astrology. By this point, it should be clear why these five planets' transits are being emphasized over the transits of the other planets, but mentioning a few examples of each should prove useful as a way of synthesizing the many ideas already mentioned.

Jupiter Transits

Jupiter's transit through any natal house may be concisely described as a time when one can: 1) gain a more comprehensive understanding of that area of life through wider experience; 2) expand the scope of that area of life and possibly improve it; and 3) act in a way that has future ramifications and/or is based on future considerations. With all Jupiter transits, there can be a tendency toward over-expansion, leading to dissipation of energy and resources. But, contrary to what many books on transits indicate, people often experience many of these transiting aspects (including the squares!) as times when they are prompted to act more confidently and to do what they have really *wanted* to do anyhow. In other words, all the expansion of personal plans and activities toward which you have long been urged can at these times be put into action because you have greater motivation to improve your current situation and also greater confidence in a positive result. It seems that more people are inclined to hold themselves back unnecessarily rather than to over-expand in daily life, and thus Jupiter transits provide a needed opportunity to break through these self-imposed restraints. Some examples of Jupiter transits may clarify these points.

With Jupiter transiting through the 1st house, one can: 1) more comprehensively understand the sort of self-expression that one really needs in order to feel vital and spontaneous; 2) expand the scope of one's self-expression; and 3) act in a way that is based on a future vision of one's ultimate, potential self-expression in the world. In my own case, I started to write an article on the astrological elements while Jupiter was in my 1st house (and opposing my natal Sun) and found that it spontaneously grew into an entire book which three different publishers offered to produce. That is how my book *Astrology, Psychology, & the Four Elements* came into being; I had not planned to write such a book at all and in fact had other books planned which were going to be my first order of business as soon as I finished my so-called article on the elements. Indeed, I was rather surprised to find that I had so much to say about the elements, but Jupiter's urge toward expansion and breadth cannot be denied at such times.

As another example of Jupiter's effect, two women clients who had severe sexual inhibitions both became much more adventurous and open-minded about sex while Jupiter was transiting through their 8th house; and both of them attained not only a much more comprehensive understanding of the sexual energy and its place in life, but also a greater awareness of their own sexual and emotional needs. Two other clients enlarged their businesses and raised their prices while transiting Jupiter *squared* natal Jupiter; and, contrary to what one might expect from certain statements about this transit in a number of books, both people experienced greater income and professional success from those expansive moves, with absolutely no negative ramifications. It is worth mentioning that the oppositions of transiting Jupiter are often more problematical than the squares. The squares are more dynamic and seem to prompt expansion, new action, or a new phase of development in a way that can be immediately acted upon. *Some* Jupiter oppositions are experienced in a similar way, as extremely positive and even "lucky" times, but others seem either to manifest as *excessive* blockage in some area or to expand the problematical expression of the natal planet being activated. For example, one man experienced severe cramps in his upper back when Jupiter opposed his natal Saturn in Leo. Another man held a sale at his business while transiting Jupiter opposed natal Venus and found that only a few people even showed up for the sale, resulting in no financial gain.

Transiting Jupiter's *conjunctions* to natal planets or to the angles of the chart are almost always powerful. Conjuncting the Sun, there is usually a gain in confidence and an increase of creative energy, even though obvious worldly success may not always occur simultaneously. (Growth in self-confidence also often accompanies the square, trine, and opposition of Jupiter to the natal Sun.) Conjuncting the Moon, there is also more confidence and a feeling of things flowing more effortlessly than usual. Some people tend to over-react to stimuli which ordinarily wouldn't affect them during this time, but that is more common when the aspect is a square or opposition. When Jupiter aspects Mercury by conjunction, there are often new plans, ideas, and rapid developments in one's educational aspirations. Jupiter's conjunction of its natal place is almost always a tremendously important period of reorientation and renewed faith, as well as increased religious feelings in some cases. This period generally lasts about a year and offers the opportunity to improve your life situation rapidly if you commit yourself to a new vision of the future. The main problematical manifestation of Jupiter's transits can be summed up in one word: *exaggeration*. If one can contain and moderate the exaggerated expression of one's energies during Jupiter transits, there is really no reason to hold oneself back from taking some big risks at such times in one's life; for there is the promise of not only large gains but also of greater self-understanding and contentment.

Saturn Transits

Since Saturn's principles and characteristics are explained quite thoroughly in Chapter 5, we only need to summarize a few key points here. The transits of Saturn in dynamic aspects to natal planets challenge you to deal with things realistically, especially those things you've been avoiding. These transits *may* correlate with problems, illnesses, delays, and frustrations, but only if you've been neglecting some responsibility to yourself or to others, or if you have not been evaluating things realistically. These transits don't *cause* problems; they simply pressure you to confront areas of your life where you lack discipline, structure, or inner strength. They test the quality of your life and your commitments, and they slow the natural rhythm of your life to the point where your experience during these periods is concentrated and deeply impressive.

Some examples of Saturn transits, other than those mentioned in Chapter 5, are in order here. Transiting Saturn's conjunction of natal Pluto is often accompanied by psychic or spiritual experiences, or at least by the inner urge to commit oneself to some form of self-transformation. There is often an increased awareness of one's deepest duties to one's own self and a strong urge to reform one's bad habits. One sixty year old woman met someone who taught her how to meditate on the day this transit was exact. A couple hours later, while at home, she sat down to try this technique of concentration, and she immediately left her body and beheld brilliant visions of light and splendor such as mystics from many cultures have described. She was filled with joy and faith more than ever before, and she described the experience as something she had been longing for her entire life! This example illustrates the fact that one's mental and psychic capacities are extremely powerful and concentrated during such times. One man experienced a variety of physical and psychological symptoms when Saturn squared his Mercury. There was a great deal of nervous tension, manifesting physically as a severe toothache (although no decay was present, according to dental examination). And during this period he was also doing a great deal of serious thinking, which, although it brought him to the brink of despondency, saved him from a lot of later trouble; for he decided at this time not to go into a business partnership that seemed to offer opportunities for financial gain. Later events, however, proved that he would have lost most of his investment and a great deal of time and energy if his practical thinking had not dissuaded him from participating in that venture. Two other people, one of whom had the conjunction and the other the square of transiting Saturn to natal Uranus, experienced frustration and a desire for greater freedom which new responsibilities were preventing. But, eventually, these people came to realize that the necessity to accept limitation at this time was a key factor in their beginning to develop a practical form of creativity and a practical application of their idealism and originality. One could say that Saturn's transits of Uranus can bring about an understanding of true, inner freedom and a deep level of excitement by your voluntarily taking on duties which will eventually give you a more structured way of using your originality.

One of the most interesting examples I have seen took place when a young man had transiting Saturn in opposition to his natal Jupiter. Saturn's transits to Jupiter usually mark periods of consolidating one's aspirations and plans for future growth and self-improvement, and his experience was no exception. However, although this type of transit is usually correlated with financial, educational, or intellectual developments, his experience was extraordinary. While Saturn opposed Jupiter, he had two separate visions on two different days, each of which seemed to impart strength and wisdom. One vision was of an American Indian who exemplified the patience and understanding which this man was noticeably lacking. The Indian seemed to be a guide, a spiritual helper who could always be counted on for help and support, especially in emergencies. The other vision was of a Viking warrior in full battle dress, which symbolized to the man the strength and courage he would need to express if he was to utilize all of his creative potentials to the full. He later summarized these experiences by saying that they gave him more *faith* (Jupiter!) and self-confidence since he then knew not only what deep resources he could drawn on (symbolized by the qualities of those archetypal figures) but he also came to know more realistically what he himself could become in the future.

Uranus Transits

I have already mentioned some of the fundamental meanings of Uranus transits in Chapter 3, and I have pointed out the correlation of Uranus with suddenness and speed. Uranus transits to any number of points in the natal chart correspond with a period in life when time passes more quickly and when the rhythm of life is speeded up in order to prompt you to take risks and to hasten experimentation and new growth. These transits don't necessarily *cause* sudden events, but they do often indicate times when we are acting unconsciously in ways that may attract such experiences. One of the best ways of expressing the essential principle involved in these transits is: that we can at this time gain a more detached, objective perspective on a particular dimension of experience *if* we allow ourselves to be open and to be freed of the encumbrances of tradition, habit, past conditioning, and socio-cultural prejudices. Like all transits of the trans-Saturnian planets, Uranus transits activate what is ready to happen *because* you've been growing. All the urges toward new growth that you haven't yet acted on (thus building up the energy into a formidable reservoir of inner tension) are confronted quickly at such times. The challenge to grow *freely* and rapidly is brought into immediate focus. In fact, Uranus transits often mark times when we realize that we have *outgrown* our old patterns of life. Of course we often tend to linger in our old ruts and routines out of fear, inertia, desires for security, or anxiety about imagined changes, even though we *have* outgrown these old ways of living. However, when Uranus transits natal planets or angles, all the changes necessary for future growth suddenly confront us. Although we may not recognize it, what happens then has been, in most cases, programmed by our increasingly discontented thoughts, feelings, and behavior. Even if we then experience something traumatic which we obviously didn't want at all (e.g., the death or move of a close friend), we may see some months or years later that it was good for us, that it freed us to become more independent and to learn how to fend for ourselves. The essential meaning of a Uranus transit is that it *awakens* us to our true state of *freedom from that which we've outgrown.* It frees us from whatever we are no longer bound to by duty, fear, karma, or necessity; and it awakens us to an independent state of being and to our unique life purpose.

Some examples should be helpful. One man quit his routine job when transiting Uranus squared his Sun, for he then realized that it was time to pursue the creative types of work which he had envisioned as a child but which he had since ignored. Another man, when Uranus conjuncted the natal Sun, was unundated with rapid instruction from other dimensions about cosmic laws, spiritual evolution, and astrological truths. He also realized that his true nature required a partner and that a real state of personal freedom was impossible for him unless he was married. And therefore, he met someone and married very quickly during this time. In each case, there was a marked awakening to the truth of the person's essential nature. A twenty-four year old woman, during transiting Uranus' square to her ruling planet Mercury, came to realize that she had outgrown many old ways of thinking, acting, and even dressing (note that the Ascendant *and* its ruling planet are related to the appearance). She cut off most of her hair, began to learn an Oriental meditative art of movement, and started working part time instead of full time in order to have more freedom to pursue creative activities. All of these realizations had been coming on for at least one or two years, manifesting as discontent and strong urges for a radical change, but the change wasn't ripe to be acted on, nor were those urges toward change given definite form and direction until the aspect got close to exact. A man who had Uranus transiting in square to his natal Saturn realized then that he was indeed free to work at what he liked and was excited about, rather than having to stick to old work patterns simply to earn money. He awakened to a sense of freedom from old duties, obligations, and fear-motivated habits; and he therefore quit his old career entirely to pursue a creative line of work full time. Before he acted on that urge, the old work was beginning to feel so boring and frustrating that he was almost on the verge of a nervous collapse.

Uranus transits of Venus and Mars are almost always felt as powerful urges toward sexual and/or emotional experimentation; and, although such experiences are often extremely threatening to established relationships (such as marriage), the objectivity gained either through acting out or at least confronting those urges in many cases enables the person to improve existing relationships afterwards. During the actual transits, there is usually considerable turmoil; and the Uranus challenging aspects to natal Mars are especially tumultuous and often manifest as violent cravings for new exciting action. But there can be an *awakening* at these times to one's true Venus or Mars needs and to new ways of expressing those energies which may never have been thought of before. And, as mentioned earlier, Uranus transits to natal Neptune are often correlated with an awakening to the reality of spiritual or transcendent levels of being, during which the person may quite spontaneously experience a level of consciousness which can only be described as mystical.

Neptune Transits

Most of Neptune's essential principles were also discussed in Chapter 3. We need only summarize here by saying that Neptune transits invariably attune a person to a realm of intangibles. Although often felt as confusing periods of great uncertainty, they can also be experienced as times of inspiration or even initiation through a refining and spiritualizing of one's self in the way indicated. These periods are potentially times of learning the subtler lessons of life and of realizing that intangible, non-material factors are more important and powerful than the mundane matters of everyday life which most people seem to consider as the ultimate reality. Through Neptune's vibration permeating one's consciousness, one can be (whether voluntarily or involuntarily) opened up to a realm of infinite possibilities which can prompt a tremendous broadening of awareness and even an attunement to universal and cosmic levels of being. Transits of Neptune give us an opportunity to refine our understanding, attitudes, and behavior based on an acute perception of intangible forces at work. We tend to be confused and spaced out at such times if we don't accept the challenge to attune ourselves to an ideal!

Some specific examples are especially necessary to enhance our understanding of Neptune transits since it is difficult to explain Neptune's transcendent vibration in any logical or systematic way. One thirty-four year old woman went through a period of deep personal changes as transiting Neptune squared her natal Sun repeatedly for over one and a half years. During this time, her husband of twelve years left her but would not commit himself to either eventually returning or wanting a permanent separation. She was therefore left up in the air, not knowing whether she should start a new life herself or wait for him to make a definite decision. She also developed an interest in astrology, reincarnation, and other related fields which helped her gain a perspective on what she was going through. These studies gave her a spiritual view of life for the first time, and in fact helped give her the strength to make the decision to divorce him and to launch out on her own path of development instead of maintaining an unhealthy dependency on him. During this period, she gained a new sense of *freedom* and individuality (the Sun); and possibilities for growth began for the first time in her life to appear wide open and highly promising. A six year old boy, while Neptune conjuncted his natal Sun, was taken to a discourse by a spiritual master from India because the boy's mother was a devotee of this master's teachings. Without warning or hesitation, the boy suddenly ran up to the master and asked for initiation, something which ordinarily is never granted to anyone under twenty-one years of age. But, in this case, it must have been the time for this boy to contact a source of spiritual inspiration, for he was promised initiation and in fact was given an inner spiritual experience that left him speechless and radiant with happiness.

Neptune transits to natal Venus are particularly important in the development of a deeper, more refined understanding of love. One woman, while Neptune opposed her Venus, met a man under very unusual circumstances. Their relationship had a "fairy-tale" beginning, as if the connection were destined to be important. The relationship was therefore surrounded by a kind of glamour, which was discovered to be an illusion only as the transit began to pass. The man was a spiritually-oriented Pisces, and through him, she became acquainted with many other people of that type. (Note that Venus deals with all sorts of relationships, not solely romantic liaisons.) Her interest in and understanding of spirituality increased at this time, although this also had an aura of glamour, rather than involving truly serious study. Through this man's influence, the woman spent a considerable amount of money for a mind control class, although she was unclear and bewildered (Neptune!) about her own motivations for being there. In the class, however, she experienced her psychic ability in an immediate and surprising way. Only toward the end of the transit did she begin to become disillusioned with the *impersonal* way in which he related to her and to realize that she was more in love with an *image* than with a *person*. And, although she felt emotionally (and to some extent materially) "ripped off" by him, she now bears no resentment toward him because she feels that the experience was an important lesson in the growth of her understanding of love.

While Neptune conjuncted his natal Venus, another person found that his current love relationship began to dissolve. His idealized view of his lover was—to say the least—undermined when he found out that she had slept with his best friend. Before that time, he had tended to think of her as his own possession; and, through considerable pain, he now had to confront the jealousy and intense possessiveness which he always felt in *any* important relationship (with men *or* women). We can thus see that this one experience contained important lessons which could be generally applied to many areas of his life. (Again, the Neptunian tendency toward universalizing.) By going through the pain, he not only gained considerable detachment from his emotions and in fact refined his entire approach to love, but he also found that his feelings were opened up to the point where he could now consider taking steps toward relating to other women.

During many Neptune transits, the imagination runs wild, and the person is often afflicted with lack of concentration and resulting inefficiency (this quality is especially marked in transits to either Mars or Saturn). But, although material affairs may suffer in this way, it is a temporary interference; whereas the inspirational and intangible experiences at such times can linger on for many years as memories which can guide the person's life in important ways.

Pluto Transits

An entire section on Pluto transits is included in Chapter 4, but we might recapitulate here the essential principles of these transits. Pluto transits confront you with the necessity to end old, outgrown chapters of life. They tell you to "let go" and, if you don't, you are often forced to let go through suffering. These transits open up previously hidden or forgotten inner resources and energies by eliminating old forms on the surface of life. Not only do Pluto transits often submerge a part of you or make something disappear entirely, but they also can bring *back* into your life people, feelings, activities, or aspects of your own nature that have been long absent. In other words, these transits have the power to strip away the old shell in order to reveal the *essence* of inner being and spontaneous creativity, joy, and freedom. They can help us to experience the kind of spontaneous energy and abilities which we felt and acted out when we were young, before they became buried under the weight of cultural patterns or the veils of karma. After a Pluto transit, with the decks now cleared, we can again experience our essential nature and begin to express it. Pluto transits in fact are often felt to be like an exorcism or a form of surgery (physical, emotional, mental, or spiritual) in which some part of ourselves is removed or radically changed.

We can gain further insight into Pluto's nature through an in-depth understanding of the sign Scorpio. The Scorpio period of the year (at least in the Northern Hemisphere) is the time when the life force withdraws from all outer forms in nature and is *concentrated* in the seed. It is striking that the cultural symbol for this time of year in the United

States is the Halloween pumpkin with its insides removed, leaving only an empty shell with a blankly staring face. In fact, the jack-o-lantern is a symbol of death, a symbolic skull with the glimmering remains of the departed life force represented by the candle within it. (Scorpionic people, in fact, often feel like empty shells, as if they were living out old compulsions while being extremely dissatisfied with such behavior.) Traditionally, the Halloween feast (the eve of All Saints Day) was a time when the dead came back to life and when human beings in the physical body could most immediately contact departed spirits of all kinds, as well as their own patron saints. It is significant that children are allowed at this time to wander out at night, past their usual bed time, and that they are not supposed to go from house to house begging for food until the Sun (the symbol of physical *life*) has completely set! Indeed, Scorpionic and Plutonian people seem to have an affinity for the dark areas of experience, whether in a constructive way or through fear mingled with fascination. Children on this night are dressed in all sorts of outrageous costumes, like so many lost souls wandering here and there in search of nourishment. In fact, even the familiar "Trick or treat!" sounds vaguely reminiscent of a Scorpionic way of demanding something. It should be apparent that Scorpio and Pluto are always concerned with death of some kind, and—if one is afraid of death—one is sure to be afraid of Pluto transits. Scorpio and Pluto represent an urge to penetrate to the core of life with great intensity, until the pure life force is experienced through merging with another source (human or divine). We can therefore gather from the above that Pluto transits have the power to put us in touch with the seed power within us, with life experiences in their most intense, concentrated, and stark form, and with our essential nature and positive potentials in their purest state. And, while all this is happening, the "old shells" of outgrown emotional and mental habit patterns can fall away or be rejected at long last.

The following examples should illustrate how such transits can operate. A forty-three year old woman experienced the death of her husband as transiting Pluto conjuncted her natal first house Mars. She had never had a decent relationship with a man until she met him, and he had helped her to gain strength and confidence in herself. They had been married only a few years when he died. The important thing about this experience was that it constituted a transformation of her own self-sufficiency, strength, and the capacity to assert herself and to direct her own life (all of which are symbolized by Mars). Even before she knew of the astrological correlations with this experience, she realized that she would from now on have to fend for herself and begin to utilize independently the inner resources that she had been developing during the past few years. A twenty-six year old woman purged herself of many old attitudes and memories as Pluto conjuncted her natal Mercury. The most outwardly noticeable manifestation of this phase was that she became more relaxed (note that Mercury rules the nervous system) and that her attitudes and thoughts were much less superficial than before. One might say that her increased relaxation came about because of both deepened perception and the release of tension that can accompany Plutonian elimination. Three different examples of how Pluto's transit in square to natal Uranus may manifest reveal how individualized astrological interpretations should be: 1) one young woman transformed her sense of what "freedom" means during this time and purged herself of her erratic expression of "freedom" through her decision not to run off and join a violent revolutionary group with which she had contacts, but instead to begin study for a career in chiropractic; 2) another woman got sick, re-met two old boy-friends she hadn't seen in years, and became more definite about the kind of personal freedom she wanted; 3) a young man found this period to be a long-lasting phase of psychic transformation and psychological turmoil, during which he had very active dreams, got interested in astrology, and started to become adept in psychological counseling and dream analysis.

As transiting Pluto squared her natal Venus, a thirty-five year old woman went through severe emotional changes, all of which were painful but which ultimately opened her up to a much more joyous understanding of love. Her husband of fifteen years left her, and— shortly afterwards—one of her closest friends became paralyzed (as Uranus opposed his natal Uranus-Mars conjunction). It was a period of stripping away her old emotional attachments, which gave her a level of depth understanding which nothing else could provide. A thirty year old man left behind the entire career which he had worked to build up for eight years as Pluto conjuncted his Sun. As the aspect became close, he got emotionally and physically sick and had to stay in bed for almost a month. But during that convalescence period, he not only realized that he simply could not continue the current work which was thoroughly exhausting him, but he also began to read many books in the field which was to become his new career. It was as if all traces of his old means of livelihood were suddenly swept away, leaving only those things which he had spontaneously done with great joy when he was younger; and it was those old, familiar abilities which he then began to use in a new vocational direction.

One last example is especially pertinent to those who are trying to follow some kind of ideal or spiritual path: Pluto's transits of natal Neptune. These transits can manifest as confusion and great discontent as old yearnings, ideals, and fantasies are brought to the surface. One can gain a great depth of insight into his or her *true* motivations, yearnings, and what were previously strong unconscious feelings that prompted unrealistic behavior. Escapist urges may be strong, but one can see at this time that there is only one true escape from what is preoccupying one's mind: facing one's real desires and needs and transforming oneself and one's ideals. In fact, vague, illusory, or escapist activities are often purged during this period; and self-deceptions are often brought starkly into the light of day. In short, the urge to reform oneself, which is present to some extent during almost all Pluto transits, is focused at this time on one's own ideals and therefore also on dealing with those areas of one's life where one has betrayed one's ideals. It is common for people to confront at this time the major ways in which they have been trying to fool themselves; and it is rare that such a transit passes without an individual having to face an important area of self-deception. Various disappointments may be apparent at these times, but they are usually a result of the person's own unrealistic dreams or self-deceptions; and such disappointments serve the purpose of teaching the person deeper and more reliable life values.

The Timing of Transits

I mentioned earlier that the timing of progressions and transits cannot be defined by rigid rules since so much depends upon the sensitivity of the individual and how quickly the person is able to assimilate the full range and meaning of the corresponding experience. For example, I have seen cases where a specific traumatic event or frustration at age fifteen (as transiting Saturn opposed natal Saturn) continued to haunt those people for the next fifteen years; and the meaning and depth of the original experience was often fully understood and accepted only at the time of the first Saturn return! Many similar patterns could be explained here; for the transits of the outer five planets all share this quality: that their impact on the individual's life is at times so profound that the person's level of awareness is not sufficient to cope with it at all, let alone integrate the experience within a short period of time. In fact, the vast majority of psychotherapeutic techniques are oriented primarily toward promoting the integration and acceptance of various experiences which could not be fully confronted at the time they happened because the pain was too overwhelming. These therapeutic techniques are quite separate from traditional astrological techniques, but both methods of understanding complement each other perfectly. (Hence, those who say that astrologers have nothing to learn from "psychology" are resigning themselves to an incomplete form of counseling which deals only with the mind but not with the emotions. Very few astrologers can become qualified therapists, but astrological counselors should at least be aware of what types of therapies are available for specific types of problems in order that they can make helpful referrals.) In fact, one of the greatest values of astrology is that it can help us to assimilate the *meaning* of any given experience more quickly and fully; it *can* be, one might say, a form of "preventive medicine" which will reduce the need for intensive psychotherapy in the future.

A knowledge of astrology is especially useful in dealing with children, either as a parent or as a professional in some field. Very few children have sufficient awareness, perspective, or strength of ego to enable them to face completely the painful experiences of childhood. Therefore, like most adults, children tend to ignore, deny, or repress their painful feelings, thus postponing until later life the need to confront those emotions. And, since very few adults have any way of knowing what the child is going through, and since most adults tend to dismiss children's feelings as rather unimportant, a child is often given the advice: "Don't worry, it's just a phase you're going through. When you're older, you'll see that this really didn't matter." But the fact is that, for the child, it does matter right now! And if the parent, counselor, teacher, or relative has the aid of astrology, he or she will be able to penetrate into the child's inner experience and thus begin to relate to it more sensitively. Many of childhood's painful experiences could be ameliorated if only the child had *someone* to talk with who really understood what was going on!

But to get back to the subject of timing specific transits, it becomes apparent that timing is more an art than a science since it is such an individual matter. However, we can outline a few guidelines which can be useful, at least until the practitioner has enough experience that he or she can *feel* the impact of various transits in a specific way. One of the most important things to take note of when working with transits, something that few books on transits mention, is the common phenomenon of a specific transit repeating three (or, in the case of Neptune or Pluto, even five) times over a period of many months. For example, Pluto may square my Moon once going direct, then go retrograde to square the Moon again, and then go back direct to repeat that square. In some cases, Pluto will then again go retrograde and repeat the aspect two more times. Occasionally, a transiting planet will reach one of its "stations" (i.e., where its apparent motion is zero as it is turning either direct or retrograde) at a point which is in close aspect to a natal planet. These periods are especially powerful! When one sees that a particular transit will be repeated over a period of many months, one should view that series of transits as representative of an entire *process* of change and transformation which will be especially deep and which will begin some time before the first exact aspect and continue for some time after the last aspect. It is as if the exact aspects during that entire time mark peaks in the intensity of energy flow that is *experienced*, although the process of change is still continuing at some level even when the planet has temporarily separated from the close aspect. Important experiences and developments will not *always* manifest when such aspects are exact, although they do more often than not. But the exact aspects are invariably "seeding" periods when the impact on awareness and consciousness is usually the most intense. As mentioned earlier, the first transit in such a series *usually* corresponds to the most striking experience of all those developments that will occur during the entire change period; and the first transit will usually correlate with the most problematical experience in the case of the dynamic aspects. (It should be pointed out, however, that if the natal planet being activated was retrograde at birth, the retrograde period of the transit series will at times signify the most obviously intense experience.) It is as if you have to clear away all the obstructions during the first transit, in order to be open to the necessary lessons during the remainder of the entire process.

With some transits, the question of orbs can be simplified by utilizing orbs of *time* rather than orbs of a specified number of degrees. As mentioned in Chapter 8, for general purposes I feel that using a maximum orb of one month before and after an exact aspect is a valuable guideline for the transits of the outer planets. This means that the transiting Moon will have conjuncted each point involved in the transit configuration twice during that period of two months. If one tries to use a rigid orb of, for example, one degree, one will often fail to see the transits which do really correlate with a particular experience, although they may not have been exact at the time of the outer development.

Since the Sun and Moon regulate the actual energy flow in our lives, we should realize that—although many transits will manifest obviously when exact to the minute—others will manifest a bit before or after the exact aspect is formed, depending on the Sun and Moon positions. The one-month orb however is a *maximum*, since in most cases a two week orb (thus comprising one complete cycle of the transiting Moon) will be sufficient to outline a time period during which a particular transiting aspect will manifest powerfully. I must repeat, however, that this is only a guideline; for, in actual practice, there are a number of specific factors pertaining to transiting planets which fit no general rule and which I will now outline in greater detail.

LUNATIONS: The New Moon closely aspecting a natal planet will often begin to manifest a few days before the exact time when the Sun and Moon are conjunct. This is explainable by the fact that, as the transiting Moon nears the transiting Sun, their energies begin to merge; and, as the transiting Moon enters the *sign* that the transiting Sun is in, the energy release is intensified even more.

MERCURY, VENUS, & MARS TRANSITS: Normally, an orb of 1° will be sufficient for understanding these transits. This means that, for example, Mars transiting in opposition to the Sun will usually manifest *strongly* for a *maximum* of three days. The only additional guideline with these transits is that their sign position alone may be symbolic of a general trend for a short period; for example, whenever transiting Venus is in your Sun sign, that period may coincide with more interest in forming relationships or in meeting new people.

JUPITER & SATURN TRANSITS: In addition to the orbs of *time* mentioned above, it should also be emphasized that the sign position alone of these transiting planets should be taken into account; for merely the presence of one of these planets in the sign you have ascending, or in the sign where you have your natal Sun, Moon, or other important planets will color the entire attitude with which you express those energies for many months, even when no specific aspect is close. For example, Jupiter's transit of your Moon sign may give you greater confidence about expressing energies with which you have *always* felt particularly comfortable, and this new feeling may last for as long as an entire year. Or the entire period when Saturn transits through your Sun sign may be characterized as a rather serious time of life when you are trying to structure the way you are using your creative energies. This urge toward structuring will simply be intensified when Saturn begins to closely aspect the natal Sun. It should also be mentioned that Jupiter's transits are often experienced as an anticipation of some large-scale future development perhaps four to six months before the exact aspect forms. (Note again Jupiter's significance as an attunement to the future!) Saturn's transits, on the other hand, often lag behind, in keeping with Saturn's traditional correlation with delay and slowness; hence, many important developments may happen during as long a period as one and a half years after an exact Saturn aspect has passed.

URANUS TRANSITS: These are to be considered important primarily when they come within 5° or less of an exact aspect; their sign position alone does not have nearly the importance that Jupiter's and Saturn's sign positions do. Uranus transits are the most accurate of all timing devices in astrology, since they seem to manifest with great *immediacy* almost always when the aspect is exact. Therefore, as pointed out by both Charles Jayne and Isabel Hickey, these transits are particularly useful for attempts at rectifying charts. Finally, it should be pointed out that an individual who is highly attuned to Uranus energy in his or her natal chart (as are most of those who are intensely involved in astrology) will be more sensitive to these transits and therefore will begin to feel their effects as a general speeding up of the pace of life considerably before the exact aspect is formed. It is primarily in these cases that the maximum orb of 5° mentioned above will be needed.

NEPTUNE TRANSITS: Again, the timing of these transits depends chiefly upon the attunement of the individual. People who are totally involved in the gross affairs of material survival and responsibilities often tend to notice these transits only when they become within a degree or two of exact; whereas those who are open to the subtleties of life tend to perceive the Neptunian vibration in their life when Neptune is as much as 5° away from forming an exact aspect. As with Uranus, the sign position alone of transiting Neptune is of little importance for individuals.

PLUTO TRANSITS: These transits can be surprisingly powerful, even when the exact aspect is some 5° or so from exact. In some ways, I feel Pluto should be given a larger "orb of influence" than any other transiting planet except Jupiter and Saturn, in spite of its small physical size. For, while the *exact* aspects of transiting Pluto to natal planets usually correlate with important changes that are noticed by most individuals, extremely powerful effects seem to be evident in many cases as much as a year before such exact aspects take place, when Pluto may be as much as 5° away from forming the exact aspect. It is as if Pluto is preparing the person for the large-scale, profound changes to come later by eroding some of the foundations of the person's old lifestyle in advance of the time when major rebirth potentials will become evident. People tend to be more open to the new when they are in a condition of disorientation; and the exact Pluto transits are often preceded by experiences of tiredness, boredom, searching, and emotional pain which affect the person deeply enough to induce an overall state of psychic disorientation. While sometimes painful or confusing, this can of course be a very fruitful experience. Although most of our educational training and cultural prejudices incline us to feel absolute terror at the thought of chaos, valuable lessons can be learned by adapting ourselves to whatever situations arise during these transition periods. As Carl Payne Tobey writes in *The Astrology of Inner Space,*

> Never fear chaos because out of chaos something is always born. Instead of worrying about a chaotic situation, I await the birth. When your mind becomes chaotic—or when my mind is—it is because it is impossible to see the whole.

Capricorn

10

The Ascendant & Midheaven: Vital Factors of Personality Structure

*The natal chart can be rightly interpreted only
by men and women of intuitive wisdom; these are few.*
— Paramahansa Yogananda

Gaining a meaningful sense of the Ascendant and Midheaven eluded me for many years, although I was reading every astrological book I could find and also attending lectures on the subject. It was only when I began to do many consultations focused on a deep exploration of the various components of a birthchart that I began to develop a feeling for the significance of these astrological factors. Until I had gained some immediate experience through one-to-one counseling, thus enabling me to observe many different people and their various ways of expressing themselves, all of the theoretical explanations of the Ascendant and Midheaven remained abstract and of little use. I feel this direct experience was necessary for two reasons. First, the *Ascendant* symbolizes a way that the entire self is expressed so immediately and spontaneously that no mere words are capable of capturing its essence. It thus has almost a transcendent significance from the viewpoint of its importance in one's total integration as a fully functioning, dynamic individual. Secondly, the meaning of the *Midheaven* seems very abstract when one is young, but—as one grows older and more fully participates in society, as one gives greater emphasis to attaining one's ambitions, and as one's personality structure becomes more established in a set pattern—the meaning of the Midheaven becomes more relevant to one's experience and thus more easily understandable. By noting the correlation of Saturn and its qualities with the Midheaven (10th house cusp in most systems), one can appreciate the connection of the Midheaven with both maturity and the pursuit of an integrated life structure.

It should also be mentioned that the research of the French statistician Michel Gauquelin confirms the astrological traditions about the importance of the Ascendant and Midheaven, particularly conjunctions to these points. However, Gauquelin's work seems to indicate that the Ascendant and Midheaven are *not* the beginnings of their respective houses, but rather important focal points of energy flow. The 1st and 10th houses seem to begin quite a few degrees before these points, as indicated by the fact that his studies showed a planet to be especially prominent when it was located in the areas that are traditionally called the 12th or 9th houses, some degrees from the actual 1st and 10th cusps. This discovery confirms what I and many other astrologers have begun doing quite spontaneously: namely, considering the cusp to be a powerful area of each house but not the absolute beginning of a house as is so often stated. However, I do not carry this so far as to say that the cusp is the middle of a house, as has also been suggested. I personally feel that the cusp and its surrounding 6° or so is the most powerful area of any house, and I therefore always use *at least* a 6° orb with house cusps. According to astrological traditions, a planet rising over the first house cusp (Ascendant) at the moment of birth was regarded as an especially powerful influence in the person's life. The reason why a planet near the horizon is so particularly prominent should be clear when we consider the following phenomenon.

The Ascendant

Any planet's position on the horizon (i.e., near the Ascendant) can be considered to indicate an unusual prominence of that planet's qualities and energies in the life of a person born at that moment. (This is also reflected in the way transits to the Ascendant are felt to be especially strong.) Since most astrology is geocentric and thus assigns importance to various celestial factors according to their appearance as observed from earth, one might expect that such a trend (drawn from astrological observation) should be evident in one's direct perception of the astronomical phenomenon itself. And indeed, this is so; for any planet on the horizon is seen to be *magnified!* Imagine a full harvest moon, glowing orange and gold just above the horizon. It looks huge, easily twice its normal diameter. Many people ascribe this apparent increase in size (which is also observed with the Sun, planets, and constellations when near the horizon) to atmospheric distortion; but, while smog, dust, and other atmospheric components give the harvest moon its golden hue, they don't magnify the image. Nor is the Moon closer when it is on the horizon, although it appears that way. (In fact, it is closest to the observer when it is directly overhead!) The surprising truth is that the increase in size is a perceptual effect, solely "in the eye of the beholder." If you photograph and measure the Moon both on the horizon and overhead, the diameters are identical; the image size hasn't changed at all. This phenomenon is therefore considered by scientists to be a "mere optical illusion." However, since in geocentric astrology the way things *appear* to us on earth (e.g., the retrograde motion of planets) is regarded as crucially important, we should see this phenomenon as symbolic of the fact that any planet near the horizon is especially prominent in our lives since its "influence" is thereby magnified!

As an example of the significance of a planet near the Ascendant, let us take the case of a man whose Sun is in Capricorn, Moon is in Virgo, and whose Ascendant is Cancer. If one were to judge his overall temperament from those three factors alone, it would be apparent that he would probably be a rather conservative sort of person: cautious, self-protective, security conscious, and perhaps even a bit skeptical of anything not rooted in cultural or familial traditions. However, if this man also has Uranus conjunct the Ascendant (whether on the 12th or the 1st house side), we begin to see an entirely new dimension of his personality. For, in spite of all the natal factors pointing toward security and traditionalism, the Uranian vibration is likely to indicate a powerful streak of experimentalism, unorthodoxy, and openness to the new and different. Rather than being a stick-in-the-mud sort of person filled with fears and self-doubt, he may well exemplify progressive thinking and even revolutionary inclinations on some level. In fact, this man could never be satisfied with a Capricornian sort of lifestyle in which the primary emphasis was upon duty and personal limitation, for he would need to not only think about but also to act out his constant urge toward variety of experience and freedom of self-expression.

As another example, suppose a woman has an Aquarius Sun, a Sagittarius Moon, and even Leo rising! This is a powerful combination of positive exuberant energies which we might expect to be expressed dynamically in a particularly overt manner. But if this woman has Pluto conjunct the Ascendant, she would most likely express herself in a manner reminiscent of those with Scorpio rising: secretive, moody, reflective, and self-repressive. Or, to state this more precisely, there might be a strong fear of allowing herself to express the kind of spontaneity that her other chart factors symbolize. In this example, the presence of Pluto near the Ascendant magnifies the Plutonian quality far more than would be the case with Pluto in other areas of the chart.

The Ascendant shows a way in which we are acutely sensitive and aware, and this is another explanation of why a transit to the Ascendant is felt to be so powerful; for it affects us in the area of our lives and in the dimension of our energy field that is most sensitive. In fact, some astrologers have said that the Ascendant shows the point where the spirit enters the body at the moment of the first breath. I do not know if this is true, but my experience in the healing arts (especially with Polarity Therapy) leads me to believe that the part of the body associated with the rising sign indicates where you are dynamically connected to your subtler bodies (or subtler energy fields) and hence where there is an inrushing of powerful energies. We might mention here some of the meanings of the Ascendant:

A. The Ascendant represents the *image* of the personality that is seen by others. This does not mean that this image is an accurate portrayal of one's total self, but it does show something which other people often notice as a first impression. The Ascendant image may, in fact, reveal personal qualities which are distinctly at variance with one's more inward orientations.

B. The Ascendant represents the way in which you actively *merge* with life in the outer world when your energy is flowing spontaneously. Hence, it reveals a general approach to life which in older astrological treatises has been called the "temperament."

C. The Ascendant symbolizes an important aspect of your personal destiny in the sense that you simply *must* live and express yourself in that way in order to feel free and whole.

D. The Ascendant (especially according to its element: fire, water, air, or earth) reveals the quality of energy flow directly vitalizing the *physical* body and thus whether there is marked conductivity (air or fire) or strong resistance (water or earth) to the spontaneous flow of the vital energies. This correlation explains why transits to the Ascendant so strongly affect your vitality, appearance, and general state of health.

E. The connection between the Ascendant and the physical body is also evident in another way: the fact that the body constitutes your most immediate physical environment. When we are born, our physical body and, to some extent, that of the mother comprise our entire environment; and, although we forget it in later years as we become more identified with the body, our physical vehicle always remains an essential part of our environment. Hence, we see why the Ascendant so often has been correlated with the quality of the early environment, for any contact with the outer world is filtered through the attunement of the Ascendant. The body (and thus the Ascendant) brings the environment into existence for us, and the Ascendant therefore colors how we see our total environment and our attitude toward the outer world in later life.

F. The Ascendant represents a dimension of one's nature which some have correlated with the ego. Although one cannot make a direct correspondence between the Ascendant and the ego, it can be stated that the Ascendant represents an important *dimension* of the ego. When one is threatened, one tends either to retreat from the form of expression shown by the Ascendant to the more secure personality center symbolized by the Sun or to further emphasize the Ascendant's qualities in order to assert one's individuality and ensure one's survival. Since the Ascendant in a natural chart correlates with the sign Aries, the Ascendant is always indicative of a way of expressing one's individuality and thus—in a sense—one's ego. However, this is not to be regarded as a negative quality unless perhaps one is overly compulsive about it.

G. The "transcendent" dimension of the Ascendant mentioned earlier can be seen in the way the Ascendant shows how we merge with life purely and spontaneously; it is a way of living and being which is beyond "understanding." Much more than the Ascendant, the Sun sign indicates how we "understand" and assimilate experience. The Ascendant rather reveals the way we feel ourselves to be uniquely ourselves, the highest point of spontaneous conscious attunement and action.

This last reference to the transcendent quality of the Ascendant may at first seem a bit far fetched or unclear, so it is worth explaining this idea in more detail. The Ascendant marks the point of separation between the 12th house (things beyond conscious control) and the lst house (forces we can consciously use). Hence, any planet on the Ascendant (either natally or by transit or progression) indicates that one is becoming aware of that function, energy, or universal law with great immediacy. The Jungian psychologist Patrick Harding further explains this point:

> ...we find the Ascendant taking up a position exactly, if the timing is really accurate, between life in the womb and life in the world outside it. It thus shows us the exact position of the timeless zone between the two. It would seem, therefore, that the timeless point may, and almost certainly does play some part in the stamping of the qualities of the rising sign upon the psyche of the child.

If we take the Ascendant as the exact mid-point between the unconscious womb world and the conscious outer world, it would then seem logical that when these are in balance or in a state of timelessness, the trinitarian principle operates and the third member of the psyche "The Collective Unconscious" comes into play. Within the collective unconscious there exist the Great Archetypes and there is some evidence to show that these are twelve in number and that they correspond to the symbolic images allocated to the signs of the zodiac.... It seems natural then, that as the child passes through the timeless zone at the moment of birth, the active archetype of that period claims it for its own and impresses its qualities upon it. (from "Time Alone Can Tell," *Journal of Astrological Studies*, Vol. 1, p. 193)

Because a planet is a much more concentrated focus of energy than is a sign, it should be pointed out here that the ascending sign alone should not be considered apart from those planets which modify, energize, or color the mode of self-expression shown by the Ascendant and the entire 1st house. There are basically two types of such planets: 1) any planet in the 1st house (which includes not only planets beneath the horizon in the traditional 1st house area—except for those within 6° to 8° of the 2nd house cusp—but also planets situated in the traditional 12th house area, within even 10° of the Ascendant); and 2) the ruling planet (or planets) of the Ascendant.

The ruling planet of the Ascendant is treated separately in the next section since a full understanding of its importance calls for some depth of explanation. However, we can rather briefly examine the significance of a planet situated in the natal 1st house. The first thing to emphasize is that a 1st house planet can overshadow the vibrations symbolized by the Ascendant, at least in *obvious* ways. The qualities represented by the ascending sign are still there and operating, but the presence of a planet in the first house (especially if it is close to the Ascendant) indicates a mode of expression which is particularly forceful. There is an especially strong contrast in cases where the 1st house planet is in a sign that is different from the ascending sign. For example, a person with Leo rising will inevitably manifest certain Leo characteristics; but the presence of a Virgo planet in the 1st house may provide enough Virgo emphasis to prompt other people to guess that the person has Virgo rising. Those whose charts contain a 1st house planet in a sign that differs from the rising sign are characterized by having a more complex overall approach to life than other people. In those cases where the 1st house planet is *in* the ascending sign, there is a double emphasis on the qualities and energies of that sign, although the specific mode of energy release will greatly depend upon which planet is so situated. For example, if one has Saturn in Aries in the 1st house and also Aries rising, the expression of the Aries energy is shown to be deeply important to the individual and something which he or she may work at with great effort. However, although the Aries qualities and urges will be strong in that person, the Saturn placement indicates that the actual release of the Aries energy may be something less than spontaneous and may in fact be somewhat inhibited. In some instances, such a person may even appear to be more of a Capricorn rising type of person than an Aries rising type.

The Ruler of the Ascendant

The ruling planet of the Ascendant, together with its house and sign position, is another factor which must be considered simultaneously with any analysis of an individual's ascending sign. In fact, one might say that there are, for example, twelve basic types of Aries rising (depending on the sign position of Mars), twelve types of Taurus rising (depending on the sign position of Venus), and so on. Both the sign and house position of the ruling planet are extremely important factors in any chart, although the house position is much more important than sign position if the ruler being considered is Uranus, Neptune, or Pluto. The position of the ruling planet signifies the primary energy and area of life experience that motivates you to act in the world. In addition, the element of the ruling planet's sign position is often indicative of the level of experience that gets your physical energy flowing. And, since the Ascendant itself represents the *generalized* experience of being yourself and realizing your individual nature most spontaneously, the house position of the ruling planet can be said to represent the *specific* field of life activity wherein you can experience your essential nature most immediately. Once you have tuned in on the field of experience and the type of energy represented by the ruling planet and its house and sign, you begin to feel more alive, more motivated to express yourself, and more inwardly secure and authentic. The aspects involving the ruler of the Ascendant are also especially important, on a par with aspects involving the Sun or Moon or the Ascendant itself. Such aspects are so significant because they indicate specific dynamics affecting the overall flow or inhibition of your self-expression. The connection of the Ascendant's ruler with the flow of physical energy and with one's state of health can hardly be overestimated, and its importance in this regard may easily be seen by watching the transits to the ruling planet. So often, such transits will correlate with marked changes in one's health, vitality, or appearance. For example, one client (a 34 year old man with Virgo rising) experienced a total nervous collapse as Uranus squared his natal Mercury. Granted that transiting Uranus being in square to anyone's natal Mercury could correlate with a period of nervous stress, such a transit would nevertheless not be so dominating a force for those who do not have Mercury as the ruler of the Ascendant.

One might ask *why* the ruler of the Ascendant is so important, more important in most people's lives than the ruler of the Sun sign in terms of profound immediate experiences and complete changes in one's attitude toward life. To answer this question, it seems to me it is necessary to return to a very ancient concept: namely, the idea of the ruling planet being the "Lord" which presides over not only one's birth but also over one's entire life. In various ancient concepts of astrological forces, the ruling planet of the Ascendant was considered to be the deity or cosmic power appointed by the Supreme Lord to preside over an individual's entire incarnation. In more modern terms, one might say that the nature of the ruling planet lends an overall tone to the person's entire life, both his experiences and his approach to interacting with the outer world. The specific sign position of this ruling planet is therefore of great importance as a symbol of the quality of experience, energy flow, and general orientation to life that will dominate the individual's way of being for this incarnation. Although I cannot claim to have enough direct experience to enable me to confirm the ancient concept mentioned above in any specific way, I have had one experience which powerfully impressed me and which might be significant in this regard. I was present at a home birth a few years ago, and I had given specific instructions to another person there to keep a record of the exact time of birth. Therefore, I know that the child who was born then has an extremely accurate birthchart. When it appeared that the delivery was imminent, I mentally calculated an approximate Ascendant and assumed that the child would have Aquarius rising. As the child was born, the room became filled with a powerful and almost tangible presence. The intensity of pressure felt in that room at that moment could only be described as a Saturnian energy and vibration, and I remarked to one of the others present that the atmosphere was charged with this powerful force. Later that night, after things had calmed down and the new baby had fallen asleep, I calculated his chart precisely and found, to my surprise, that he had 28° of Capricorn rising. His ruling planet was therefore Saturn, and I could not have imagined a more Saturnian birth experience nor a more Saturnian vibration in the air than that which accompanied his arrival. Since birth into the material world is of course a rather Saturnian event, I cannot say whether or not the same experience would have occurred if the child had, for example, been ruled by Venus or Jupiter. But I feel this instance is worth mentioning in order to encourage people to pay attention to the vibrations that may be felt during the birth of other souls into the physical plane.

It should be apparent by now that no consideration of the Ascendant is complete without simultaneously including the entire complex of factors which are closely related to the Ascendant. In other words, the qualities of the rising sign and its ruling planet (including its sign and house), as well as any 1st house planet, all show urges, needs, and orientations which form one of the most crucial combinations of energy in your life. All these factors together constitute a key fulcrum upon which the entire personality structure is balanced, and they reveal a theme which colors how the whole of one's self is projected. If one is not able to express these energies with ease, a generalized tension develops and, in many cases, a feeling of being bored, lifeless, and lacking direction and purpose. To give an example of how so many factors might be combined in interpretation, let us take the case of the above-mentioned child whose "Ascendant complex" contains the following factors:

1) Capricorn Ascendant
2) Ruling planet Saturn in Gemini and in the 5th house, conjunct Venus and Mercury.
3) Jupiter in Aquarius in the 1st house

We might describe this combination as follows:

> A need to approach life with caution (Capricorn rising) and with in-depth creativity (Saturn in 5th), both mentally and emotionally (Mercury and Venus conjunct Saturn); a need to think deeply and to communicate his thoughts in a serious way (Saturn in Gemini, conjunct Mercury); and a need to see tangible results from his organized, self-disciplined efforts (Capricorn rising and Saturn in 5th), all infused with an independent faith and an expansive, optimistic generosity toward others (Jupiter in Aquarius).

Aspects to the Ascendant

One additional factor which participates in the Ascendant Complex mentioned above is any close aspect to the Ascendant. Traditionally, such aspects have been said to influence one's character and temperament, although very few books include guidelines for interpreting these aspects. In this brief section, I do not propose to give a systematic list of "interpretations" for such aspects. However, there are a few key points to keep in mind in order to recognize those Ascendant aspects which are most important in a particular chart. As a general rule, the Ascendant aspects show how one most characteristically expresses himself or herself in the outer world, either easily and naturally (certain conjunctions, the sextiles, and—most of all—the trines) or with some degree of stress, tension, inhibition, or extraordinarily strong ambition (squares and oppositions). In other words, aspects to the Ascendant reveal whether various dimensions of oneself (symbolized by natal planets) are in harmony or discord with the mode of expression toward which the Ascendant's energies constantly urge us.

The OPPOSITIONS with the Ascendant in some cases reveal an inner division in the individual, a state of being wherein the person endures an almost constant tension since there is a strong urge toward modes of activity which are in many ways completely opposite. This inner tension can generate great energy and manifest as a particularly complex type of consciousness. Oftentimes, such a person will alternate between the two life orientations over a number of years, at times giving conscious emphasis to one mode of self-expression and at other times focusing on the other orientation. It often seems that the progressed Moon or transiting Saturn and Jupiter periodically bring out one side or the other of the person's nature.

The SQUARE to the Ascendant is often symbolic of some quality in the person's early environment, usually having manifested either as a type of oppression or inhibition (especially when the planet involved is in the 4th house) or as an unusually strong pressure toward achievement or recognition (often when the planet involved is in the 10th house). In other words, there are basically two types of squares with the Ascendant, which may be classified as follows: 1) the 4th house type of square often indicates emotional patterns that hold us back from reaching the spontaneity of expression shown by the Ascending sign; and 2) the 10th house square often reveals forces within us that pull us onward toward some kind of achievement.

The SEXTILE with the Ascendant generally shows that the energy of the planet involved may be put into operation quite smoothly once a period of learning has taken place. Some small adjustment may have to be made before that dimension of experience becomes fully integrated with the energy of the Ascendant, but the transition period is usually rapid and encouraging.

The CONJUNCTIONS and TRINES with the Ascendant should be treated together due to their participation in an important—but rarely mentioned—astrological phenomenon. This phenomenon is the triangle formed by the "fire houses" (Houses I, V, and IX). The triangle formed by the fire *signs* is of course mentioned in most basic textbooks of astrology, as are the triangles (or trinities) associated with the signs of the other elements. But the triangle of the fire *houses* has been mentioned in very few books. The reason for this apparent neglect is that this triangle represents a pattern of energy flow which in many cases verges on the transcendent. I have already mentioned how the Ascendant can

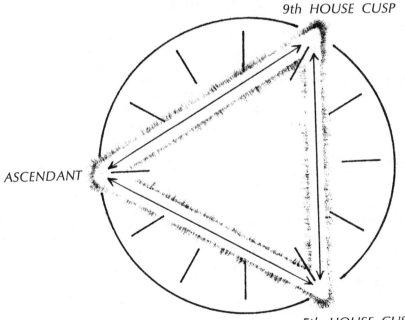

9th HOUSE CUSP

ASCENDANT

5th HOUSE CUSP

A CIRCUIT OF FIERY ENERGY:
Spirit, inspiration, being, becoming, joy, & faith

be seen as representing a mode of expression and energy release which is timeless, spontaneous, and so natural that it eludes our capturing its essence in words. And, in a general way, this quality applies also to the entire triangle of the fire houses; for the fire houses deal with pure being and becoming. The purity of self-expression represented by them can in some cases be accurately classified as spiritual (mainly in those cases where the person has ceased to identify his ego with the creative forces flowing through him and instead sees himself only as a channel for the manifestation of a greater power). I stumbled on to the importance of the fire houses early in my astrological studies, years before I had ever seen mention of this phenomenon in print. This realization occurred when I drew up and studied the charts of about a dozen spiritual masters. When I tried to discover common factors in all of their charts, it became apparent that the only thing that was regularly emphasized in the majority of those charts was the emphasis on the fire house placement of planets. After trying to understand this pattern, without much success, I had a vivid dream in which I was shown a flow of fiery energy circling around the triangle formed by the Ascendant and the 5th and 9th houses. The immediacy of realization that accompanied that dream is impossible to describe in words, but it was a direct and profound lesson about the energy flow represented by these houses. The diagram of the "Fiery Triangle" in this section is an attempt to convey that dream image.

The practical application of this idea is recognizing the potential shown in a chart where natal planets are located in close trine to the Ascendant or in conjunction to it. This does not mean that such planetary placements always indicate great spirituality, for—in most cases— emphasis on these houses cannot accurately be labeled a "spiritual" orientation since most people are undeniably egocentric. In general, however, there is a particularly dynamic flow of creative energy which can be expressed spontaneously and powerfully. Whatever dimension of experience is symbolized by a planet closely trining or conjuncting the Ascendant may be put into active expression with a degree of naturalness, immediacy, and positive energy greater than that represented by most other astrological factors. For example, one who has Mars either conjunct the Ascendant or in trine to it from either the 5th or the 9th house areas may be a natural leader and be characterized by a marked degree of courage and maybe even a certain roughness of demeanor. Or one who has Saturn in a similar position may be characterized by a sense of practicality, a capacity for good timing, and the expression of wisdom far beyond his or her years.

Although each of the fire houses may be differentiated from the others and given its own set of meanings, we should be aware of the fact that any planet situated within this dynamic triangle will be likely to exert a powerful impression on the individual's orientation to life. In fact, one of the simplest ways of characterizing the fire houses as a group is to say that the signs on the 1st, 5th, and 9th house cusps, together with the planets located in those houses (especially those closely aspecting the Ascendant), signify dominant qualities in the individual's overall attitude toward life! Since our attitude toward life determines a great many of our experiences (for you attract what you express in life), one can easily see why these factors in any chart play such an important role in the person's overall life pattern. The other point to be considered is that our attitude toward ourselves is inseparable from our attitude toward life in general. In fact, one might say that they are the same thing. It is obvious that our overall attitude toward life emanates directly from our attitude toward ourselves; and the opposite is also true, for we have all seen the transformation in self-confidence that an individual can experience when a positive life philosophy has been adopted. The fiery triangle thus symbolizes *the essential quality of our innermost sense of self*, as well as indicating our general approach to life itself.

The 1st house and its planets can indicate either a spontaneous flow of vital energy with such positive vibrations that the person is characterized by an almost radiant aura *or* a high degree of self-centeredness and often excessive pride. Naturally, these two ways of being represent the extreme manifestations of such energies, but it is not uncommon to find people who clearly exemplify these extremes. Any planet *conjunct the Ascendant* can indicate that we have considerable pride in that part of ourselves. For example, the Sun conjunct the Ascendant frequently correlates with a child-like simplicity and generosity in some cases, or with a childish glee in showing off one's abilities through dramatic displays (and often both). The Sun conjunct the Ascendant is similar to Leo rising in many ways, although the arrogance and self-centeredness found so often in those with Sun conjunct Ascendant is usually much more blatant than in those who have a Leo Ascendant. Another example might be the person who has Mercury conjunct the Ascendant, where we often find a considerable pride in one's learning and intellectual abilities. In some cases with the Mercury conjunction, a tendency to try to figure out every little thing causes unnecessary problems and constant worrying. These people often have particularly sharp minds and the ability to verbalize ideas with an extraordinary sense of drama, although their opinions can be their worst enemy.

The 5th house and its planets reveal creative resources which can be tapped in abundance, as well as being key symbols of the person's level of self-confidence, or at least what he or she feels must be done in order to attain real self-confidence. Since the 5th house corresponds to the Sun's own sign, Leo, it is not surprising that I have gradually become inclined to consider this house as the strongest house in the chart after the 1st; for the 5th house emphasizes not only the individual's creative potentials but also vibrations that characterize the person's overt way of pouring forth his or her energies spontaneously. And, in actual practice, any planet in the 5th house (especially if in close trine to the Ascendant) may color a person's entire scope and method of self-projection just as strongly as a planet in the 1st house.

The 9th house and its planets signify creative, future-oriented beliefs and aspirations. The 9th house's connection with one's general attitude toward life may be more obvious than that of the 1st or 5th house, since the 9th house has traditionally connoted one's religious or philosophical orientation. As many books have stated, the 9th house and its planets are related intimately with the higher mind; and since our higher aspirations and beliefs are among the most dominant factors in forming our life attitudes, one can see how readily 9th house factors harmonize with the overall orientation of the fire house triangle.

Of these three, the 5th house has been most misunderstood, due to the common practice of emphasizing only its connection with children, gambling, love "affairs," and other pleasures. However, the 5th house has deeper connotations which are closely related to the transcendent meaning of the fire triangle we've been discussing. I must say that it is quite surprising to me that generations of astrologers can continue to place so little relative emphasis on the very house that corresponds to the Sun itself! Although 5th house energies often *manifest* as speculation, love affairs, sensual pleasures, and childish self-centeredness, all of these activities are rooted in the urge to take some risks in order to let a greater power manifest through the individual personality. As has been stated, the 5th house shows either the power of love or the love of power. At best, it indicates one's capacity for letting God's love and light flow through you and a simple trust in the goodness of life itself. It is related to our ability to allow the creative forces of life to manifest *through* us, as shown by its connections with children of both mind and body (the desire to have something greater than our limited ego be born through us). Both children and true creativity teach us the lesson that we must do what we *love* to do in order to attain a joyous sense of vitality. This kind of joy is a gift or an act of divine grace, not a "pleasure" in a sensual way. By far the best presentation of this dimension of the 5th house appeared in Dennis Elwell's article on the subject in the *Journal* of the British Astrological Association in the summer of 1973. In this insightful piece of writing, he states:

> The fifth house...represents a barometer of our confidence in life, and particularly in its incalculable elements; and of the extent to which life secures us in the sense of our own worth by little signs of approval which arrive like a gift, an unsought blessing.

Some of these "little signs" might be "falling in love," which is of course quite beyond our control, having a child or a creative work be born through us (which again we cannot control), or even winning at gambling. Elwell points out that love is perhaps blind, as is so often said, but he goes on to clarify the spiritual meaning of the 5th house and Sun principles that are symbolic of this kind of love:

> Perhaps it is only when we are "in love" with someone that we see them as they should be seen!...When we fall in love our temperatures get reversed: now we regard ourselves coldly, and our shortcomings become all too obvious, while we feel warmth, admiration, and enthusiasm for someone else.

When in love, the sky is bluer, all life experiences are intensified, and everything looks better because we are then seeing things as they are; for the fire of love has burned away our ego! We might therefore say that the 5th house principle represents either the *fire of ego,* or the *fire of love* which burns up the ego. And, in a general way, *the entire triangle of the fire houses comprises this essential significance!* Planets in these houses therefore are almost always of great importance, and particularly those which closely aspect the Ascendant can be considered as indicators of extraordinary developmental power!

The Midheaven & Its Aspects

Almost all astrological texts mention the Midheaven as an important point in the natal chart, but very few give what I would consider practical guidelines for understanding its significance. In general, I have found various 10th house (or Midheaven) factors to share one common meaning, and this applies to not only the sign on the Midheaven but also to the ruling planet of that sign and any planets in the 10th house: all these factors indicate ways of being, personal capabilities, or personality qualities which one tends to admire, respect, and work hard at trying to develop and become. The Midheaven's sign symbolizes something that we spontaneously flow toward and grow toward *as we get older* (although we may exhibit some of those qualities in "seed form" while we are young), but it does often require effort to attain the optimum expression of those qualities. For example, Aries on the Midheaven may indicate that the person admires strength and courage and thus feels impelled to work at developing his or her assertive qualities. Taurus on the Midheaven may show that the person looks up to an image of serenity, ease, and beauty and thus puts forth effort to develop those qualities personally. Scorpio on the Midheaven may reveal that the person respects charismatic and powerful qualities in others and therefore seeks to use his or her own similar capacities to the utmost. Pisces on the Midheaven can indicate that the individual admires compassionate and intuitive qualities in others and therefore consciously seeks to cultivate those qualities.

The ruling planet of the Midheaven sign is primarily important due not only to its general symbolic meaning but more specifically due to the fact that *its house position so often shows where your real vocation comes into clearest focus.* The word *vocation* means literally "that toward which one is called," and not only the Midheaven sign itself but also other 10th house factors are closely related to what sort of vocation you feel pulled toward. But the most useful factor in my experience seems to be the Midheaven ruler's house position, for so often that house represents a field of experience which feels like your true calling at a very deep level. You may feel that you have finally come home to do what you were really meant to do when you begin to realize your true vocation. It is curious that the Midheaven is located at the top of one's chart and that it and its ruling planet symbolize the "summit" of your meaningful attainments and ambitions.

Another way of expressing the meaning of the Midheaven and 10th house factors is that these factors in a chart symbolize what is *important* to you. This terminology is especially relevant to the meaning of planets that fall in the 10th house (especially those which conjunct the Midheaven—even from the 9th house side). Such a planet represents ways of being, qualities, or types of activities that are extremely *important* to the individual and which he or she respects. Due to this feeling of respect, people will often exhibit those qualities or express those energies publicly in order that others might think well of them. (Hence, the connection of the Midheaven and 10th house with one's "reputation.") Some examples might help to illustrate this point:

> If Mercury is in the 10th house, it is important to the person to be educated and knowledgeable. If they themselves don't have the education that they respect, they may either work hard at attaining it or try to push others into achieving it.

> If Venus is in the 10th house, beauty in general (including artistic expression) and one's personal appearance in particular are felt to be important, and much money and energy may therefore be expended in these directions.

> If Saturn is in the 10th house, some tangible form of achievement is extraordinarily important to the person, for he or she tends to have a lot of respect for work, endurance, and the capacity to handle responsibilities.

> If Uranus is in the 10th house, it is important to the person to be independent and independent-minded.

> If Pluto is in one's 10th house, it is important to be authoritative, powerful, and to wield some influence.

Similar phrases could be presented for the other planets as well, but that would be belaboring the point. But it should be pointed out that the general meaning of, for example, *Venus in the 10th house* is similar to the meaning of *Venus as the ruler of the 10th house* (i.e., Taurus or Libra on the Midheaven). For another example, the general meaning of *Mars in the 10th house* is similar to the meaning of *Mars ruling the 10th house* (i.e., Aries on the Midheaven). In both cases, there is an extra importance and seriousness attached to those values, qualities, etc. which the relevant planet symbolizes. The only difference is that a planet actually placed in the 10th house should be seen as a more specific and concentrated focus of energy.

Other than the conjunction which we have already mentioned, aspects to the Midheaven can be treated together. These aspects are almost completely ignored in most textbooks, and the only available specialized study of this subject which I know of is Vivia Jayne's *Aspects to Horoscope Angles*. In that book, she states that the precise type of aspect (i.e., whether a sextile, trine, square, etc.) to the Midheaven is much less important than the specific planet making that aspect. I tend toward the same conclusion from my experience, although I do feel that the trine to the Midheaven is second in power only to the conjunction due to the fact that such a planet is usually in the same element as the Midheaven itself. Jayne's book lists the general meaning of each planet's aspects to the Midheaven, so there is no need to repeat them here. In addition to the traditional correlation of such aspects with "influencing" your public self-expression, career, and vocational goals, we need only say that any planet in a *close* aspect with the Midheaven usually indicates a type of energy and orientation which is essential in the structure of your position in the world at large and instrumental in what you will contribute to society.

The Four Angles in Comparisons

Few books on chart comparisons sufficiently emphasize the importance of aspects between one person's natal planets and the other person's Ascendant, Midheaven, or their ruling planets. One of the few exceptions is Lois H. Sargent's *How to Handle Your Human Relations*, in which she makes repeated reference to the Ascendant and its ruler. Here are a few of her comments:

> Most important in judging attraction is the aspect between the ascendant of one chart and the planets of the other. This is true not only for marriage but for all comparisons.
>
> Sun, Moon, Venus or Mars in one horoscope in the sign ascending or descending in the other horoscope is an astrological testimony of a strong attraction.
>
> Unless the ascendant or descendant of one horoscope does combine with the planets of the other by sign it is doubtful that the attraction would result in marriage. So far as my own experience has been concerned in testing this rule, I would say that an attraction would never result in marriage unless the ascendant or descendant of one or both horoscopes is so involved.
>
> It is the ascendant, symbolizing personality of the individual, that determines the real power or magnetism of the attraction. The ascendant of one chart in aspect to planets of the other chart confirms and supports any congeniality and compatibility as read in the aspects formed between planets in the respective horoscopes.

I refer the reader to Sargent's book for more detailed information about the Ascendant and its ruler in chart comparisons. In the first part of her book, she lists many of the possible combinations (with sample charts) that may be formed between the Ascendant, Descendant, and both their ruling planets. Those comments, and in fact her entire book, are well worth studying. I primarily want to emphasize how overridingly important *all* aspects to *all* four angles are in comparisons, for only rarely does one do a chart comparison for two people involved in a particularly close or important relationship where there is no close aspect involving one of the four angles.

Sargent's book, however, does not place much importance on the aspects to the Midheaven (and thus to its opposite point, the I.C.). Although I agree with her that the aspects involving the Ascendant and Descendant are more apparent and more generally important than those involving the Midheaven, my experience indicates that aspects involving the Midheaven are still extremely significant. The aspects involving the *Ascendant* are so important because, if for example someone's natal Sun or Jupiter conjuncts or trines my natal Ascendant, that person's influence on me will be—at least in part—to encourage me to express *my entire self* naturally, spontaneously, and dynamically. That person's impact on my life, in other words, will be most immediate at a personal level which colors my self-expression and my overall attitude toward life. All aspects involving the Ascendant in chart comparisons have this common feature: they all signify a powerful impact on one's feelings of spontaneity, vitality, and authenticity in every dimension of experience. (Aspects involving the Descendant are also extremely powerful but tend to indicate a focus upon *relatedness*.) The *Midheaven* aspects in comparisons are, on the other hand, indicative of more specific types of interaction, and they are most often found in relationships wherein there is a definite pattern of one person wielding authority in the life of the other person. This pattern is not, as might be thought, limited to relationships dealing solely with career, employment, or interaction between parents and children. Similar patterns are often found in comparisons between lovers, marriage partners, or close friends.

A general guideline for understanding Midheaven aspects in comparisons is that they usually indicate one of two dominant patterns: 1) either the person whose planet aspects your Midheaven helps you to manifest your achievement potential in some clear way; or 2) that person quite noticeably holds you back through some form of domination from pursuing the ambitions toward which you are drawn. Since the Midheaven is correlated with Saturnian qualities and activities, anyone whose natal planets strongly aspect your Midheaven usually plays a strong formative (Saturn!) role in your life, either helping you to come into your own as a productive member of society or inhibiting your achievement through authoritarian methods of influence. If someone's natal planet closely aspects my Midheaven (especially if it is a conjunction), I will very likely feel considerable respect for some quality or ability that that person exemplifies. I may greatly admire that person, although if my admiration is too excessive, I may unknowingly place myself under his or her power to an extent that I may later regret. From the viewpoint of karma, an emphasis on Midheaven or 10th house factors in a comparison (similar to Saturn interchanges in comparisons) may often be taken to reveal a pattern of one person holding power or authority over another. In some cases, such an emphasis (which of course automatically implies a 4th house emphasis also, symbolic of the family) seems to correlate with past familial ties wherein one person was the child of the other.

An example might help to clarify these points. If someone's natal Sun conjuncts your Midheaven, you may find that that person not only encourages your ambitions and may even take definite steps to advance your career goals, but also that he or she wants to "take you under his wing" in a very paternal way. In fact, each person may feel extraordinarily protective of the other in a way reminiscent of a parent-child relationship. Through this association, you may be *encouraged* (the Sun in particular is the planet of *encouragement;* if another planet were involved, the quality of the impact on your life would be different) to develop more confidence in *your own* ability to achieve your goals and ambitions.

One last chart comparison factor to pay special attention to is the situation where you find the two people's ruling planets (i.e., the rulers of their Ascendants) in a *close* aspect. The exact type of aspect is not so important as the fact that there is *some* close relationship between such individually dominant life orientations. (But it should be pointed out that the conjunctions or flowing aspects do *in most cases* indicate a more harmonious mode of interaction; when the aspect between the ruling planets is more challenging, there may be a certain type of conflict, barrier, or frustration inherent in the relationship, even if the people get along extremely well and even if they maintain their relationship for many years.) I always take an aspect between the ruling planets as a testimony to the fact that the two people are likely to have a relationship of extraordinary intensity and importance. They often have extra strong karmic ties with each other, and the fact that such a comparison factor is much rarer than simply a case where one person's Ascendant or Descendant is in the same *sign* as the other person's natal planets should induce us to pay extra attention to these special cases. The close interaction of the ruling planets' energies can be seen as indicative of a particularly *specific* symbol of how the two people interact with each other and what they see in each other that is especially stimulating. In the vast majority of such cases, all of the other levels of interaction shown in a comparison will be secondary to the intense type of interchange symbolized by the aspect between the rulers. It is as if the entire relationship revolves around that one pivotal energy exchange, and how the people deal with that energy is crucial to the development of the relationship.

Aquarius

11

Concepts of Astrology
in the Edgar Cayce Readings

*As to appearances in the earth,—these have been quite
varied. All of these may not be indicated in the present, for—
as given—each cycle brings a soul-entity to another cross-
road, or another urge from one of several of its activities in
the material plane. But these are chosen with the purpose to
indicate to the entity how and why those urges are a part of
the entity's experience as a unit, or as a whole. For, one enters
a material sojourn not by chance, but there is brought into
being the continuity of pattern or purpose, and each soul is
attracted to those influences that may be visioned from
above. Thus THERE the turns in the river of life may be
viewed.*
— Edgar Cayce's Reading #3128-1

The Edgar Cayce psychic readings contain a formidable amount of
information related to astrology, and it is my feeling that people engaged
in all branches of astrological studies can benefit from a study of the
Cayce material. The depth and breadth of all Cayce's work is astounding, and the fact that his psychic readings were so rigorously recorded
and documented makes his work all the more valuable for research
purposes. Edgar Cayce consciously had no belief in astrology when he
started to give "Life Readings" in an effort to explain people's past life
influences and karma. These particular readings, however, almost always
included references to astrological "influences" of a type that might
seem unusual to those familiar with traditional Western astrology. Although the language of the readings (as can be seen from the above
quotation) is often convoluted and sometimes even a bit confusing due
to the fact that Cayce was trying to communicate with several different
dimensions of life simultaneously, we can here try to clarify the readings'
primary concepts related to astrology and explain what their
implications are and how they expand our understanding of more traditional astrological tenets. I will examine two types of ideas found in the
Cayce readings: 1) those which clarify astrological traditions either by
explaining the mode of operation of astrological "influences" or by
defining the scope of astrology's application; and 2) those which contrast
with (or even contradict) traditional astrological theories.

A thorough treatment of all Cayce's concepts which relate to astrology
would require an entire book, and in fact one already exists: Margaret
Gammon's *Astrology and the Edgar Cayce Readings*, in which the author

systematically examines what Cayce had to say about each planet's nature and compares it to the way that planet is usually explained in traditional astrology books. In addition, she goes into detail about Cayce's readings on "aspects," "houses," and other specific chart factors. I highly recommend Gammon's book to all those who are interested in the deeper dimensions of astrology, but I do feel that it is worthwhile to point out here some specific ideas in the readings which can be immediately integrated with common astrological practice. For Cayce's readings in general are often impenetrable, and his statements about astrology in particular are often unusual enough to bewilder any astrologer trying to find simple and direct correlations between Cayce's assertions and birthcharts as we now understand them. I personally visited the Cayce Library (at the Association for Research and Enlightenment Headquarters in Virginia Beach, Virginia) in order to study the original readings first hand. The birth data for many people for whom Life Readings were given are included in the files, and therefore it was possible in numerous cases to draw up the accurate birthcharts in order to attempt to establish correlations between specific chart factors and the statements found in Cayce's readings. After considerable time and effort, I found that I could use only some of Cayce's information in my practice, whereas other ideas were either totally incomprehensible to me or were obviously based on an ancient system of astrology (either Persian or Egyptian) which no longer exists in any accessible form. Nevertheless, since it is well proven how accurate Cayce's information was in thousands of psychic readings on other subjects, I personally feel that one must assume that his astrological information was just as accurate, whether or not our level of understanding enables us to fathom it. Hence, the following is an attempt to present whatever of value I have been able to glean from his readings.

First of all, it must be stated that all of Cayce's readings were placed in the context of reincarnation, karma, and the individual's potential for spiritual growth and higher consciousness. Therefore, many of his ideas are particularly attuned to the primary topics of this book. Cayce emphasized that each lifetime comprises the sum total of all previous lifetimes, in the sense that each of us is simply "meeting self" in all of our experiences in this life. What we are *now* is a composite of what we have been; and everything which has been previously built, both good and bad, is contained in this life's opportunities. Cayce urges us to recognize that what we are today is the result of what we have done about our ideals and our knowledge of God (or "the Creative Forces") in past lives. As mentioned in the quotation at the beginning of this chapter, the soul is "attracted to those influences that may be visioned from above." In other words, each of us is drawn toward those astrological vibrations, aspects, etc. which most nearly fit our development. Cayce's readings give strong support to the ancient idea of the microcosm-macrocosm correspondence, for he states, "All those essential forces which are manifest in the universe are manifest in the living man, and above that the soul of man" (Reading #900-70). The oneness of all creation was one of Cayce's most basic teachings, and this oneness was not viewed as an ethereal, vague dream, but rather as an absolute fact of life:

> There are, as set in the beginning, so far as this physical earth plane is
> concerned, those rules or laws in the relative force of those that govern
> the earth, and the beings of the earth plane. These same laws govern the
> planets, stars, constellations, groups, that which constitute the sphere,
> the space in which the planet moves. These are of one force.... (Reading
> #3744-4)

In addition to Gammon's book mentioned above, another treatment
of Cayce's approach to astrology is found in *There is a River,* Thomas
Sugrue's beautiful biography of Cayce. Sugrue explains that the solar
system in Cayce's conception is viewed as a cycle of experiences for the
soul. It has eight dimensions, corresponding to the planets (excluding
the primary energizers, the Sun and Moon). The planets represent focal
points of these various dimensions of life, as well as symbolizing the
various levels of consciousness* through which the soul passes between
earthly incarnations. The earth is conceived of as the third dimension
and as a sort of laboratory for the entire system, because only here is free
will so dominant. On the other planes, more control is kept over the soul
to see that it learns the proper lessons. According to the Cayce readings,
whatever is learned by the soul must be built into the life upon the physical plane, for soul growth must be made while on the earth plane
through effort and applied will.

According to Cayce, the innumerable arrangements of stars and
planets represent soul patterns, and the signs of the Zodiac are twelve
fundamental patterns from which the soul chooses when coming into
the earth plane for a new incarnation. They are patterns of temperament,
personality, and mental attunement; and the physical body is considered
to be an objectification of the soul pattern, a reflection of "the individuality of the soul." As Cayce said:

> The signs of the Zodiac are Karmic Patterns; the Planets are the Looms;
> the Will is the Weaver. (Reading #3654-L-1.)

As in many occult traditions, Cayce correlated the planets with the
various *chakras* (or energy centers) within us, and with their corresponding endocrine glands. Seemingly, astrological "influence" and our particular karma is manifested in part through these glands and these energy
centers, which affect not only the physical body but also the emotional,
mental, and vital "bodies." One particularly interesting reading presents
Cayce's definitions of *personality* and *individuality,* terms which have
often been correlated with the Moon and Sun principles in astrology:
"Your personality, then, is the material expression; and your individuality is the personality of the soul" (Reading #2995-1). To me, this statement indicates that the complex of tendencies and emotional patterns
represented by the Moon and often called the "personality" is immediately related to our experience in the material plane. Indeed, the Moon
has often been said to reveal the "pull of the past" and the conditioning
patterns from past lives. Seemingly, the Cayce readings agree with what

---

*These "levels of consciousness," "planes of being," or "dimensions" are all terms applying
to the same reality. I have come to use the term "dimensions of experience" to explain
what the planets symbolize because that term seems most descriptive of what I experience, and it avoids the connotation of a limited two-dimensional view of personal development.

I have written in previous chapters, i.e., that the Moon's qualities are a direct emanation of our karmic inheritance. The Sun, on the other hand, has been correlated with "individuality" in many astrological books. Obviously, the Sun cannot be said to represent the actual soul itself, nor can the Sun-*sign* be correlated with that essence within each of us which makes us all One and which thus connects us with the Lord, since each Sun-sign is but a twelfth of the Whole. However, to say that the Sun and its sign represent the "personality of the soul" is to me a strikingly accurate and incisive statement, for our Sun-sign qualities have so much to do with our way of *being* and are so often those aspects of our nature which are most radiant, creative, and dynamic.

The subject of karma is explained at length throughout the Cayce readings, and there are in fact entire books dealing with Cayce's statements about reincarnation and karma. The best of them are Gina Cerminara's *Many Mansions* and Noel Langley's *Edgar Cayce on Reincarnation.* Certain of these ideas are especially appropriate for an understanding of questions that are fundamental to astrology. For example, the entire question of why and how one incarnates at a particular time and, thus, with a particular natal chart can be clarified by a study of the Cayce readings. Choice of incarnation, it is said, is *usually* made at conception, when the channel for expression is opened by the parents. A new pattern (similar to Rudhyar's "seed pattern" which the birthchart symbolizes) is made by the mingling of the parents' soul patterns. It seems that the parents' interaction and conception set up a specific vibration (or complex of vibrations) which attracts a soul who is at a state of development that is appropriate for that pattern. In spite of this fact, however, Cayce insists that the chart most symbolic of one's nature and most useful for self-analysis is one drawn for the actual physical birth rather than conception.

Cayce's readings are also replete with references to all types of cycles, and we have already quoted some of his statements about seven-year cycles in Chapter 5. A few more quotations from the readings can give further perspective on life cycles, which are so important in work with transits and progressions and which often serve as a foundation for astrological counseling.

> The purpose for each soul's entrance is to complete a cycle, to get closer to the infinite, that it may know the purpose with the entity in the earth. (Reading #3131-1)

The idea of our needing to complete various cycles during any given incarnation might well explain the nature of different aspects to us. Cayce indicates that the position of the planets show the individual's "rule upon the planet, rather than the planet's rule upon the entity...." In other words, the position of the planets (particularly by aspect) perhaps shows how well we have mastered various tests and how thoroughly we have completed various cycles of experience and learning. This idea coincides with the belief held by some astrologers that the "stressful" or challenging aspects in a chart reveal unfinished business and incomplete cycles of realization rather than simply weights tied to the soul to hamper its expression for no reason or purpose. In fact, Cayce says, "Ye are a god in the making." Perhaps our birthcharts show us at what stage in the making we are and specifically what cycles of learning and development we are now working to complete.

One other type of cycle that is mentioned numerous times in the Cayce readings is the phenomenon of a soul incarnating in successive lives at times when similar astrological forces were in effect.

> For as we find in this particular entity, and oft,—ones that enter an experience as a complete cycle; that is, upon the same period under the same astrological experiences as in the sojourn just before (that is, being born upon the same day of the month....though time may have been altered); find periods of activity that will be very much the same as those manifested in the previous sojourn, in the unfoldment and in the urges latent and manifested. (Reading #2814-1)

If this type of cycle is true, then it certainly contradicts what has always seemed to me a rather simplistic attempt to correlate astrological factors with reincarnation patterns: the notion that, if one is an Aries Sun type in this life, he or she will then have, for example, a Taurus Sun or perhaps Aries rising in the next life. There are many such theories thrown about in astrological writings or teachings, but they have always seemed to me to be utterly unrealistic and of dubious validity. There are no doubt definite *patterns* in the way astrological attunement varies through successive lifetimes, but I would think that any person's particular pattern would have to suit his or her individual nature and reflect how quickly he or she was learning the necessary lessons.

Cayce also mentions another type of pattern of karmic experience which may be helpful in understanding astrological cycles and individuals' experiences as one chapter of life ends and another begins to open. This kind of pattern is explained as follows in Thomas Sugrue's book *There is a River:*

> The incarnations which influence the personality reflect their patterns in the person's life. Sometimes they intermingle: a child's parents may re-create the environment of one experience, while his playmates will re-create the environment of another. Sometimes the influences work in periods: home and childhood may re-create the conditions of one incarnation, school and college those of another, marriage those of a third, and a career those of a fourth....[The karmic] problems are presented to him as he is prepared to meet them. (p. 319)

"Planetary Sojourns"

The concept most fundamental to an understanding of Cayce's ideas about astrology is also the most strikingly different from traditional astrological teachings. In fact, Cayce's description of "planetary sojourns" is a revolutionary idea which could potentially place all theories of astrological "influence" in a new and exciting perspective. I have always felt that one of the weakest links in the structure of both traditional and more contemporary astrology was the absence of a meaningful and convincing theory of how and why astrological factors relate to our lives on earth. However, Cayce's concept of "planetary sojourns" could fill this need perfectly. What indeed are these "sojourns" he refers to? I mentioned earlier in this chapter that each planet can be seen as representing an entire "level of consciousness" or "dimension of experience"; and, in the context of reincarnation, the soul is seen as passing through these various dimensions after it leaves the physical body. Cayce repeatedly asserts that astrological "influences" are a fact of life because, between earthly incarnations, each individual soul has passed through, dwelt in, and become attuned to these various subtler dimensions of being symbolized by the planets.

> Astrological urges are not existent just because of the position of the Sun, Moon, or any of the planets at the time of birth; but rather because the soul of the entity is part of the universal consciousness, and *has dwelt in those environs.* (Reading #2132-L-1)

Cayce's readings therefore indicate that our astrological attunement is a direct result of our soul actually journeying through these various dimensions. Seemingly, by our dwelling in (or sojourning through) these different planes of being, we become attuned to the various vibrations and qualities symbolized by the planets. And, in fact, the dimensions through which the soul may pass are not limited to the planets in our solar system alone, for many of Cayce's readings mention various stars and constellations as also having similar "influence" on our lives:

> Also we find that the experiences of the entity in the interims of plane-tary sojourns between the earthly manifestations become the innate mental urges, that may or may not at times be a part of the day dreaming, or the thought and meditations of the inmost self.
> Hence we find astrological aspects are an influence in the experience, but rather because of the entity's sojourn in the environ than because of a certain star, constellation or even zodiacal sign being in such and such a position at the time of birth. (Reading #1895-1)

Cayce's readings also refer repeatedly to the planet from which "the soul took flight," which means the latest plane of consciousness or dimension of experience where the soul sojourned before the present incarnation. In many cases, this planet from which the soul "took flight" is the planet nearest the Midheaven, although there seem to be other factors also at work which prevent us from making this guideline into a definite law that has no exceptions. But a study of many Life Readings in comparison to the birthcharts of those for whom the readings were given *does* indicate that the planet nearest the Midheaven is very often symbolic of the latest dimension through which the soul has passed before this lifetime, and therefore representative of specific qualities to which that person is strongly attuned.

The Cayce readings indicate that our needs for future soul-growth, as well as the type of life we led during our most recent incarnation, explain why at death one soul may be pulled toward Uranus, for example, and another soul may be drawn toward Venus. Whatever has been built into us through our thoughts and actions and whatever we have assimilated during the most recent lifetime all act as a powerful motivating force as we leave the physical body and pass through other dimensions.

> Immediately after death, there is a period of unconsciousness, the duration of which is governed by the spiritual development of the entity. After death, the soul and spirit *feed upon—and in a sense are*

possessed by—what was created by the mind during the recent Earth experience. Whatever has been gained in the physical plane must be used. (#3744)

Cayce's concept of the soul's dwelling in other dimensions between lifetimes on the earth can perhaps explain much about how the planets "influence" us in this lifetime. If we indeed merged our very being in those dimensions of the universe at some time in the past, we can see that our present attunement to those dimensions has not come about by accident or by some mysterious action of "planetary rays" alone; for we actually assimilated those qualities and became attuned to those energies during our sojourn in the various planetary dimensions.

It took me by surprise to find similar descriptions of planetary sojourns in the psychic pronouncements of the famous medium Arthur Ford in Ruth Montgomery's book *The World Before*. In fact, the information in that book, claimed to have been psychically transmitted by Ford after his death, coincides with Cayce's concepts very closely. In Chapter 13 of the book, entitled "Planetary Visits," we find descriptions of how the soul can journey into the environment of other planets while out of the body and even to Arcturus and other stars. These "readings" also emphasize that the earth is the best place to evolve spiritually but that the entire cosmic environment about the earth is part of a vast system for soul-growth and development.

If one achieves near perfection in physical living, these planetary visits are painless, for one walks unchallenged through tests that for another are frighteningly real. [These visits are necessary] to face self. To compensate for injuries to others and rid self of egotistical attitudes and superiority complexes. They are a leveling process. Again and again we tell you: Face oneself while in physical life. Take stock. Improve, and attempt to undo wrongs of thought or action committed against others, because it is far easier to accomplish it there than to undergo the spiritual tortures of these planetary visits. Why not take the time now to begin this process of cleansing the akashic record? Assess the harm done to others, and straightaway commence to undo it by atonement, or helpfulness to those who are afraid of you. What matter if they have harmed you? That is not your karma, but their's, and when they meet self they will be required to atone for it; so leave it to them, but help whenever possible by forgiving and forgetting. It is easy to do this in physical life, and so strenuous after passing into spirit. Ease the faults while there is yet time, and make the most of that opportunity in the flesh. (p. 164-165)

Ford's readings further describe how these planetary visits are experienced:

To experience this novelty we venture onward and outward, willing ourselves to be in the area of Mars or Neptune or Uranus, for instance. First, we "think" ourselves there. Then we are as pinpoints of light which pierce the gloom, and before we know it we are there on the surface, let us say, of Mars. (p. 159)

Arthur Ford's view of Saturn is particularly interesting when contrasted with the old-fashioned concepts of Saturn as representing only negative qualities and personal hardship:

Saturn is where one goes for spiritual uplift, and it is reserved by most until the other planetary influences have been met, for to achieve

perfection Saturn is so important...that (most are) not yet ready for that
ultimate testing of the soul and would first run the course of the others.
(p. 164)

Ford's view of Saturn is confirmed by Edgar Cayce's statement that Saturn
is that planet "to which all insufficient matter is cast for its remoulding."
This association of Saturn with "remoulding" sounds similar to my
analogy in Chapter 5 of Saturn's influence often being experienced as
"cosmic hands" reaching into one's life to remake and remould one's
way of being.

Both Cayce and Ford refer to Arcturus as an important dimension in
relation to spiritual growth and heightened consciousness. Ford states
that "Arcturus is an interesting example of a star which has a decided
effect on our spiritual growth"; and Cayce expands this reference by
stating that Arcturus represents not only a high state of consciousness
but also the "door out of this system" whereby the soul can journey
beyond this solar system into other systems in the universe. In a reading
for a particularly developed soul, Cayce described this phenomenon:

> Not that the Sun which is the center of this solar system is all there is. For
> the entity has attained even to the realm of Arcturus...that center from
> which there may be an entrance into other realms of consciousness.
> And the entity has chosen in itself to return to the earth for a definite
> mission. (Reading #2823-L-1.)

Cayce's Reading #630-2 provides us with a concise summary of his view
of astrology and specifically of planetary sojourns:

> In giving that which may be helpful to this entity in the present
> experience, respecting the sojourns in the earth, it is well that the
> planetary or astrological aspects also be given. It should be understood,
> then, that the sojourning of the soul in that environ (planetary), rather
> than the position (square, trine, etc., of planets at birth), makes for a
> greater influence in the expression of an entity or body, in any given
> plane.
>   This is not to belittle that which has been the study of the Ancients,
> but rather it is to give the understanding of same. And, as we have
> indicated: it is not so much (important) that an entity is influenced
> because the Moon is in Aquarius or the Sun in Capricorn; or Venus or
> Mercury in that or the other house or sign; or the Moon in Sun sign; or
> that one of the planets is in this or that position in the heavens. But
> rather because those positions in the heavens are from the entity having
> been in that sojourn as a soul!

Although Cayce's view of astrology differs markedly from traditional
approaches, he nevertheless urged people to investigate astrology *if
they would study it and understand it properly.* For, in that way, it could
be of greatest benefit to individuals who were trying to gain more self-
knowledge. In a few readings, he even gave what could be regarded as
pointers for interpreting charts.

> The strongest of such powers in the destiny of man is: first, the Sun.
> Then the planets closer, or those coming to ascendency at the time of
> birth.
>   The inclinations of man, then, are ruled by the planets under which
> he was born. To this extent the destiny of man lies within the scope or
> sphere of the planets..., *without regard to the power of the will, or
> without the will being taken into consideration.* [my italics] (Reading
> #3744)

The emphasis on the power of the will is a theme found throughout the Cayce readings, for Cayce sought to place astrological "influences" in proper perspective by repeatedly warning people that they should try to take their lives into their own hands as much as possible through effort rather than relying too much on planetary influences.

> As has been indicated by some, ye are part and parcel of a Universal Consciousness, or God. And thus (part) of all that is within the Universal Consciousness, or Universal Awareness: as are the stars, the planets, the Sun and the Moon.
>
> Do ye rule them or do they rule thee? They were made for thine own use, as an individual. Yea, that is the part (they play)....For ye are as a corpuscle in the body of God; thus a co-creator with Him, in what ye think and in what ye do....(#2794-3)

One might then ask how one should study astrology and use it for optimum benefit, or indeed whether one should study it at all if a temptation then develops to rely upon it too greatly. In Reading #3744, this question was asked: "Is it proper for us to study the effects of the planets upon our lives, in order to understand our tendencies and inclinations better, as they are influenced by the planets?" Cayce's answer was as follows:

> When studied right, (it is) very, very, very much worth while. Then how studied aright? By studying the influence (of the planets) in the light of knowledge already obtained by mortal man. Give out more of that knowledge—giving the understanding that the will must ever be the guiding factor to lead man on, ever upward.

It is my feeling that the most valuable aspect of Cayce's readings on astrology is that they help us place astrology in the perspective of spiritual development, seeing this ancient art and science as a practical tool for self-understanding. In addition, through Cayce's statements we can gain insight into not only the inner workings of astrology but also into its limitations. If we take to heart the essence of Cayce's inspiring admonitions, we will use astrology with a bit of detachment and humility, always emphasizing to ourselves or to clients that effort and will are crucial in the way we meet our karma in daily life. The use of astrology, either in our private lives or in a professional practice, should be viewed with an inner seriousness; for it is not just a toy or a parlor game to be dragged out at any moment to entertain or to satisfy mere curiosity. Our own birthcharts reflect what we are, what we have been, what we can become, and—as Cayce often points out—what we have done about our highest ideals in past lifetimes. Surely nothing is more personal and serious, and therefore worthy of respect and even awe. The next chapter presents an exercise which any of us may use in attempting to clarify our highest ideals in *this* lifetime, and Cayce's readings continually insist upon the great importance that should be attributed to our ideals.

> As to whether a soul is developed or retarded during a particular life depends on what the person holds as its ideal, and what it does in its mental and material relationships about that ideal.
>
> Life is a purposeful experience, and the place in which a person finds himself is one in which he may use his present abilities, faults, failures, virtues, in fulfilling the purpose for which the soul decided to manifest in the three-dimensional plane. (from *There is a River*)

Pisces

12

The Astrologer & Counseling

"Rabbit's clever," said Pooh thoughtfully.
"Yes," said Piglet, "Rabbit's clever."
"And he has Brain."
"Yes," said Piglet, "Rabbit has Brain."
There was a long silence.
"I suppose," said Pooh, "that that's why he never under-
stands anything."
— A.A. Milne, *The House at Pooh Corner*

"Everybody is all right really."
— Pooh, *ibid.*

Since writing the chapter called "The Uses of Astrology in the Counseling Arts" in my book *Astrology, Psychology, & the Four Elements,* a great many things have occurred to me concerning astrology and counseling which I would like to share. Many issues have recently become clarified in my mind, and this increasing clarification is leading me to a new and healthier perspective on my work, my sense of purpose and motivation, and the practice of astrology and counseling in general.

Many years ago, when I was just beginning to study astrology, I felt that I had to work with people in some intimate capacity, but I had no idea what form it was to take. I knew that astrology could be a valuable *tool* in almost any kind of work with people, but I had no desire to be or to be known as an "astrologer." In fact, I resisted accepting that label for many years, and—in some ways—I still do. Although by now, after earning my living exclusively through activities associated with astrology for many years, I am used to being known publicly as an "astrologer"—and indeed I have become fairly comfortable with (or at least resigned to) that label—I still insist that my main function in one-to-one dialogues is that of counselor or consultant; and I just happen to use astrology as a primary tool in that work. With many planets in the seventh house of my natal chart, one-to-one counseling comes easily, naturally, and has been quite a vitalizing part of my life as well as a profound learning experience. And I am seeing more all the time that, even if I had never become acquainted with astrology, I would nevertheless be dealing with many people in an immediate and personal way. These thoughts have recently been growing from the increasingly distinct awareness that it is not the astrology that matters so much as the astrologer. The practice of astrology is an individualized art, and the "astrologer" is first and foremost a human being to whom others, for various reasons, look for help, guidance, and clarification. I will return to this line of thought shortly, but first, it may be helpful to some younger students of astrology to mention briefly the process I went through in my search for a meaningful work-structure and a significant approach to astrology and counseling in general.

Since, as I mentioned, I had no desire to be known as an "astrologer," with all the unrealistic, depreciating, or inflated connotations that term has for many people, I quite naturally thought that I should get a Ph.D. in psychology, become a "psychologist," and—thus having my identity in society confirmed and a secure niche carved out—thereafter do the kind of counseling and therapy work I wanted, with or without the aid of astrology. Hence, I started graduate school in psychology with the idea that I would continue on for the Ph.D. It soon became apparent, however, that even the "liberal" and "open-minded" professors with whom I had to deal simply could not handle the whole idea of astrology and all of its ultimate ramifications. They became somewhat nervous when I talked about it, and it was clear that they suffered from a sort of mental and emotional indigestion when confronted with the need to assimilate an idea so foreign to their usual way of thought. The main cause of such indigestion, I feel, is simply the rigidity of ego that becomes built up when one's life is based on the unexamined assumption that one is *in control* of all aspects of one's destiny.

To make a long story short, I finished the MA program only through incredible persistence and utilizing all my powers of persuasion (as the progressed Sun squared natal Saturn), and through the help of one somewhat sympathetic professor (a *triple* Cancer!). I then resigned myself to the strong probability that no Ph.D. program in the country would suit my rather rebellious and questioning nature. I had also seen that, of all the "personality theories," therapeutic techniques, and experimental studies that were dealt with in academic psychology circles, perhaps only ten percent of them had any relevance to what I was perceiving as real life. This is not to say that astrologers should not study this ten percent; in fact, I feel they not only should, but that they are likely to be very poor counselors if they don't. I personally have heard many astrologers say things like: "Well, don't you think astrology includes all of psychology?" Of course astrology, since it is a comprehensive symbolic language of life, does ultimately have the tools to *symbolize* all phases of psychological experience. But the implication of statements or questions such as the above is: since astrology is so great, wouldn't it be easier to just ignore this annoyance called psychology? It is like saying that you prefer Christianity to Hinduism. After all, they both supposedly deal with God, don't they? Such statements are based on the inference that astrology is a *belief*, like religion. You simply choose one and reject the others. This attitude ignores the fact that astrology and psychology are simply different approaches to life, to understanding the individual's inner workings. They can contribute a great deal to each other, and the work of many of the most innovative and pioneering astrologers proves the value of this dynamic intermingling of the two disciplines.

I would be the first to admit that many psychological theories and therapeutic systems are based on assumptions which are untrue or even rather ridiculously limited. So often they merely reflect the particular bias of the theoretician who developed them, and—if you share that bias, that approach to life—you may find that person's ideas compatible with your own. Much psychological theory is based not on cosmic truth but rather upon *projection* of one's inadequacies and half-truths. This is inevitable when any person attempts to design a theory or system to describe and explain human functioning, if that person has no universal perspective upon which to base his concepts. Hence, although I feel that many astrologers could benefit from more psychological sophistication and from an acquaintance with certain psychological theories, the idealization of psychology should not be allowed to occur. Psychologists as a group are stumbling around in the dark more than astrologers are. In most cases, the birth-chart can illuminate the *facts* of experience but not the ultimate causes, and psychological theories rarely reveal the ultimate causes either! For when it comes to ultimates, when it comes to answering the deepest *why* of the client, that is the moment when the practice of astrology becomes an art of counseling, the moment when the particular religious, spiritual, and philosophical assumptions or beliefs of the astrologer have their impact. And, the more the practitioner realizes this fact, the more he or she can take full responsibility for the quality of the work, and the more he or she can begin to open self to an immediate realization of a greater purpose at work.

My attitude toward my work at this time is difficult to express. I don't identify with the term "psychologist," nor do I identify with the label of "astrologer." I see my work with clients as that of counselor, someone who points others in the direction of seeing the deeper meanings of their life experience, a function which I believe should be one of the primary purposes of any astrologer's work. I see astrology as an incredibly valuable, awe-inspiring tool for helping one to live life and to understand life more fully, but it is not for me a religion or even a way of life. It is an individualized art and, just as our use of astrology can help others to perceive with sharpened clarity their individual uniqueness, creative capacities, and growth potential, so *it can help the practitioner to discover in himself that essence of creative purpose which inevitably transcends all labels or professional pretensions.* In other words, I feel that anyone who finds that his creative purpose *compels* him toward the practice of astrology as a profession should realize that he is privileged to serve as a guide for others struggling to find their way amidst the storms, whirlpools, and shipwrecks of life on the material plane. What label is worn really matters very little. One could be called a psychologist, astrologer, counselor, consultant, guide, friend, good neighbor, or servant. What matters is the quality of the work, the quality of consciousness that pervades and hopefully illuminates one's in-depth personal encounters with others.

So now, when my students ask me how to go about becoming a professional astrologer, whether there are schools to go to, courses to attend, organizations to join, or tests to pass, I tell them: It is YOU that matters. It is not the astrology itself, isolated from you. You are not to become a computer filled with meaningless data and thousands of blips of information. Certainly you should learn the basics, become familiar with the various branches of astrology and the diverse schools of thought that deal with different approaches and interpretive methods. But all that is simply background, a foundation upon which you build your self, your work, your essential structure through which your personal creative energy may flow. By doing the work, you learn to do the work that is required of you. By being what you are, you become what you are. There is no magic moment when all the magic measurements fall into place and confirm that you are now designated a real live astrologer. If you are to make your living doing counseling with others, they will come to you because *you are what you are* more than simply because you know what you know. As Jung said, it is the personality of the "doctor" that has or does not have a curative effect. The "system" you use ultimately becomes irrelevant, for what becomes important is the fact that you are using your personal system, born of your experience: *YOU are the system*, the channel through which your consciousness flows.

My experience and most recent feelings impel me to say that astrology must be seen and used as part of counseling, not as something self-contained and isolated from the intimate dialogues of the helping professions. Astrology, unless it is applied to a *specific* person and to a *specific* situation, cannot be used to its full potential. In fact, I feel that many astrologers (and every practicing astrologer has experienced this to some extent, whether or not he or she recognized what was happening) lose perspective on what they are doing and what their essential purpose is by getting too absorbed in astrological details, mind games, or endless mathematical or "esoteric" technicalities. It is difficult to hold in mind at all times a myriad of details and *apparently* unrelated facts while at the same time maintaining a focus on the wholeness of the person we are dealing with and on the ultimate effect and implications of our statements. The great thing about Dane Rudhyar's work is that he keeps reminding us of the greater purpose of astrological work and the wholeness of the individual person. But all too often we say, "That's a great idea!" and then go on to forget to *live* this realization in our work. People are creatures of habit and, unless the astrologer continually examines himself and continually redefines and clarifies the purpose of his work, it is almost inevitable that he will fall into some rut of habit which will eventually inhibit him from maintaining the openness required for incisive and helpful counseling work.

This openness is so necessary because, I feel, the astrologer serves as a channel to a dimension of order, knowledge, and insight that is normally inaccessible to other counselors. Through the lens of the birth-chart, the astrologer can learn to focus his consciousness in such a way that he begins to know things or at least to sense the possibility of things that he cannot logically calculate, no matter how many mathematical formulae he may use. As the practitioner continues to use astrology diligently and deeply for a number of years, he finds that the intuition can be sharpened, the psychic sensitivity can be increased, and his sense of wonder can exceed all boundaries. In a sense, the astrological counselor often functions as a medium, an antenna stretched out to the cosmos, attuned to dimensions of experience for which there are often no ready psychological terms, or, at times, even logical explanations. Hence, the ideals, values, purposes, motivations, and—in general—the purity of the channel have a great effect. This, more than any other reason, is why the practice of astrology, *at its best*, is a completely individualized art which can never be computerized, dogmatized, or—perhaps surprisingly—taught in the way that other "subjects" are taught.

Astrology used in the way mentioned above thus serves the practitioner as a method of personal refinement and evolution, a means of developing those inner powers and faculties that lie dormant in most human beings. But how does one begin to achieve this attunement to other dimensions (symbolized in the astrologer's birth-chart by a strong accent on the trans-Saturnian planets)? The answer, I believe, is *openness* (which necessarily precludes too much ego-involvement or arrogance) combined with thorough and continual *practice*. One must maintain the attunement through constant use of those developing faculties, or else, if one were to "do a chart" only once a month or so, all momentum in the growth of these new faculties would be lost. Hence, when students of mine who want to be "professional astrologers" express this desire to me, I often ask how many charts they are doing per week. Are they simply reading books, or are they beginning to apply the theories in an immediate way, testing everything and assimilating the essential meanings of astrological factors through personal experience? If they say they are doing two charts a week, I ask them to do three or four. It is only by constant and in-depth practice that an art so transcendent and demanding as the practice of astrology can become thoroughly accessible and practically useful.

One doesn't get something for nothing. It is very difficult for a weekend astrologer to be sufficiently attuned and to gain sufficient experience to do high quality work. For example, if you are sick, would you want to go to a doctor who only practices medicine in his spare time? I don't want to get too dogmatic on this point, but it does seem clear to me that, in order to achieve the highest level of astrological practice, one must have a great deal of practical experience to provide the background and breadth necessary to attain an accurate perspective on individual clients' situations. If we have done only a dozen charts in our lifetime and all of them are those of friends or relatives, we really have very little experience to draw upon. Hence, if for example someone asks us what to expect when Uranus transits the descendant and the only experience we have with that factor is having seen Aunt Mollie divorce Uncle Bill, we may easily emphasize the possibility of divorce as the likely manifestation of that time period, ignoring the fact that a revolutionary change in attitude toward partnership may indeed be good for that person's marriage. Likewise, it is easy for astrologers to fall into the habit of expecting the most sensational, problematical, or traumatic manifestation of any astrological configuration. This predisposition toward a negative attitude arises because the astrological counselor—like others in the helping professions—is naturally confronted with the problematical side of things. Most astrologers' clients want a consultation because they feel there is a problem, a hard decision to make, or a feeling of discontent or anxiety that they want to clarify. But what about all those other millions of people who never request assistance, who never make an appointment with *any* person in the helping professions? Surely they have their ups and downs also, their crises, their conflicts. And surely they go through periods of the outer four planets' transits and the progressions that are often said to be "difficult." What do they *experience* during these cycles? I feel it is required of the conscientious astrologer to make an active effort to seek out people other than clients, to do their charts, and to establish a dialogue with them in order to test what the other possible manifestations of these "crisis" periods may be and in order to question them as to their personal *experience* during these important change periods. Anyone in the helping professions can easily develop a rather lopsided view of other people if he is not careful to maintain a balance between his dealings with those who have obvious problems and fairly normal friendships which are totally separate from his work.

In fact, the entire problem of the isolation which often becomes the lot of those in the helping professions is dealt with in great depth in the book *Power in the Helping Professions* by Adolf Guggenbuhl-Craig. The author is the President of the Curatorium at the C.G. Jung Institute in Zurich, Switzerland, and his extensive experience in the dialogue process of counseling and therapy is evidenced in the profound depth and insight that illuminates this entire book. The author clearly shows how the role of counselor, doctor, or healer can severely damage one's relationships in private life and how it can and very often does lead the person unknowingly to become the very kind of "charlatan" or "false prophet" which he feels that *others* are. Other chapters of the book deal with such important topics for counselors as: how to cope effectively with the problems created by the role of "healer"; the necessity for self-knowledge and honest self-examination if one is to remain personally integrated as well as effective in work; and the problem of sex and eros in the counseling situation. In short, Dr. Guggenbuhl-Craig's book is a complete discussion of almost all the common problems that a counselor has to deal with, not only in his professional work but also in his private life. I highly recommend it to anyone who maintains or plans to develop a personal counseling practice. (The book is published in Switzerland and is not easy to find in American bookstores, but it may be obtained for $6.50 from CRCS Publications, the publisher of this book.)

Before moving on to discuss other considerations relevant to the topic of astrology and counseling, it seems appropriate to mention a quotation that arrived in the mail today as part of a letter from a distant correspondent. It could certainly be considered a synchronistic phenomenon that, while I was writing this chapter, the letter arrived with the following excerpt quoted:

> Counseling is as effective as the therapist is living effectively....If counseling is not a way of life, then it is a game of techniques. (from *Beyond Counseling & Therapy* by Carkhuff and Berenson)

I think we could likewise say that the practice of astrology as a person-to-person art is only as effective as the astrologer is living effectively and that, if our astrological practice is not integrated with our way of life, then it becomes merely a game of "techniques," techniques which, although perhaps curious and diverting, are ultimately meaningless.

The Art of Not Giving Advice

Although many astrologers would likely consider it one of their primary duties to give specific advice to their clients, and although many people no doubt think they are going to an astrologer for advice, I have some serious reservations concerning the practice of too glibly advising someone what to do or what not to do. First of all, we must ask ourselves honestly whether we really know what a particular person should do. As Jung wrote:

> It is presumptuous to think that we can always say what is good or bad for the patient. Perhaps he knows something is really bad and does it anyway and then gets a bad conscience. From the therapeutic, that is to say empirical, point of view, this may be very good indeed for him. Perhaps he *has* to experience the power of evil and suffer accordingly, because only in that way can he give up his Pharisaic attitude to other people. Perhaps fate or the unconscious or God—call it what you will—had to give him a hard knock and roll him in the dirt, because only such a drastic experience could strike home, pull him out of his infantilism, and make him more mature. How can anyone find out how much he needs to be saved if he is quite sure that there is nothing he needs saving from? (*Civilization in Transition*, Vol. 10, Collected Works)

The wisdom of this statement has been brought home to me many times in my work. For example, I have often seen clients months after our encounter, and have discovered that either they didn't follow my oh-so-clever advice (whether or not they still think they should) or that something happened shortly after our dialogue which put all of their problems in a new light or in a radically different context.

What then, one might ask, does an astrologer do? What is his purpose? What can he legitimately offer people if not specific advice? He can offer his insight, his understanding, and his support; and he can provide, with the help of astrology, clarification, a sense of order and meaning, a possibility of gaining higher awareness, and a sense of the ultimate implications of the present situation. Astrology used in this way provides a means by which people can more effectively deal with their lives by recognizing their participation in cosmic cycles, thus helping them to gain a true *perspective* on themselves and their dealings with the outer world. A birth-chart is not a static thing that one simply "gets done." It is rather a map which can help the person along the road of self-discovery and self-realization. The higher purpose of astrology is not to try to *change* one's destiny, but rather to *fulfill* it through growing in awareness. Even if all aspects and implications of an individual's situation seem perfectly clear, there may still be factors which complicate the attempt to give advice. Again to quote Jung:

> The great decisions in human life usually have far more to do with the instincts and other mysterious unconscious factors than with conscious will and well-meaning reasonableness. The shoe that fits one person pinches another; there is no universal recipe for living. Each of us carries his own life-form within him—an irrational form which no other can outbid. (*The Practice of Psychotherapy*, Vol. 16, Collected Works)

The Importance of Ideals

Another factor which has a strong impact on not only what we say to a client but also on *how* we say it is the person's values and ideals. Jung often pointed out that a counselor or therapist should never damage, criticize, or deprecate the important values of an individual. The person must be worked *with,* not worked *on.* There is no place for preaching of any kind. However, many people who request astrological assistance are suffering from a lack of values, from the absence or at least the unconsciousness of a guiding ideal. Almost everyone acts in relation to some ideal; but most people have never clarified for themselves what this ideal is that so forcefully motivates or confuses them. I began to realize the importance of the individual's guiding ideals through a long-term study of the Edgar Cayce psychic readings. Cayce's readings repeatedly emphasize the importance of becoming conscious of one's own ideals. In fact, Cayce often advised people to perform a simple exercise to help in this clarification process, and I often mention this to clients. (It is a particularly useful exercise when transits to natal Neptune or of transiting Neptune are in effect; for only an awareness of a higher ideal or of a transcendent, non-material reality can give one a sense of order at those times.) The exercise is simply this:

1. Take a sheet of paper and draw upon it three columns with the headings *spiritual, mental,* and *physical.*

2. After some thought (it could even take a few days), write in each column as precisely as you can what your ideal is in that area of life. In other words, what do you want to be like spiritually, mentally, and physically?

3. Take some definite steps to bring those ideals into reality by consciously assimilating or practicing that which will make you more like your ideal. For example, if you want to be physically stronger and more energetic, perhaps you'll begin an exercise program or improve your diet. If you want to be more loving and God-minded, perhaps you'll learn to meditate and practice it regularly.

4. Keep in mind that your ideals will change and evolve as time goes by. What you wanted to be when you were twenty-one is not

necessarily what you want to be when you're fifty. Hence, as changes in your ideals become apparent, feel free to alter or define what you've written.

5. The main thing is to work *toward* the ideals, realizing that they are *ideals* and that, if you had totally attained those qualities, they would no longer serve as guideposts in your growth.

I mention this material on the need to clarify one's ideals not only as a useful "technique" that astrological counselors might want to try, but also as an introduction to the fact that all "advice" given clients should be in accord with the clients' ideals, with what they are trying to be and become. In fact, any advice given that is not in accord, at least generally, with the individual's higher ideals will not harmonize with the person's deepest nature and hence will be worse than useless. Not only will the counselor's advice be ignored or rejected, but it may even at times introduce a new discordant note into the person's already troubled life. In short, if the astrologer remains true to his personal ideals and is sensitive to the ideals and values of his clients, his work as a counselor will often be rewarded with immensely revealing and beautifully subtle experiences.

FINIS

Bibliography & Suggested Readings

Arguelles, Jose & Miriam
  Mandala
Arroyo, Stephen
  Astrology, Psychology, & The Four Elements
Baba, Meher
  Life at Its Best
  Listen, Humanity
Benjamin, A.
  The Helping Interview
Carter, Charles E. O.
  The Astrological Aspects
  Encyclopedia of Psychological Astrology
  Essays on the Foundations of Astrology
  Principles of Astrology
  Some Principles of Horoscopic Delineation
  Zodiac and the Soul
Cooke, Joan (Hodgson)
  Wisdom in the Stars
Cerminara, Gina
  Many Mansions (Cayce's Reincarnation Readings)
Cunningham, Donna
  An Astrological Guide to Self-Awareness
Davidson, Dr. William
  Lectures on Medical Astrology
DeVore, Nicholas
  Encyclopedia of Astrology
Dobyns, Dr. Zipporah
  The Astrologer's Casebook
  Finding the Person in the Horoscope
  Progressions, Directions & Rectification
Gammon, Margaret
  Astrology & the Edgar Cayce Readings
Guggenbuhl-Craig, Adolf
  Power In The Helping Professions
Greene, Liz
  Saturn, A New Look at an Old Devil
Hall, Manly P.
  Healing, the Divine Art
  Man, the Grand Symbol
  Reincarnation, the Cycle of Necessity
  The Secret Teachings of All Ages
  Self-Unfoldment
  Twelve World Teachers
Hand, Robert
  Planets in Transit
Head & Cranston
  Reincarnation, An East-West Anthology
Hickey, Isabel
  Astrology: A Cosmic Science
  Minerva/Pluto: The Choice Is Yours
Jansky, Robert C.
  Interpreting the Aspects
Jayne, Charles
  Horoscope Interpretation Outlined
  Progressions and Directions
  The Technique of Rectification
Jayne, Vivia
  Aspects to Horoscope Angles
Johnson & Vestermark
  Barriers & Hazards In Counseling
Jung, Carl G.
  Civilization in Transition (CW, Vol. X)
  The Development of Personality (CW, Vol. XVII)
  Dreams
  Essays on a Science of Mythology
  Four Archetypes
  Man and His Symbols
  Mandala Symbolism
  Memories, Dreams, Reflections
  Modern Man in Search of a Soul
  Mysterium Conjunctionis (CW, Vol. XIV)
  On the Nature of the Psyche
  The Practice of Psychotherapy (CW, Vol. XVI)
  Psychological Reflections
  Psychological Types
  Undiscovered Self
  Symbols of Transformation

Koch, Walter A.
  Birthplace Table of Houses
Langley, Noel
  Edgar Cayce on Reincarnation
Layman, Dr. Marvin
  Interviewing & Counseling Techniques for Astrologers
Lewi, Grant
  Astrology for the Millions
May, Rollo
  The Art Of Counseling
Mayo, Jeff
  The Astrologer's Astronomical Handbook
  The Planets and Human Behavior
Montgomery, Ruth
  Born to Heal
Moore, Marcia
  Hypersentience
Moore, Marcia & Douglas, Mark
  Astrology, the Divine Science
  Diet, Sex, & Yoga
  Reincarnation, Key to Immortality
  Yoga, Science of Self
Oken, Alan
  As Above, So Below
  Astrology, Evolution, & Revolution
  The Horoscope, the Road & Its Travelers
Pagan, Isabel
  From Pioneer to Poet
Robertson, Marc
  Cosmopsychology: The Engine of Destiny
  The Eighth House
  Sex, Mind & Habit Compatibility
  The Transit of Saturn: Critical Ages in Adult Life
Rudhyar, Dane
  Astrology & The Modern Psyche
  The Astrological Houses
  An Astrological Study of Psychological Complexes
  Fire Out of The Stone
  From Humanistic to Transpersonal Astrology
  The Lunation Cycle
  New Mansions for New Men
  The Planetarization of Consciousness
  The Practice of Astrology
  The Pulse of Life
  Triptych
Ruperti, Alexander
  Cycles of Becoming
Sargent, Lois
  How to Handle Your Human Relations
Schulman, Martin
  Karmic Astrology: The Moon's Nodes & Reincarnation
Sharma, I. C.
  Cayce, Karma & Reincarnation
Sheehy, Gail
  Passages
Singh, Maharaj Charan
  The Path
  Spiritual Discourses
Sugrue, Thomas
  There Is A River
Tyl, Noel
  Astrological Counsel
  The Expanded Present
  The Horoscope As Identity
Watters, Barbara
  Sex & The Outer Planets
  What's Wrong With Your Sun Sign?
White, Stanley
  Liberation of The Soul
Wynn
  The Key Cycle
Yogananda, Paramahansa
  Autobiography of a Yogi

CRCS PUBLICATIONS

ASTROLOGY, PSYCHOLOGY & THE FOUR ELEMENTS: An Energy Approach to Astrology & Its Use in the Counseling Arts by Stephen Arroyo
.... $7.95 Paperback; $14.95 Hardcover
An international best-seller, this book deals with the relation of astrology to modern psychology and with the use of astrology as a practical method of understanding one's attunement to universal forces. Clearly shows how to approach astrology with a real understanding of the energies involved. Awarded the British Astrological Assn's. Astrology Prize. A classic translated into 8 languages!

ASTROLOGY AND THE MODERN PSYCHE: An Astrologer Looks at Depth Psychology by Dane Rudhyar .... 182 pages, Paperback $8.95
Deals with Depth-Psychology's pioneers with special emphasis on Jung's concepts related to astrology. Chapters on: Psychodrama, Psychosynthesis, Sex Factors in Personality, the Astrologer's Role as Consultant.

ASTROLOGY, KARMA, & TRANSFORMATION: The Inner Dimensions of the Birth-Chart by Stephen Arroyo .... 264 pages,10.95Paperback; $17.95 Deluxe Sewn Hardcover
An insightful book on the use of astrology as a tool for spiritual and psychological growth, seen in the light of the theory of karma and the urge toward self-transformation. International best-seller.

CYCLES OF BECOMING: The Planetary Pattern of Growth by Alexander Ruperti
.... 6 x 9 Paperback, 274 pages,$12.50
The first complete treatment of transits from a humanistic and holistic perspective. All important planetary cycles are correlated with the essential phases of psychological development. A pioneering work!

AN ASTROLOGICAL GUIDE TO SELF-AWARENESS by Donna Cunningham, M.S.W.
.... 210 pages, Paperback $6.95
Written in a lively style by a social worker who uses astrology in counseling, this book includes chapters on transits, houses, interpreting aspects, etc. A popular book translated into 3 languages.

RELATIONSHIPS & LIFE CYCLES: Modern Dimensions of Astrology by Stephen Arroyo
.... 228 pages, Paperback $7.95
A collection of articles and workshops on: natal chart indicators of one's capacity and need for relationship; techniques of chart comparison; using transits practically; counseling; and the use of the houses in chart comparison.

REINCARNATION THROUGH THE ZODIAC by Joan Hodgson ..... Paperback $5.50
A study of the signs of the zodiac from a spiritual perspective, based upon the development of different phases of consciousness through reincarnation. First published in England as *Wisdom in the Stars.*

LOOKING AT ASTROLOGY by Liz Greene .... 8½ x 11, $6.95
A beautiful, full-color children's book for ages 6-13. Illustrated by the author, this is the best explanation of astrology for children and was highly recommended by *School Library Journal.* It emphasizes a healthy self-acceptance and a realistic understanding of others. A beautiful gift for children or for your local library.

A SPIRITUAL APPROACH TO ASTROLOGY by Myrna Lofthus ... Paperback $12.50
A complete astrology textbook from a karmic viewpoint, with an especially valuable 130-page section on karmic interpretations of all aspects, including the Ascendant & M.C. A huge 444-page, highly original work.

THE ASTROLOGER'S GUIDE TO COUNSELING: Astrology's Role in the Helping Professions by Bernard Rosenblum, M.D. .... Paperback $7.95
Establishes astrological counseling as a valid, valuable, and legitimate helping profession, which can also be beneficially used in conjunction with other therapeutic and healing arts.

THE JUPITER/SATURN CONFERENCE LECTURES *(Lectures on Modern Astrology Series)* by Stephen Arroyo & Liz Greene .... Paperback $8.95
Transcribed from lectures given under the 1981 Jupiter Saturn Conjunction, talks included deal with myth, chart synthesis, relationships, & Jungian psychology related to astrology.

THE OUTER PLANETS & THEIR CYCLES: The Astrology of the Collective *(Lectures on Modern Astrology Series)* by Liz Greene .... Paperback $7.95
Deals with the individual's attunement to the outer planets as well as with significant historical and generational trends that correlate to these planetary cycles.

CHILD SIGNS: Understanding Your Child Through Astrology by Dodie & Allan Edmands 150 pages, 12 photos of children .... Paperback $7.95
An in-depth treatment of a child's developmental psychology from an astrological viewpoint. Recommended by *Library Journal,* this book helps parents understand and appreciate their children more fully. Nice gift!

DYNAMICS OF ASPECT ANALYSIS: New Perceptions in Astrology by Bil Tierney. Groundbreaking new work! .... 288 pages, Paperback $8.95
The most in-depth treatment of aspects and aspect patterns available, including both major and minor configurations. Also includes retrogrades, unaspected planets & more!

ASTROLOGY FOR THE NEW AGE: An Intuitive Approach by Marcus Allen ....
.... Paperback $6.95
A highly original work with an uplifting quality. Emphasizes self-acceptance and tuning in to your own birth chart with a positive attitude. Helps one create his or her own interpretation.

THE PRACTICE & PROFESSION OF ASTROLOGY: Rebuilding Our Lost Connections with the Cosmos by Stephen Arroyo .... Paperback $7.95
A challenging, often controversial treatment of astrology's place in modern society and of astrological counseling as both a legitimate profession and a healing process.

HEALTH-BUILDING: The Conscious Art of Living Well by Dr. Randolph Stone, D.C., D.O. Approx. 150 pages, Paperback $7.95
A complete health regimen for people of all ages by an internationally renowned doctor who specialized in problem cases. Includes instructions for vegetarian/purifying diets and energizing exercises for vitality and beauty. Illustrated with drawings & photographs.

POLARITY THERAPY: The Complete Collected Works by the Founder of the System, Dr. Randolph Stone, D.O., D.C. (In 2 volumes, 8½ x 11), $25.00 per volume.
The original books on this revolutionary healing art available for the first time in trade editions. Fully illustrated with charts & diagrams. Sewn paperbacks, over 500 total pages.

A JOURNEY THROUGH THE BIRTH CHART: Using Astrology on Your Life Path by Joanne Wickenburg...168 pages, Paperback $7.95
Gives the reader the tools to put the pieces of the birth chart together for self-understanding and encourages creative interpretation of charts by helping the reader to think through the endless combinations of astrological symbols. Clearly guides the reader like no other book.

THE ASTROLOGY OF SELF-DISCOVERY: An In-Depth Exploration of the Potentials Revealed in Your Birth Chart by Tracy Marks.......
288 pages, Paperback....................................$8.95
A guide for utilizing astrology to aid self-development, resolve inner conflicts, discover and fulfill one's life purpose, and realize one's potential. Emphasizes the Moon and its nodes, Neptune, Pluto, & the outer planet transits. An important & brilliantly original new work!

THE PLANETS & HUMAN BEHAVIOR by Jeff Mayo...180 pp, Paperback $7.95
A pioneering exploration of the symbolism of the planets, blending their modern psychological significance with their ancient mythological meanings. Includes many tips on interpretation!

ASTROLOGY IN MODERN LANGUAGE by Richard B. Vaughan...340 pp, $9.95
An in-depth interpretation of the birth chart focusing on the houses and their ruling planets–– including the Ascendant and its ruler. A unique, strikingly original work! (paperback)

THE ART OF CHART INTERPRETATION: A Step-by-Step Method of Analyzing, Synthesizing & Understanding the Birth Chart...by Tracy Marks
Paperback $6.95
A guide to determining the most important features of a birth chart. A must for students!

THE SPIRAL OF LIFE: Unlocking Your Potential With Astrology.....
by Joanne Wickenburg & Virginia Meyer...paperback..........$6.95
Covering all astrological factors, this book shows how understanding the birth pattern is an exciting path towards increased self-awareness and purposeful living.

NUMBERS AS SYMBOLS FOR SELF-DISCOVERY by Richard B. Vaughan..$7.95
A how-to book on personal analysis & forecasting your future through Numerology. His examples include the number patterns of a thousand famous personalities. 336 pages.

PLANETARY ASPECTS––FROM CONFLICT TO COOPERATION: How to Make Your Stressful Aspects Work for You by Tracy Marks, 225 pages...$8.95
This revised edition of How to Handle Your T-Square focuses on the creative understanding and use of the stressful aspects and focuses on the T-Square configuration both in natal charts and as formed by transits & progressions.

THE ASTROLOGICAL HOUSES: The Spectrum of Individual Experience by Dane Rudhyar...216 pages...Paperback....................$7.95
A recognized classic of modern astrology that has sold over 100,000 copies. Required reading for every student of astrology seeking to understand the deeper meanings of the houses. Probably the most accessible and practical of Rudhyar's books, it interprets each planet in each house.

PRACTICAL PALMISTRY: A Positive Approach from a Modern Perspective by David Brandon-Jones...268 pages...Paperback.............$8.95
This easy-to-use book describes & illustrates all the basics of traditional palmistry and then builds upon that with more recent discoveries based upon the author's extensive experience and case studies. A discriminating approach to an ancient science. Many original ideas!

HELPING YOURSELF WITH NATURAL REMEDIES: An Encyclopedic Guide to Herbal & Nutritional Treatment by Terry Willard, Ph.D. (One of Canada's Foremost Experts), 144 pages, paperback...$8.95
This easily accessible book blends 20th Century scientific & clinical experience with traditional methods of health maintenance. Allows the reader to select natural remedies for over 100 specific problems, all arranged in alphabetical order & with a complete index!

THE FOOD ALLERGY PLAN: A Working Doctor's Self-Help Guide to New Medical Discoveries by Dr. Keith Mumby, 210 pp, paperback, $5.95
A current best-seller in England! A step-by-step guide that helps the reader identify and eliminate those foods which cause distress, anxiety, irritation, or symptoms of illness.

TAI CHI: Ten Minutes to Health by Chia Siew Pang & Goh Ewe Hock
131 pages, **sewn paperback, 295 diagrams & 590 photos,**...$12.95
A detailed and clear presentation of the short form of T'ai Chi' Chuan. An excellent book for those seeking an alternative form of excercise. Received excellent reviews in many magazines.

CHINESE VEGETARIAN COOKERY by Jack Santa Maria, 164 pages...$8.95
VEGETARIAN magazine called this "the best" of all the books on Chinese vegetarian cookery. It is by far the most accessible for Westerners and uses ingredients that are easily found.

For more complete information on our books, a complete booklist, or to order any of the above publications, WRITE TO:

CRCS Publications
Post Office Box 1460
Sebastopol, California 95473
U.S.A.